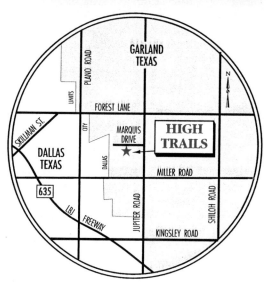

Rivers and Rapids

Your Guide to Floating and Fishing the streams of Texas, Arkansas and Oklahoma

Bob Narramore (stern) and Ben Nolen

Bob Narramore and I (Ben Nolen) started canoe racing together in 1961. By training together, a minimum of four days per week, we were putting in a lot of paddle time. Initially we raced the traditional "stump thumpers," but quickly made the transition to the more sophisticated U.S.C.A. and pro model canoes. In 1966 and 1967 we were Texas State Champions, competing regularly in marathon races in Texas, New Mexico, and Louisiana. We entered the Texas Water Safari twice, finishing sixth in 1967, after leading the race from San Marcos to Cuero, and "wrapping" our canoe during the second night. The Safari race course, in 1967, stretched 400 miles, from San Marcos to Freeport.

Henry "Hank" Stowers, then the Outdoor Editor for the Dallas Morning News, recruited us to help document, and expose, some of the pollution problems on the Trinity River immediately below Dallas. While working on this project, Hank suggested we put all our "trip time," and accumulated "river knowledge" to good use, and publish a river guide. Over the years, "Rivers and Rapids" has evolved from that meager beginning, and is now recognized as one of the premier river guide books in the country.

Bob now owns and operates High Trails Canoe Outfitters in Garland, one of the oldest and largest in Texas. He is also the manufacturers rep. for Old Town Canoes, covering Texas, Oklahoma, and Kansas. He is still actively working with canoe clubs and river runners in north Texas, Oklahoma and Arkansas. I now live in Bandera, Texas, and own the publishing company, Ocean-graphics, which is responsible for putting "Rivers and Rapids" together. I still spend all the time I can fishing and floating the Medina, Guadalupe, Llano, and Devils Rivers in the Texas Hill Country. I am active with the Hill Country Paddlers in Kerrville and the Alamo City Rivermen in San Antonio.

Cover Photos courtesy of Gaylon Wampler, The Houston Post .

Rivers and Rapids

ISBN: 0-9632403-8-2

Liability Waiver

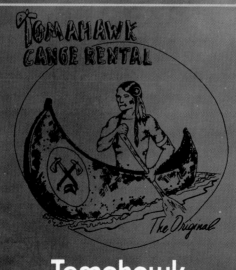

HANS WEICHSEL, JR.

Hans Weichsel, Jr. has, since our initial printing in 1972, been at the top of our "river consultants" list. His ideas, suggestions, corrections, and up-to-date information have been consistently dominant factors in upgrading this publication. For his continued unselfish support, we are proud to dedicate our 1992 "Rivers and Rapids" to this legendary riverman.

For Hans, his love of the outdoors and canoeing started around the age of six. During the summer months he and his folks lived high on a cliff overlooking the Merrimac River, about 30 miles from St. Louis. His first canoe was a wooden Old Town. As a kid, he remembers that paddling the Merrimac was the social "in" thing for that area in the 1920's. Each weekend saw hundreds of canoes making the scenic float on the Merrimac between Valley Park and Castlewood Beach. The canoeing fad of this period centered around groups with elaborate facilities, including canoe storage buildings, dressing rooms and clubhouses. Due to the rarity of automobiles and good roads in the 1920's, canoes were hauled upstream in the baggage cars of the local shuttle trains.

Prior to the age of 10, Hans and his close friend, Parker Matthews, were canoeing the Upper Merrimac. Before long, they were making the first canoe explorations of the Current, Jack's Fork, Eleven Point, Gasconade, Big Piney, the North Fork of the White, and other Missouri rivers. The locals were dumbfounded that these two boys were foolish enough to run these rivers in a small fragile canoe. According to them, these rivers could only be safely navigated by the large, cumbersome jon boats. To use anything smaller and less stable was totally foolhardy. In 1936, the St. Louis newspaper ran an article about these "two crazy kids" canoeing "uncanoeable" streams. The story was read by Dr. Earhart, owner and operator of a wilderness camp in Wisconsin which catered to "problem children." The good doctor called Hans, checked out his credentials and hired him as a guide and trip counselor for northern Wisconsin and the upper peninsula of Michigan. After his second summer in the North Lakes Country, Dr. Earhart called Hans and his friend into his office. He showed them a series of old trip diaries detailing canoe trips from the Eagle Lake area (Lake Superior) to St. Louis. This is a 1,300 mile trip covering part of the upper Mississippi. Consecutive trip logs showed the distance being covered in progressively faster times. The boys, excited by the old trip logs, decided to go for the record - paddle the entire trip in 19 days. Their plan was to use an 18½ foot canoe with three canoeists. Two would paddle while the other slept. This routine would be followed 24 hours a day for the entire 1,300 miles. Naturally, things didn't go as well as the old diaries depicted. At Princeton, Iowa they were jailed for one night as vagrants. After reaching the Mississippi, they found a series of

dams had been constructed since the early log entries. After portaging the first dam, a friendly dam-keeper suggested that the boys get a whistle and paint a number on the bow of the canoe. At subsequent dams, they blew the whistle and the locks

Courtesy Linda Clark

were opened; they quickly paddled in and were lowered to the downstream level. This technique worked great until they came to a "private" dam. That dam-keeper was not about to let three young vagrants through his locks. However, the status of the young canoeists rose appreciably when the senior law student in the group, spouting "river and dam" law, confronted the dam-keeper. The dam-keeper was so impressed that he treated the boys to a steak dinner and a 100+ mile shuttle in exchange for them conveniently forgetting the whole incident. They did make it in the 19 day, record-breaking time. In 1991, 53 years later, Hans again challenged the Mississippi. He successfully made the 110 mile trip from Greenville to Vicksburg. This fulfilled his teenage ambition to paddle both the upper and lower sections of the Mississippi.

These days, Hans is still running rivers. In the backyard of his home in eastern Fort Worth, live a dozen or so canoes and kayaks plus a storage building crammed with enough equipment to outfit a Boy Scout troop. In the house is one office devoted entirely to canoeing, camping and hiking. A half dozen file drawers bulge with documentation covering various rivers and trips.

On December 31, 1984, Hans retired after a 34 year career with Bell Helicopter Textron. At retirement, he held the position of Senior Vice President and General Manager of the Customer Support and Service Division. While with Bell Helicopter, he was instrumental in the development of the Cobra attack helicopter, initially used in Vietnam. Hans attributes most of his successes to his friends and supporters. He says, "I find whatever you do in life, you really have to have a group of true friends, supporters, a nucleus of folks. I have a great support group, people from all walks of life, working at all kinds of professions."

Making friends and having fun is what Hans does for a living now. According to him, "This kind of living keeps a person young forever."

Hans, we thank you for everything and may you really stay "forever young!"

FISHING and FISH

Our rivers and streams have long been recognized as places to "wet your hook" for catfish - channel cats, yellow cat or blues. However, catfish represent only a small number of the finny residents of our rivers. As overcrowding and the escalating costs of "big lake" equipment continues, it becomes more difficult for the average fisherman to spend a lot of time on our large impoundments. More and more are returning to the fishing holes of their youth - rivers and streams which produce a wide variety of fish which can be caught consistently on average equipment.

River and stream fishing is simple, productive and exciting! River fish come in all kinds and sizes. You may not know immediately if you're fighting a largemouth, a smallmouth, a spotted bass, a jumbo sunfish or a rod bending channel cat. Yes, river channel catfish consistently strike artificial lures. This uncertainty is an exciting ingredient of stream angling. Where else can you catch such a varied stringer of fish, largemouth, smallmouth, spotted bass, white bass, catfish, striped bass, numerous perch and a tremendous variety of sunfish - all with little change in tackle or lure presentation. However, you may have to adjust your style just a little. "Tried and true" angling techniques generally used on the large lakes won't always work in the constant motion of a river/stream environment . Rivers and streams, for the most part, have a continuous current. This current dictates how you fish, where you fish, the equipment you use and what baits you use.

River fish, especially bass, are different. Biologically they may be the same as their lake bound relatives, but there is a drastic difference in their habits and behavior. They must continually deal with the constant pull and push of the current. They have to feed more often and more effectively to replenish the energy sapped by the ever present current. Current, simply, is the one factor which sets river fish apart from their impounded cousins.

River fish are generally smaller, but much stronger, for a given age class. A couple of reasons, the continuous energy expended by living in the current and a shorter high volume feeding season due to the shallow streams becoming cold sooner, keeps their weight below that of lake fish.

FOOD CHAIN

One very important key to putting fish on the stringer lies in knowing the predominant foods available. Overall, streams will have a smaller food chain than large impoundments. For example, schooling baitfish such as shad are very seldom found in streams. However, shiners, small fish and a variety of minnow species flourish in moving waters. Depending on the season, grasshoppers and a multitude of insects, small snakes, lizards, worms and small animals fall or drop into the stream from the overgrown banks.

Crawfish are generally more plentiful in the rocky, gravel reaches of streams than they are in lakes with mud bottoms. For best fishing results, live bait or artificial lure presentation should closely resemble the natural forage of the stream.

FISH LOCATION

River fish are much more hard structure (logs, boulders, etc.) orientated than lake fish. Lake fish use structure for comfort and ambushing food. Likewise for river fish, but the desired "hard structure" will break the force of the current. In effect, river fish hold in places to rest, while at the same time, taking advantage of the current bringing food to them. At least 90 percent of the time fish are holding just out of the current behind, under or in some form of hard structure. Finding these "current breaks" is the key to successful stream fishing. You should look for downed timber, the bigger and older the better, tree roots, rocks and boulders, irregular rocky ledges and tributary entries having undercut banks and protected still water - all adjacent to moving current. Small bays or coves, especially if they have water protected by a point, should never be overlooked. Cross current channels, holes and depressions in the river bed will usually yield fish. Shade is also a major factor in stream angling. Always fish the shade on bright sunny days and especially during those "high sun" hours. When fishing deep water pools, take note of the adjoining landscape, as river bank topography will usually continue on down below the stream's surface. An almost sheer rocky hillside suggests that the water is deep and that numerous rocks are spread randomly along the river bottom. Likewise, eroded banks where the current has cut away a hillside denotes deep water. These areas offer good angling, especially if there is hard structure to break the flow of the current.

WHAT FISH, WHERE

Each specific area will dictate the type and size of fish to expect. The largemouth will hold in the deeper slower waters. The preferred structure in these areas will be logs, brush piles and undercut banks topped with heavy grass or brush cover. The smallmouth and spotted bass will stay close to swift water. Shaded

undercut banks, holes and depressions, drop-offs, irregular rocky outcropping and large rocks in the current afford an easy ambush site protected from the current. Perch and sunfish prefer areas of shaded and protected shallow water. The water will seldom be over four feet deep and will usually have a minimum to slow current. Striped and white bass are found most often in the swift tailrace below the large lake dams such as Lake Whitney on the Brazos and Lake Texoma on the Red River.

EQUIPMENT

Nothing really exotic is needed for successful stream fishing. However, rods and lines need to be lighter than those used on the large lakes. Accuracy in lure placement is mandatory to successful stream angling. You'll catch some fish by just chunking the lure, but as you become more accurate, your quantity and quality of fish will increase. Usually your cast will be less than 50 feet. This tends to help you some on accuracy and eliminates the need for a long rod and heavy test line A short light rod is best for the short casts and works best in tight places. Due to the clarity and the shallow depth of most of our streams, light test, low visibility line in the 6 to 10 pound range gives the best performance. Our rivers and streams are a dream come true for the ultra-light angler.

Lures, if kept on the small side will ALL work. On our streams, it's not the lures that make the difference, it's how and where they're used. In streams with current, a lure looks natural if it comes from upstream. For hard structures such as rock ledges, logs or boulders which cross the current flow, a retrieve parallel to the structure can be very productive. Another good approach is to retrieve the lure down current and cross over where the current meets slower downstream water. Dropping a jig or worm over a drop-off, into holes under structures or into underwater depressions will initiate smashing strikes. Small spinner baits, worms and jigs, imitation floating minnows, small topwater plugs, plastic grubs and crawfish imitations are always good lure choices. When selecting lures, remember that the lures which are easy to cast and control in moving water will be the most productive.

Not only does river or stream fishing offer an ever changing, private fishing environment, a wide variety of fish, beautiful scenery and country quiet, it will have a lot of shade. Shade is something you definitely do without on our large lakes. And it's sure nice to have on one of those long, hot summer days.

LARGEMOUTH BASS

The largemouth bass, or black bass, is native to all the streams and lakes in our area. Although the largemouth is called "bass," it is actually our largest member of the sunfish family. It is generally green in color with dark mottled blotches forming a dark stripe lengthwise along its side. The dorsal fin is almost divided. The soft rear "half" of the fin contains 12 to 13 rays. When the mouth is closed, the upper jaw extends back beyond the rear margin of the eye. Although lake largemouth commonly exceed 12 pounds, expect the largest river largemouth to be in the 5 to 7 pound range. Their life expectancy will generally range between 6 and 8 years.

SPOTTED BASS

Also known as the Kentucky bass, the spotted bass is native to the majority of our fast flowing streams. The spotted bass can be distinguished from the largemouth by several characteristics. Above the lateral band there are dark markings. Below the lateral band there are definite linear streaks. The dorsal fin is not as deeply notched as that of the largemouth. The upper jaw of the spotted bass does not extend beyond the rear margin of the eye when the mouth is closed. Although not as big as the largemouth, it is a first class game fish. It will generally be caught in or just off the current. Pound for pound, it will out fight the largemouth. River spotted bass usually average between one half pound to two pounds. A three pound spotted bass is considered a big fish.

GUADALUPE BASS

This stream-adapted fish inhabits many of the Texas Hill Country streams and rivers of central Texas. The Guadalupe has a distinctive black, diamond shaped pattern along its sides and rows of spots which form stripes on its belly. The Guadalupe does well in fast flowing streams. Because of its total adaptation to current, it is tremendously strong for its size. At this printing, the Texas record is 3 pounds 11 ounces. Its lifetime in a continuous current has made it strong and aggressive. It is generally caught around or behind river cover which protects it from the current. The Guadalupe bass positions itself so the current can bring the food to it. Fish with this in mind and you won't be disappointed.

SMALLMOUTH BASS

The smallmouth is one of the most exciting and aggressive fish in our rivers. Found predominantly in extremely fast water, it uses the force of the water when hooked. Although smaller than it largemouth relative, it is stronger and has more endurance when hooked. The distribution of the smallmouth, however, is fairly limited. It is found in the Devils and Pecos Rivers of Southwest Texas and a number of the fast flowing streams of Arkansas and Oklahoma. It is easily recognized by the motley vertical bars along its sides and brownish green color. In some instances this color will vary from a dark golden brown to almost black. The white belly area does not extend far up the sides. The average size is one to three pounds.

WHITE BASS

White bass are widely distributed throughout the lakes and rivers of the South and Southwest. A member of the true bass family, its colors are dark gray to black on the back, bright silver on the sides and white on the belly. Several incomplete dusky stripes run the length of the body. The first anal spine is only half as large as the second, and the second anal spine is only half as large as the third. Large schools of white bass migrate up rivers each spring. Aggressive feeders, they can be caught, sometimes two at a time, on small white or yellow jigs, small spinning baits or live minnows. They are determined fighters at the end of your line and excellent eating. They do not jump but fight doggedly with deep long runs. Average size is 1 to 1½ pounds. Fish going over 2 pounds are considered large.

GREEN SUNFISH

General distribution over the entire South and Southwest. The green sunfish is most easily identified by its large mouth, bass-shaped body and the yellow-orange color bordering the dorsal, anal and tail fins. This sunfish is dark green above, shading to lighter green on the sides and yellowish below. There are faint vertical bars on the sides. Some scales are tipped with turquoise, giving the appearance of rows. This is a fun fish to catch on fly fishing equipment or ultra-light tackle. Although the average size is four to eight ounces, they are super fighters. They will strike almost any small artificial bait offered when they're in the mood.

YELLOW SUNFISH

This sunfish is found almost everywhere in the South and Southwest except the far west and southwestern Texas. Although this fish does possess a yellow belly (sometimes orange or rusty color), it might have been better named the "longear." In adults, the "ear" (opercle flap) often reaches a length of an inch or more. It is narrow and usually not wider than the eye. The yellow belly is one of our larger sunfish, occasionally attaining weights of a pound or more. Although both males and females have the yellow or orange belly, the male is much brighter. They can be caught on small spinning baits, small plastic grubs, small jigs rigged with spinners and the small ultra-light swimming/diving minnow imitations.

ROCK BASS

Also known as the warmouth, this fish is large mouthed and heavy bodied. The adults are dark in appearance with a heavy mottled brown coloration on the back and sides. The lower sides and belly are golden colored. The male has a bright orange spot at the base of the dorsal fin. The rock bass prefers the cover of weed beds, sunken longs and brush rather than the open water. They can reach sizes of up to a pound, but the average weight will be around eight ounces. Although found all over our area, they are more abundant in east Texas and Louisiana. A common slang name for this sunfish is "goggle-eye." They can be taken on almost all types of light tackle and baits. Sometimes they'll surprise you and hit larger bass tackle.

BLUEGILL SUNFISH

Abundant throughout the South and Southwest, the bluegill is probably better known than any other sunfish. The adult is practically oval in shape, having an almost round outline with a flat compressed body. Its most distinguishing characteristics include a dark spot at the base of the dorsal fin, vertical bars on its sides and a small mouth. Colors vary greatly but the throat is often yellowish or rust colored; especially on the male during spawning season. Sides may be green with some lavender, brown, copper or orange. Bluegills reach weights over a pound, but the average size will generally be four to six ounces. They still can be a lot of fun on fly rods or ultra-light tackle. Due to their exceptionally small mouths, be sure to use small baits.

RIO GRANDE PERCH

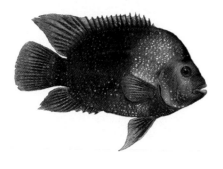

Found primarily in the Rio Grande, San Marcos, Guadalupe, Llano and Colorado Rivers of south and southwest Texas. The Rio Grande ranges in color from almost black to light olive. They will always have cream and turquoise spots, however. This fish is basically ugly with rough feeling scales and a disposition to match. It is not a sunfish, but a member of the Cichlid family. It is tropical in nature and cannot survive temperatures below 49 degrees. Adults can weigh up to 3 pounds. When the black lining of their abdominal cavity is removed before cooking, they are considered a fine eating fish. They are exceptionally strong and can be exciting when taken on light tackle. They are considered a serious predator as far as eating the eggs of other fish.

CRAPPIE

Both the white and black crappie have achieved wide distribution throughout the South and Southwest. The white crappie has silvery green shading to darker green on the back. The belly is bright silver or white. The sides have several vertical bars. The black crappie can easily be confused with its white relative, however, it is deeper bodied and has seven or eight spines in the dorsal fin, whereas the white crappie has only six. The sides of the black crappie have irregular black blotches rather than vertical bars. Both species average from ¾ to 1½ pounds. These 2 are probably the most popular panfish in our area. In rivers they are found in still, deep waters in holes along the bottom or along deep drop-offs.

FLATHEAD CATFISH

Also known as the yellow cat and opelousas, it is found in almost every river in our area. The flathead's color will vary greatly according to its watery environment. In clear waters, it is a dark olive to brown with mottled splotches. The belly may be creamy white to pale yellow. In muddy waters, it will be much lighter. The head is very broad and flat. Its mouth is almost as wide as the head. The flathead is our second largest freshwater sports fish. The average size will run around 20 pounds, but some have been caught weighing over 100 pounds. They can reach the 50 pound mark in 8 to 10 years. The 80 to 100 pound fish are probably 18 to 20 years old. Flatheads are caught in deep quiet pools along rock shelves, long jams or in areas with deeply undercut banks. They will take only live bait.

CHANNEL CATFISH

These catfish are native to all our rivers and lakes. The channel cat has a forked tail and a small narrow head. The coloration is silvery gray above, shading to silvery white on the belly. Its sides are usually marked with small black spots which become obscure or absent in adults. The dorsal and pectoral fins all have a first spine which is extremely sharp. If handled improperly, these spines can cause a very painful wound. Channel catfish can be caught on almost anything - alive or dead. Night is the best time to fish, even though channels are often caught in the daytime. Although they may reach weights exceeding twenty pounds, they will average between 2 and 3 pounds. They are considered an exceptional food fish and are raised commercially for their excellent taste.

BLUE CATFISH

The blue cat is found in most of our major rivers and streams. This fish is slate blue above and shaded to white on the belly. Its tail is deeply forked like that of the channel cat. The upper jaw protrudes slightly beyond the lower. Often the blue catfish is confused with the channel cat, however it can easily be identified by the 30 or more soft rays in the anal fin. The channel cat never has more than 29. This is the largest freshwater sports fish in our area. It has been known to reach weights of over 150 pounds, however these extremely large fish area becoming quite rare. They commonly reach sizes of 20 to 40 pounds. The blue cat, like the channel, will eat almost anything. Even though it does well in moving water, it prefers that the water be deep.

ALLIGATOR GAR

Found in all the warm rivers of the South and Southwest, the alligator gar is the "big boy" of the gar family. The alligator gar can exceed weights of 300 pounds and will be over eight feet long. The gar is a relic of a large group of primitive fishes. They are distinguished by very hard, interlocking, diamond shaped scales covering a long cylindrical body. The snout is beak-like and lined with rows of needle sharp teeth. The gar is an "air-breather" and can survive in stagnant water that would support few other fish. Gar were once considered real villains by the fishing fraternity, but biologists now believe that gar may be beneficial as predators in keeping down the number of rough forage fish.

LONGNOSE GAR

Also known as the needlenose and fish gar, this is the one we see most in our local rivers and streams. This gar does much better in flowing streams than does the alligator gar. The longnose is more at home in clear streams, feeding in the eddy water just off the current or in protected coves along the river shoreline. Although these gar may reach the 20 pound plus class, few this size are ever caught. Most average 5 to 10 pounds. Gar fishing can be extremely exciting. One of the most popular rigs is medium to heavy tackle using a jig made with white nylon strings approximately four inches long. No hook is needed. The gar's teeth become entangled in the nylon. Gar are edible, but very difficult to clean because of their armor like scales. Keep your fingers away from their mouth, especially if they're still alive!

RIVERS
RAPIDS
& RATINGS

Although most of our local streams cannot be considered "big water," there are still many rapids which deserve respect, and are severe enough to be rated.

The following is a brief description of Class I through Class VI per the International Scale of River Difficulty (ISRD). Texas doesn't have many past the Class IV rating, so rest easy.

CLASS I: Moving water with a few riffles and small waves. Few or no obstructions.

Upper Guadalupe, Class I

CLASS II: Easy rapids with waves up to 3 feet, and wide, clear channels that are obvious without scouting. Some maneuvering is required.

Picture Book Rapid, Mulberry River - Class II

CLASS III: Rapids with high, irregular waves often capable of swamping an open canoe. Narrow passages that often require complex maneuvering. May require scouting from shore.

Rust Falls on the upper Guadalupe, Class II-III

CLASS IV: Long, difficult rapids with constricted passages that often require precise maneuvering in very turbulent waters. Scouting from shore is often necessary, and conditions make rescue difficult. Generally not possible for open canoes. Boaters in covered canoes and kayaks should be able to Eskimo roll.

Rockslide, Santa Elena Canyon on the Rio Grande - Class IV-V

CLASS V: Extremely difficult, long and very violent rapids with highly congested routes which nearly always need to be scouted from shore. Rescue conditions are difficult and there is significant hazard to life in the event of a mishap. Ability to Eskimo roll is essential for kayaks and canoes.

CLASS VI: Difficulties of Class V carried to the extreme of navigability. Nearly impossible and very dangerous. For teams of experts only, after close study, and with all precautions taken.

Remember, rising water levels will usually upgrade any rating. Also, when you canoe in water below 50°, or in an extreme wilderness area, increase the class scale by one rating.

9

CANOES

Confused about canoes and paddles - what to buy and what not to buy? Join the thousands who have gone before you!

The traditional canoe is available in a variety of lengths, styles, widths, colors, weights and materials. Somewhere in this jumble of dimensions, load capacities, hull designs and price ranges, is a boat which will fill your needs without flattening your pocketbook.

Lets start with the basics: the canoe with a greater length to width ratio (long and narrow) is faster and will hold its course better, but will be harder to turn or maneuver. A short canoe (15') is slower and will have less load carrying capacity, but will turn easily, and is light to portage.

What we're looking for is a compromise between the two extremes - a canoe with adequate load capacity, fast enough to cover the long stretches at less than a snails pace which will also perform well in whitewater. For overall general canoeing, a QUALITY seventeen footer can usually get the job done.

Equipment becomes more specialized only as need demands it, i.e. extensive use in whitewater, long float trips, cold water/cold weather canoeing, or trips with many or long portages. When these extremes are determining factors, don't stop short of obtaining equipment designed for that specific purpose.

Which is the best material? Alcoa will argue aluminum, Dow Corning's choice is fiberglass, DuPont's favorite is Kevlar 49, Royalex prefers ABS (Acrylonitrile-butadiene-styrene), Old Town touts the advantages of their cross-link polyethylene, and the romantics wax poetic over original wood or wood/canvas combinations. All these fill the needs of a specific river runner somewhere. The following are what we believe to be the pros and cons of each material. When you make your final selection, take into consideration how often and when the craft will be used, under what conditions, how much carrying will be involved, how and where the canoe will be stored, and if it will have room for the kids.

ALUMINUM-

Advantages: comparatively inexpensive, generally in the $500.00 plus range. Will take a lot of abuse. Virtually maintenance free.

Disadvantages: does not lend itself to slick hull design. All hulls are symmetrical. Extremely noisy. Hot in the summer, cold in the winter. Uncomfortable. Heavy. Noisy. Retains dents and creases. Colors chip off easily. Limited models.

FIBERGLASS-

Advantages: low to medium cost, $500.00 - $1,200.00. Wide variety of models and hull designs. Broad choice of colors and will retain color. Easy and economical to repair. Comfortable and quiet.

Disadvantages: chips easily and comes up a little short on impact strength. Brittle and will self-destruct if "wrapped." The higher quality glass boats are a little on the heavy side.

POLYETHYLENE-

LINEAR POLYETHYLENE:

Advantages: inexpensive, ranging from $500.00 - $700.00. Variety of colors. Colors are permanent. Good impact strength.

Disadvantages: more flexible and harder to repair than fiberglass. Usually needs some type of structural support to reduce hull flexibility. More susceptible to sunlight deterioration than fiberglass.

LAYERED OR CROSS-LINK POLYETHYLENE:

Advantages: priced about the same as linear polyethylene. Produces a stronger canoe which does not need a keel or frame for structural strength. Molded in colors. A variety of hull designs and lengths. Usually returns to original shape after wrapping.

Disadvantages: low abrasion strength. Usually heavier than fiberglass. Bow entry wide because of mold construction. Slower than fiberglass, but faster than aluminum.

ROYALEX -

Advantages: mid price range, $650.00 - $1,200.00. One of the toughest canoes on the river. Reformable after wrapping. A variety of hull styles, lengths and molded-in colors. Low noise level.

Disadvantages: inside slick when wet. Low abrasion strength. The bottom will flex in some models.

KEVLAR -

Advantages: extremely light. Wide variety of designs and lengths. Molded-in colors. Exceptionally strong with tremendously high resistance to puncturing or cracking (bullet proof vests are made from this stuff.)

Disadvantages: very expensive with some models selling for around $2,000.00. More difficult to repair than fiberglass. Unless correctly reinforced, have a tendency to be flexible, especially in the ultra light weight models.

WOOD-WOOD/CANVAS-

Advantages: lightweight; nothing to match it's beauty. Will have beautiful, natural wood finish or permanent canvas colors. Low noise transmission. Comfortable and easy to repair. An heirloom!

Disadvantages: Very expensive generally running $1,200.00 - $3,000.00. Count on continued maintenance. Naturally, they are easily damaged.

SHORT COURSE IN CANOE DESIGN,
(COURTESY OF WE-NO-NAH CANOE, INC.)

To untrained eyes all canoes look much the same when, in truth, many subtle differences have a major impact upon paddling performance.

To begin at the beginning, consider bow sharpness. The sharper the better for streamlining and tracking. From the bow back, inspect how quickly the hull widens out. This affects speed, capacity and stability. For efficiency, a hull should widen slowly and smoothly. For more stability and capacity, the hull must widen sooner and stay wide longer. A hull that is moderately wide over a longer distance can be more stable than one with greater width but over a shorter span. This aspect of a hull is called its (fullness.) Unfortunately, extra fullness creates higher paddling effort. But if the transition from a sharp bow to a full middle is very smooth, the loss can be small.

The same rules apply to the stern as the bow. Fullness aft of center is good. So is a sharp stern exit line. Thus the transition here must be smooth, too. Many canoes have their fullest point aft of center. Called "asymmetrical," it makes the bow smoother at the expense of the stern but gives a net gain in efficiency.

The curve in the bottom is called "rocker" and plays a major role in canoe performance. A hull with lots of rocker turns on a dime. With rocker, the bow and stern draw less water than the center does. They present less hindrance to turning and give less help to going straight. Rocker makes a hull act shorter than it is and increases maneuverability but lessens streamlining.

Cross-sectional hull shape is difficult to explain yet is very important as it's the major factor governing stability and safety. Some hulls feel very steady at their normal attitude. Many people take this as proof of high resistance to capsizing. This can be a total illusion. Initial stability is a hull's steadiness when upright or near it. Final stability, by contrast, is resistance to capsizing as he hull nears that point.

Which is more important? If a hull favors one form - as often it must - higher final stability is the safer choice. Flat bottom hulls have little final stability. They feel steady when level, but capsize suddenly on waves or if leaned beyond a critical angle. Many

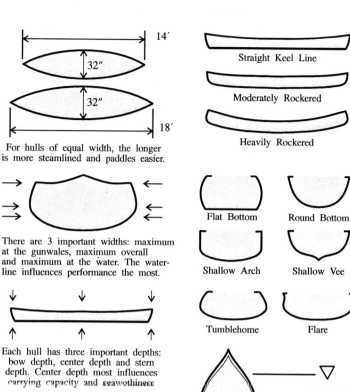

For hulls of equal width, the longer is more steamlined and paddles easier.

There are 3 important widths: maximum at the gunwales, maximum overall and maximum at the water. The water-line influences performance the most.

Each hull has three important depths: bow depth, center depth and stern depth. Center depth most influences carrying capacity and seawothiness.

Two canoes that look much the same from above may have completely different shapes at the waterline

Straight Keel Line

Moderately Rockered

Heavily Rockered

Flat Bottom   Round Bottom

Shallow Arch   Shallow Vee

Tumblehome   Flare

Tumblehome and flare can sometimes be combined into the same hull to achieve the benefits of both

Only you can decide what shape a hull must be to work for you. The first step is to anticipate how you'll use the hull and what aspects of performance you value most. If you'll take scenic trips and carry little gear on fairly calm water, for example, you'll seldom need high capacity or seaworthiness. You'll want paddling ease and can sacrifice hull volume in order to get it.

Think also about the paddlers' sizes and levels of experience. New canoeists who are large need a deeper, more stable hull simply to accommodate their own weight and the fact that they may err in balancing the hull.

When comparing canoes, look at all parts of a hull to predict how they'll effect performance. Also look for contradictions that hint the hull wasn't designed for performance but for ease of manufacture or some other reason.

Paddle each canoe you are considering. You'll be surprised at the differences. To analyze stability, capsize the hull. To assess paddling ease, see how far the hull glides after you stop paddling. Portage it too, since you'll eventually need to carry the canoe alone.

Typically, people buy one - perhaps two - canoes in a lifetime. It's sad if they spend 20 years living with one canoe's failing when some analysis at first could have saved the problem.

Paddles

Paddles, like canoes, come in a wide variety of materials, lengths, widths, bent shafts, straight shafts and so on. Like most things, you get what you pay for, but why pay for the most expensive if you don't really need it! Buy a paddle, a quality one of course, to fit your specific needs, build and strength. Talk to your favorite outfitter. Let him know your style and type of paddling. He will fit you to a paddle that will fill both your specific needs and bank account. To cover some of your options the following is a quick rundown on types of paddles, materials and general pricing.

Paddles are available in two basic designs: the straight shaft and the bent shaft. The straight shaft is what all of us grew up with; a straight handle going into a straight blade. The bent shaft, usually with a 12-15 degree bend, has a forward bend in it immediately above the blade. Technically it lets you present the flat side of the blade in a vertical position during the exact power part of your stroke. In layman's language, it is just more efficient and better balanced once you get accustomed to the feel of it. Some of the materials and prices you'll run into:

WOOD - good wooden paddles are multi-laminates with special blade coatings. The straight shaft, wooden paddle will range from $15.00 - $25.00 each. The wooden bent shaft from $19.00 - $150.00.

PLASTIC (ABS): These are very popular, fairly inexpensive and extremely durable. Although they aren't quite as aesthetic and generally don't fit as well as the more expensive paddles, they are work horses. These paddles have proven themselves in all types of situations. They will usually have a specially formulated synthetic blade, tempered aluminum shaft (some polyethylene coated for comfort) and either "T" or palm-shaped synthetic grips. Their cost will usually range from $15.00 - $25.00 each.

COMPOSITE: these are the ones used by many of the purists, by hard-core racers or those who want the ultimate in performance and quality. Many will be a composite of Kevlar, graphite and foam or similar materials. They will be very well balanced, extremely light (usually under a pound), unbelievably durable and tremendously expensive. A good composite paddle will run somewhere between $85.00- $250.00.

paddlers don't know it's hull shape that causes this stability problem. So, as with most aspects of hull design, the best solution lies between the extremes. Here, it is the "shallow arch hull." Compared with a flat bottom it trades off some initial stability for more final stability and predictability.

The remaining type of hull is often called a "shallow Vee." It's much like a shallow arch but with a ridge (like a keel) running along the center. Compared with a true shallow arch of similar shape, the stability of a shallow Vee is about the same, but the ridge increases water resistance and creates some of the same problems as a keel.

So far we've explored the part of the hull that's in the water. Shape above the water is important, too. Canoes function in active conditions; if the hull meets a wave or tips due to movement of the paddlers, it immerses a different area than it ordinarily does. So by planning shape above the water line, designers impart extra safety that comes into play only if needed.

One idea is flaring the hull out near the gunwales to deflect waves and give extra resistance if a capsize threatens. Flare is often given to canoes for rapids or wind-driven lake waves. Its penalty is that flare forces you to reach farther out to paddle.

Tumblehome is the opposite of flare. It's useful for marathon hulls as they seldom encounter waves and the paddlers want maximum comfort to perform strokes perfectly.

Sometimes flare and tumblehome can be built into one hull; the sides can turn in near the paddlers and can turn out elsewhere. For greatest effect, the hull needs wood gunwales as aluminum ones can't hold the odd shape required to combine significant tumblehome and flare into different areas of one hull.

MAPS

There are two types of maps used by most river runners to get in and out of the hard to find places.

One type is the U.S. Geological Survey Topographical Map. This shows elevations, cliffs, valleys, creeks, structures, pipeline crossings, and other topographical landmarks. For plotting accurate river mileage this map is always the best.

The second type is the county road/highway map. This is a map of each separate county showing most existing highways and roads. Although not as accurate as the topographical map in plotting river mileage, it is more accurate and informative on road numbers, descriptions, and locations.

These maps may be purchased by mail or over the counter from Ferguson Map Co. (see adjoining ad.) or The Distribution Section, U.S. Geological Survey, Federal Center, Denver, Colorado 80225. If you need Arkansas maps, we recommend the following: for county maps write Map Sales, Room 203, Arkansas State Highway and Transportation Dept., P.O. Box 2261, Little Rock, Arkansas 73302. For topos, write Arkansas Geological Commission, Map and Publication Sales, 3815 W. Roosevelt Road, Little Rock, Arkansas 72204. An "Index to Topographic Maps for Arkansas" is available free from the Commission. Some of the best reference sources for the "back roads" that we have found are "Roads of Texas" and "Roads of Arkansas." Both are published by, and available from, Shearer Publishing, see adjoining ad.

These maps, especially the topos, will give you a greater understanding of the terrain along and surrounding the river. Actually, it is a lot of fun to plot your progress on the map and pick out reference points for future trips.

OFF SEASON CANOEING

Some of the years best canoeing is done in the early winter months, and canoe-camping in this off-season can provide extra pleasure.

The summer green is gone from the trees but the reds and yellows remain. The air around you is virtually bug free. The sun sets early, leaving more time around the fire, and the long nights are cold, but cozy, in a warm sleeping bag.

Short canoe runs on familiar rivers are suggested for these cooler months. Brisk weather invites brisk activity, but it is important not to over-tax your endurance. On a lengthy trip rest often to avoid cramping, but take care to keep dry getting in and out of your canoe.

Dress depends on the temperature, whether or not you are likely to be wet, and whether you are paddling a kayak or canoe. If a kayak is your choice, a wet suit is almost mandatory for keeping warm. Canoeists usually prefer warm, light clothing, and the layered style of dressing. Hooded rain gear is available either poncho style or in regular rain suits. Always provide yourself a full change of clothing, either waterproofed and carried in your canoe or in the car at the take out point.

If you don't plan a meal during a winter trip, but you have a small stove, include it (and matches in waterproof packets), with your gear, along with packages of instant hot chocolate, coffee or tea. Chocolate bars and other high energy foods such as dried beef jerky or protein bars can provide that extra push you might need.

Even if you prefer to leave most of the whitewater to summer, canoeing is a year round activity - no sense putting your boat out to pasture or in the garage during the winter season.

SAFETY AND SENSE

PREVENTION

1. Wear life preservers at all times. All children should be equipped with a well-fitting life preserver.

2. Distribute your weight and gear evenly for a safe and comfortable trip.

3. Tie in and waterproof all necessary and valuable items.

4. Carry a knife and a rope at all times (preferably a 50' length of nylon or plastic).

5. Test a new canoe or kayak and spray cover in flat water before taking it out into whitewater.

6. When you reach water you feel may be unsafe, always beach your boat and plan your route carefully before you begin your run.

7. Currents are always stronger than they look - never underestimate them.

8. Learn to heed natural danger signals. Learn to read the water, its current, flow direction, and natural hazards.

9. Recognize your own strength, endurance, and abilities.

10. Never stand up in a canoe in moving water.

11. Do not grab or try to hold onto fixed objects (limbs, rocks, vines, etc.) while in moving swift water.

RESCUE

1. Stay with your overturned boat if possible. It has flotation and will help you stay afloat until you reach shallow water.

2. If separated from your boat, swim for an eddy before you try to stand up.

3. Never attempt to stand up in a fast moving current.

4. Keep your feet high and pointed downstream if you are adrift in moving water.

5. Walk only when the river is too shallow for swimming or if you are held by a rope.

6. If you must rescue your boat, be belayed from upstream with a rope.

7. When attempting to rescue a victim who is caught in a crevasse with his head above water, support the head before doing anything else.

8. If the head is under water take immediate steps to get the head above water. Every second counts!

9. During a long and heavy rapid, paddlers can quickly get physically exhausted. Take the rapids one boat at a time with some of your group ashore.

10. While seated in your canoe, you can rescue a swimmer who has capsized by letting him hold your stern rope, then go to shore, or ride out the rapid if there is no other choice.

11. If a victim is trapped underwater, a rescuer may be belayed from upstream with an extra rope to be tied to the victims waist.

12. In any rescue, stabilize the victim's position, and centralize rescue efforts from the bank where there is firm footing.

SURVIVAL

(Not Necessarily a Do-It-Yourself Project!)

Most paddlers are acutely conscious of water safety, particularly in turbulent or hazardous waters. As the paddler becomes more water-wise, he becomes aware of the responsibility for the safety of his partner, or other river runners who might be in trouble. Many times, self-rescue is impossible. Then the canoeist must rely totally on others for help.

Even a sizable group - immobilized with fear or panic, will be unable to save a trapped or drowning companion. To avoid such tragic situations, know the proficiency of your fellow river runners and their limitations. Have a group discussion regarding safety precautions and rescue procedures before you start.

CANOE CLUBS AND ORGANIZATIONS

TEXAS

ALAMO CITY RIVERMEN CANOE CLUB
P. O. Box 171194
San Antonio, Texas 78217

AMERICAN CANOE ASSOCIATION
7432 Alban Station Blvd., Suite B-226
Springfield, Virginia. 22150

BAY AREA ROWING CLUB OF HOUSTON
P. O. Box 57508
Webster, Texas 77598-7508

BAYOU CITY WHITEWATER CLUB
P. O. Box 980782
Houston, Texas 77098-0782

BIG THICKET VOYAGEURS
P. O. Box 186
Mont Belvieu, Texas 77580

DALLAS DOWNRIVER CLUB
P. O. Box 595128
Dallas, Texas 75359-5128

HILL COUNTRY PADDLERS
808 Lazy Lane
Kerrville, Texas 78028

HOUSTON CANOE CLUB, INC.
P. O. Box 925516
Houston, Texas 77292-5516

NORTH TEXAS RIVER RUNNERS
215 Lakeshore Dr.
Waxahachie, Texas 75165

TEXAS RIVERS PROTECTION ASSOCIATION
P. O. Box 2622
Austin, Texas 78767

TEXAS RIVER RECREATION ASSOCIATION
P. O. Box 12734
Austin, Texas 78711-2734

TEXAS WATER SAFARI
Rt. 1, Box 55-R
Martindale, Texas 78655

UNITED STATES CANOE ASSOCIATION, INC.
4169 Middlebrook Drive
Dayton, Ohio 45440-3311

ARKANSAS

ARKANSAS CANOE CLUB
P. O. Box 477
Russellville, Arkansas 72801

THE ARKANSAS PADDLER
P. O. Box 1843
Little Rock, Arkansas 72203

OKLAHOMA

DUST BOWL CHAPTER OF ARKANSAS CANOE CLUB
4606 E. 11th Street
Tulsa, Oklahoma 74112

TULSA CANOE & CAMPING CLUB
4606 E. 11th Street
Tulsa, Oklahoma 74112

MISSOURI

OZARK MOUNTAIN PADDLERS
P.O. Box 1588-555
Springfield, Missouri 65805

To Harry Roberts.

As editor of "Canoesport Journal," "Paddle Magazine," and "Wilderness Camping," Harry made many impressive contributions to our sport of river running. For this dedication, Harry's own words seem most appropriate. He wrote, " a person is walking to a lake, approaches the shore, and wants to keep on walking. That's really where it starts." "The seeking of perfection is its own reward, it imposes human dimensions on a universe otherwise too vast for comprehension. Make each word right, one word at a time. Make each prayer right, one prayer at a time. Make each stroke right, one stroke at a time."

CREDITS

Hans Weichsel, Jr., Leonard and Martha Hulsebosch, Roger Bills (Old Town Canoe), Linda Clark, John Harvey, Gene and Donnie Coleman, Janie Johnson, Max Wellhouse, John Hanlon, Fred and Marie Hurd, Laird Fowler (Texas Parks & Wildlife), Johnny Blass, Jack Richardson, Howard Pitts, John Parks, Dick Leech, Jr., Mike Mills, Genie Strickland, Billy Fuller, "Doc" John Baker, Wayne Thompson, Darrell Leidigh (Mohawk Canoe), Harrold (Joe) and Patsy Little, Nick Rodes, Max and Luella Rhodes, Jerry Gumm, Brad Wimberly, Mike Cichanowski (We-No-Nah Canoes), Louis Aulbach, Steve Wright, John Carter, Ben and Cynthia Fruehauf, Jim McGee, Hill Country Paddlers, Dallas Downriver Club, Houston Canoe Club, J.W. and Reba Collins, David Claunch, Carol Bishop, Dan Hatfield, and last, but certainly not least, Travis Redman.

EQUIPMENT CHECKLIST

Float trips require as much planning and pre-trip preparation as that "once-in-a-lifetime" vacation. In some instances they require more. Example: no matter where you vacation, it's usually possible to pick up a toothbrush round the next corner. Not so when you're camping on gravel bars in the middle of nowhere.

The following is a very general check list which can be applied to trips lasting two or more days. Just a helpful hint on meal planning - prepare each meal, on paper, for the entire trip. This will let you work out a good variety, will eliminate duplication of foods and also ensure that you do not leave that one special ingredient, for that super special meal, at home.

Canoe Gear

- [ ] CANOE
- [ ] PADDLES PLUS SPARE
- [ ] BOW AND STERN ROPES
- [ ] FLOOR RACK
- [ ] PATCH KIT OR DUCT TAPE
- [ ] MAPS
- [ ] FIRST AID KIT
- [ ] COMPASS
- [ ] DRY BAGS
- [ ] WATERPROOF CAMERA CASE
- [ ] _____

Camping Gear

- [ ] TENT (OPTIONAL)
- [ ] TARP/GROUND COVER
- [ ] SLEEPING PADS/AIR MATTRESSES
- [ ] SLEEPING BAGS/BLANKETS ETC.
- [ ] STOVE
- [ ] BOTTLED OR LIQUID FUEL
- [ ] LIGHTS/LANTERN/WITH EXTRA MANTLES
- [ ] WATER
- [ ] EATING AND COOKING UTENSILS
- [ ] ICE CHEST/COOLER (OPTIONAL)
- [ ] FOOD (BY THE MEAL PLUS SNACKS)
- [ ] MATCHES/LIGHTER

- [ ] KNIFE
- [ ] TOILET PAPER
- [ ] SCRUB PAD
- [ ] TRASH BAGS
- [ ] EXTRA ROPE (CLOTHES LINE ETC.)
- [ ] OVEN MITT
- [ ] PAPER TOWELS
- [ ] _____

Personal Gear

- [ ] TOOTH BRUSH/TOOTH PASTE
- [ ] SOAP
- [ ] SHAMPOO
- [ ] DEODORANT
- [ ] COMB/BRUSH
- [ ] MIRROR
- [ ] WASH CLOTH
- [ ] TOWELS
- [ ] NAIL CLIPPERS/EMERY BOARDS
- [ ] PRESCRIPTION MEDICATION
- [ ] SMALL FIRST AID KIT
- [ ] ASPIRIN AND ANTIHISTAMINE
- [ ] CHANGE OF CLOTHES
- [ ] EXTRA SHOES OR CAMP THONGS
- [ ] EXTRA SOCKS
- [ ] SHORTS/BATHING SUIT
- [ ] CAP/HAT
- [ ] SUNGLASSES
- [ ] SUN BLOCK
- [ ] CAMERA/FILM
- [ ] INSECT REPELLANT
- [ ] LIGHT WEIGHT RAIN GEAR
- [ ] REQUIRED LICENSES, PERMITS AND I.D.
- [ ] PERSONAL FISHING GEAR
- [ ] _____

15

WHATZIT?

BACKWAVE: An act of saying "bye, bye" as you plummet down a Class V rapid. Not really, it's a large wave found at the bottom of a ledge or chute. The flow in this wave is opposite to the river current.

B.C.: Before the Corps (of Engineers).

BEAM: The transverse measurement at the canoe's widest point or the drink of choice after a Class V.

BOIL: Water heated at sea level to 212 degrees or, as it pertains to streams, a stream's current which has met an underwater obstruction and is forced upward into a convex mound on the surface. Visually, it resembles the 212 degree water.

BROACHING: Out of control and turning broadside to the current. Usually accompanied by total panic and your entire life flashing before your eyes.

BOTTOM OUT: An abrupt collision with the river bottom, usually at the end of a chute or the base of a drop off. Not to be confused with the "flap" being down on your longjohns.

BUNGY CORD: A great tie down made from parallel rubber strands and covered with a stretchable cloth sheath. Also used for restraint when jumping off high places.

CFS: Not Chicken Fried Steak. Actually, it's water flow measured in cubic feet per second.

CHUTE: A narrow, swift channel flowing between obstructions that has a faster, steeper and stronger current than that of surrounding water.

COOL DUDE: Anyone who has just finished running a Class IV rapid in January, especially if they ran it without a spray cover.

CRATER: A dimple in the moon. Also describes the act needed to totally demolish a canoe or kayak.

DAMITOL: A non-prescription tranquilizer as well as a frequently used canoeing term.

DECKED CANOE: A canoe which has been fitted with a commercial, or homemade, deck/cover to facilitate running turbulent rapids without swamping.

DORK: Synonymous with turkey or clunk. A river runner who consistently does the wrong thing at the wrong time for the wrong reason.

DROP: A portion of a stream where the flow runs vertically but does not free fall.

DUCT TAPE: Tape designed and marketed for sealing air conditioning ducts, but serves exceptionally well as the "best band-aid for banged boats" available.

EDDY: An area of water downstream from an obstruction or on the inside of a bend in which the current is reversed or is circular.

EDDY LINE: The usually well defined boundary separating the reverse flow of the eddy from the primary current direction.

ESKIMO ROLL: Not to be confused with sweet rolls made in an Eskimo bakery, it is the technique used by paddlers remaining in an overturned craft to right the canoe or kayak.

FALLS: A drop carried to the extreme. The water actually falls free.

FERRY: Lateral movement of your boat across current by paddling at an angle upstream. The current will actually push the boat sideways.

GRADIENT: The rate of descent of a stream or river specified in feet per mile.

HAYSTACKS: Not a place to look for a needle, but large waves found where fast, shallow water meets slower, deeper water.

HYDRAULIC CURRENT: A reverse surface current, predominately found below a drop or falls, which flows directly back toward the falling water. A very dangerous place to be.

LEAP YEAR: Comes around every four years and allows an extra day for canoeing in that specific year.

LEFT BANK: The river bank on the left when facing downstream. Opposite from right bank.

LINING: Not what's behind dark storm clouds. It's working a boat downstream around an obstruction or danger spot by the use of ropes from the shore.

LOCALS: Persons living close to the river and having varied opinions as to the exact distance to your take out.

PAINTER: Not to be confused with someone who applies paint. It's really a rope attached to the bow and/or stern of your boat.

PILLOW: A portion of water being forced upward over an underwater obstruction creating a smooth mound or "pillow" on the surface.

POOL: A section of river which is deeper and slower than those areas above or below it.

PORTAGE: To manually carry all gear, equipment and boat around an obstacle which makes this section of the stream non-navigable. A task best handled by your partner while you scout ahead.

RAPIDS: A section of river characterized by fast currents, white water, turbulence and obstructions.

RIFFLE: A baby rapid. Riffles are recognized by shallow flow over gravel bars, ledges or sand and characterized by small waves.

ROCK GARDEN: A typical Texas Hill Country garden where rocks seem to proliferate. Also, a treacherous rapid having many exposed rocks and poorly defined channels.

ROCKER: Recommended for a tired or retired canoeist. Also, the amount of outward curve of the canoe keel from bow to stern.

ROLLER: Same as a back wave. An extremely large one can be termed a "high roller".

SHUTTLE: The moving of one or more vehicles to the take out point. Prevents hitch-hiking.

STANDING WAVE: A large wave immediately downstream from an underwater obstacle. As its name implies, it just stands there, never moving downstream.

STRAINER: An obstruction in a stream such as downed trees, brush or bridge pilings which allow the flow go through, but catch and hold anything the current brings along. These are exceptionally tough on boats and bodies.

TANDEM PADDLES: Not two tanned Democrats paddling. That would be double Dork (see Dork for definition and double it). Seriously, it's a paddle with blades on each end used primarily by kayakists.

TRIM: The angle to the surface at which a boat rides. Good trim makes for easier paddling, better maneuverability and faster speed. The boat should be only slightly higher in the bow for best overall paddling.

U. S. CORPS OF ENGINEERS: A governmental agency seemingly dedicated to dam(n)ing any water which moves.

WHITE WATER: Water containing a large volume of air bubbles. It's generally associated with rapids or any type of stream turbulence. It offers poor support for a boat and decreased paddling efficiency.

Question: Can muddy streams have white water?

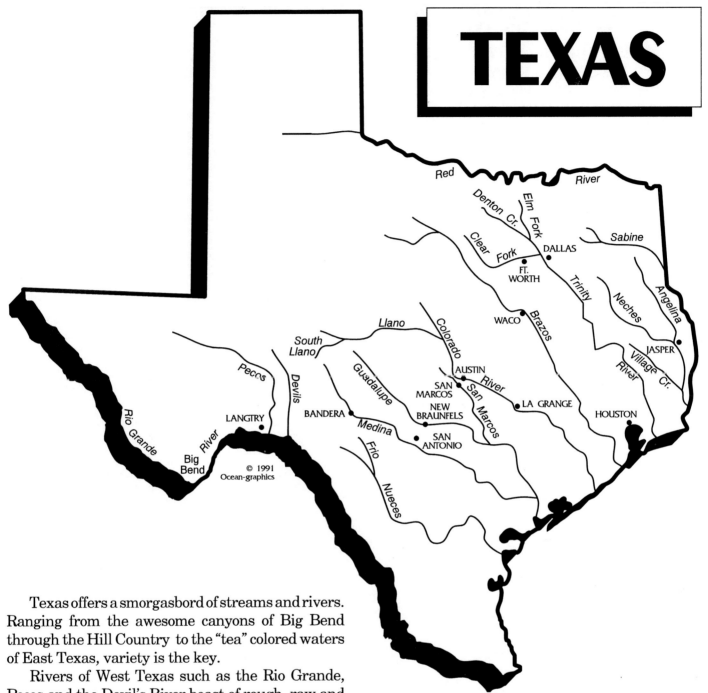

TEXAS

Texas offers a smorgasbord of streams and rivers. Ranging from the awesome canyons of Big Bend through the Hill Country to the "tea" colored waters of East Texas, variety is the key.

Rivers of West Texas such as the Rio Grande, Pecos and the Devil's River boast of rough, raw and remote environments. Whitewater rapids, desolation and the grandeur of the Texas West are all native to these rivers.

Hill Country streams such as the Frio, Medina, Llano, Guadalupe, and San Marcos are all spring fed, scenic, fast flowing and fun. Rapids rarely exceed the Class II rating, but there are a lot of them.

Rivers of the flatlands, the Brazos, Colorado and Trinity are generally easy going, wide and comfortable. They offer the laid back, take-it-easy type of river trips which everyone can enjoy. Large sand and gravel bars are common as the streams create shallow shoal areas between intermittent deep, quiet pools.

The streams of East Texas have their own unique characteristics. The Angelina, Village Creek, the Sabine and the Neches all have the "tea" colored water created by the tannic acid which is formed by the deterioration of the abundant pine needles. These streams run deep and slow between earthen banks shrouded with dense stands of timber. Snow white sandbars and a wide variety of colorful flowers decorate the majority of East Texas streams.

Whatever your river running preference, you can surely find it in Texas!

ANGELINA RIVER

SAM RAYBURN DAM TO BEVILPORT
18.0 MILES

PHYSICAL LOCATION: Jasper County, southeast Texas. Houston 100 miles, Tyler 115 miles, Dallas 210 miles, and Waco 175 miles.

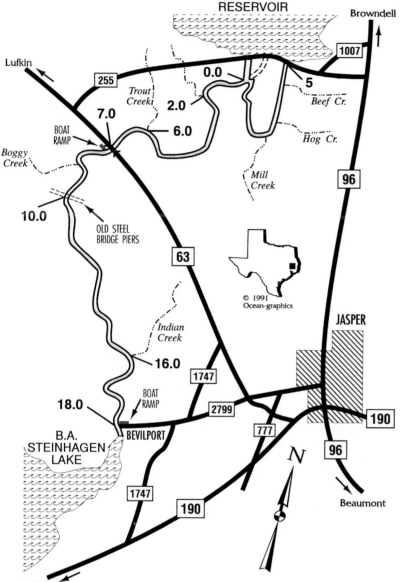

GENERAL COMMENTS: The Angelina is deep, clear and scenic. The left hand channel at the put in below Sam Rayburn Reservoir is a serene, five mile section of the old river channel. It is shallow in places, but can easily be negotiated in a canoe. Bordered by typical east Texas pine and hardwoods, the river is generally well protected from high head winds. The right bank, from the put in to the old steel bridge piers at 10.0 miles, is the south eastern boundary of the Angelina National Forest.

WATER QUALITY: Clean and clear as it comes off the bottom of Sam Rayburn Reservoir. The tannic "tea-colored" water prevalent on most east Texas streams is absent from this section of the Angelina.

WATER FLOW: There will be a current only if water is being released through the dam. Even when no water is being released, the river is extremely deep.

PREFERRED SEASONS: The Angelina offers good conditions year round. The bank vegetation is especially beautiful in spring and autumn. Expect some power boat traffic up from B.A. Steinhagen Lake on weekends during the summer.

HAZARDS: This section has no natural hazards.

PUT IN: South of FM 255 immediately below the dam, or for the lower section, at the boat ramp adjacent to the Hwy. 63 crossing. There is good access and adequate parking areas at both locations.

TAKE OUT: For the upper section take out at the Hwy. 63 crossing. For the lower 11 miles, take out at the Texas Parks & Wildlife boat ramp at Bevilport - 18 miles.

CAMPING: There are no public camp sites along the river. However, there is a limited primitive area at Bevilport. The Martin Dies Jr. State Park, located on Hwy. 190 and B.A. Steinhagen Lake offers 182 camp sites, some with water and electricity, 46 screened shelters, restrooms, showers, dump station, and dining hall, (409) 429-3491.

CANOE RENTAL AND SHUTTLE: None at this printing.

DISTINGUISHING FEATURES: The overall scenic beauty of this river with its multitude of pines and hardwoods, clear deep waters and white sand, has made this portion of the Angelina one of the most popular canoe trips in the state. River access is easy, the tree-covered banks offer protection from the wind and the feeder creeks are serene and scenic side trips.

FISHING: The Angelina is regarded as a top notch fishing stream. Its waters are generally deep and have a lot of natural cover. Fishing for black bass is usually good to great! It is best during non-generating times. Due to the extreme depths of the water, deep running crank baits, floating-diving crank baits, large spinner baits, and plastic worms all produce well. Catfishing is usually good on live bait, especially a few days after a natural rise which gets the water just a little "off color."

AREA ATTRACTIONS: The live, authentic Indian shows presented at the Alabama and Coushatta Indian Reservation located halfway between Woodville and Livingston on Hwy. 190. Entertainment, souvenirs, tours, and food are available.

MAPS: Jasper County highway map and the Pacehill, McGee Bend and the Ebenezer, Texas quadrangles.

RIVER FLOW INFORMATION: Ft. Worth Corps of Engineers, (817) 334-2214 or (817) 334-2196.

ARMAND BAYOU

CLEAR LAKE TO
NORTH OF THE BAY AREA BLVD.

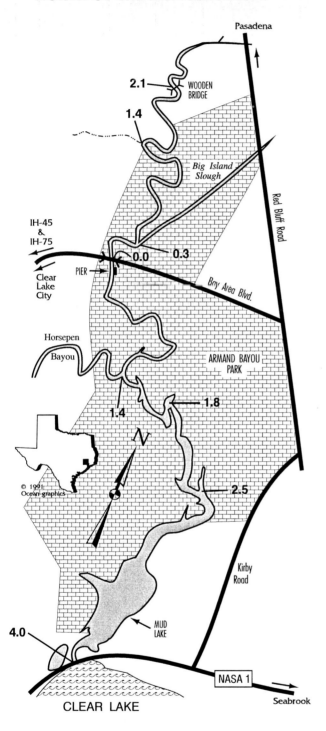

WATER FLOW: There will be no current flow unless there have been exceptionally heavy rains. An above average tide will create some flow going upstream.

PREFERRED SEASONS: Armand Bayou offers good conditions year round. Due to the extreme variations in bank vegetation, spring always offers the most scenic beauty.

HAZARDS: No physical hazards on the bayou.

PUT IN: The put in point is the public ramp, adjacent to the pier, in Armand Bayou Park or other access points in the park. Canoeing either up or down the bayou is enjoyable.

TAKE OUT: Take out at the NASA-1 Road or paddle a turn-around trip, whether going downstream to Clear Lake or upstream to the wooden bridge at 2.1 miles.

CAMPING: There are excellent camping facilities in Armand Bayou Park. Restrooms and adequate camp sites are available.

CANOE RENTAL & SHUTTLE SERVICE: A to Z Action Sports in Seabrook is the closest rental agency, (713) 474-3079.

DISTINGUISHING FEATURES: Armand Bayou is unique in that it represents an unspoiled area of vegetation containing oaks, palmettos, Spanish moss, and many flowering plants.

AREA ATTRACTIONS: NASA Space Center, San Jacinto Monument and the fun things of Houston, including the Astrodome and Astroworld. The beach and ocean at Galveston.

MAPS: Harris County Road Map and the League City topographical quadrangle

WATER FLOW INFORMATION: None needed.

PHYSICAL LOCATION: Harris County in southeast Texas. Houston 20 miles, Galveston 18 miles.

GENERAL COMMENTS: This is an excellent place for the novice or family looking for a fun outing. Easy access, good facilities, and a wilderness atmosphere are all ingredients for a great day or weekend adventure.

WATER QUALITY: Typical coastal bayou water, high in salt content and also murky.

BRAZOS RIVER

HWY. 16 TO HWY. 180
38.7 MILES

PHYSICAL LOCATION: Palo Pinto County in North Central Texas. Ft. Worth 75 miles, Dallas 140 miles, Waco 100 miles, Austin 180 miles, and Houston 250 miles.

GENERAL COMMENTS: Out where "The West Begins," this area is rich in the history of roving Comanches and early Texas settlers. There is little commercial development along the river in this area. Much of it remains the same as in the time of the Comanche and Texas cowboy.

WATER QUALITY: Exceptionally good, cool and clear as it comes off the bottom of Lake Possum Kingdom. It remains good as it flows over rock, gravel and sand for the entire trip.

WATER FLOW: Totally dependent on water release through the generating station at the dam. At low water levels the trip is possible, but there will be a lot of places where walking is necessary.

PREFERRED SEASONS: Spring and late autumn are best. There is not a lot of shade on the Brazos. The summer months are usually too hot for an enjoyable trip, especially if the water is low.

HAZARDS: There are relatively few natural hazards on either of these trips. Common sense and planning will get you down the river safely. The one hazard which might pose a problem is the rapid immediately below the Hwy. 4 bridge. The pilings below the bridge can easily "wrap" a canoe. Look it over before running and if in doubt, portage to the left.

PUT IN: Launch below the Hwy. 16 crossing downstream from Lake Possum Kingdom dam. For an alternate trip, put in at the Hwy. 4 crossing at 19.5 miles.

Dark Valley Bridge (Hwy. 4) take out

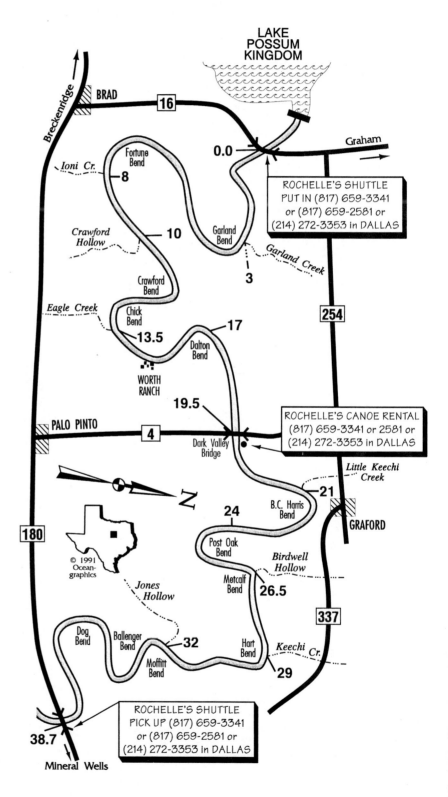

TAKE OUT: For a leisurely two-day float, take out at the Dark Valley Bridge - the Hwy. 4 crossing, 7 miles north of Palo Pinto. If you want to complete the 38.7 miles, count on two more days and take out at U.S. Highway 180, three miles west of Mineral Wells.

CAMPING: There is a limited primitive camping area at the Hwy. 16 put in. Rochelle's offers primitive camping facilities and is located at the northeast corner of the intersection of Hwy. 4 and the river. Natural campsites are plentiful along the river. Be sure to pitch camp ABOVE the generating level of the river.

CANOE RENTALS AND SHUTTLE: Rochelle's at the Hwy. 4 crossing offers both rentals and shuttle service.

DISTINGUISHING FEATURES: This is one of the most scenic and exciting trips the Brazos has to offer. The surrounding countryside is rugged, rocky and isolated. Spectacular rock outcroppings, massive bluffs and boulders frame the solitude of this trip.

FISHING: Black bass and spotted bass are abundant on this trip. However, sufficient water must be released to get them in a feeding mood. Spinners, plastic worms and grubs, small top waters and imitation floating/diving minnows are generally producers. Fish for the spotted bass in or just off the current at drop-offs, ledges or undercut banks. The blacks will hold in the deeper, slower water especially in shaded areas where cover is handy. Catfishing for yellow and channel cats is fair depending on the water flow and season. Trout have been stocked below the dam, but their numbers and size are small.

AREA ATTRACTIONS: The 1,615 acre, Possum Kingdom State Park is located 18 miles north of Caddo on Park Road 33, just off U.S. Hwy. 180. Offers all amenities, plus its own herd of Longhorn cattle. Ft. Richardson State Historical Park is on U.S. Hwy. 281, one mile south of Jacksboro. The old fort facilities include a guard house, hospital, morgue, commissary, barracks, bakery, officers quarters, and magazine.

MAPS: The Palo Pinto County highway map and the Palo Pinto, Texas and Mineral Wells, Texas, topographical quadrangles.

RIVER FLOW INFORMATION: Phone Rochelle's at (817) 659-3341, the Brazos Cooperative - Waco, (817) 752-2501 or the Brazos River Authority - Waco, (817) 776-1441.

21

BRAZOS RIVER
HWY. 180 TO C. J. YOUNG CAMP
33.0 MILES

PHYSICAL LOCATION: Palo Pinto County, North Central Texas. Ft. Worth 70 miles, Dallas 100 miles, Mineral Wells 3 miles (Hwy. 180 crossing), Austin 180 miles, and Houston 250 miles.

GENERAL COMMENTS: This, like the section above it, remains largely in its natural state. The surrounding countryside is rugged, rocky and isolated. There are numerous islands, sand bars, and scenic views of the Palo Pinto Mountains. Although this section will sustain more flow at low generating levels, the river bed is generally wide and unprotected. Navigating into a strong head wind will be tough.

WATER QUALITY: Although not as clear as the previous section, the quality is excellent.

WATER FLOW: Generally low under normal conditions but usually adequate for float trips. Expect some walking in the shallows or shoal areas.

PREFERRED SEASONS: Spring and fall are the optimum seasons. Expect low water and hot days during the summer months.

HAZARDS: The river, under normal conditions, is virtually hazard free, however, the lower trip of this section is long. Prepare and plan accordingly.

PUT IN: For either a short, one day, trip or for the total trip put in below the Hwy. 180 bridge crossing west of Mineral Wells. To run the lower section, launch at Oaks Crossing or the private camp at 12 miles. Although it can be made in 2 days, this lower section should be considered a 3-4 day float.

TAKE OUT: For the short upper section, take out at Oaks Crossing (8.5 miles) or the private camp (12 miles.) For the long, lower float, take out at C. J. Young's camp at 33.0 miles, (817) 325-6052. Alternate take out is the Hwy. 129 crossing at Palo Pinto Creek (37.0 miles), south of Brazos, Texas.

CAMPING: Castle Canoe Rental at the put-in offers camping. The natural camp sites along the river are plentiful and adequate. Be sure to camp above the generating high water mark. Private camps at 12.0 and 33.0 miles offer primitive camping facilities. Lake Mineral Wells State Park, 4 miles east of Mineral Wells and 15 miles west of Weatherford, offers 90 camp sites, restrooms, water, electricity, dump station, concession, and showers, (817) 328-1171.

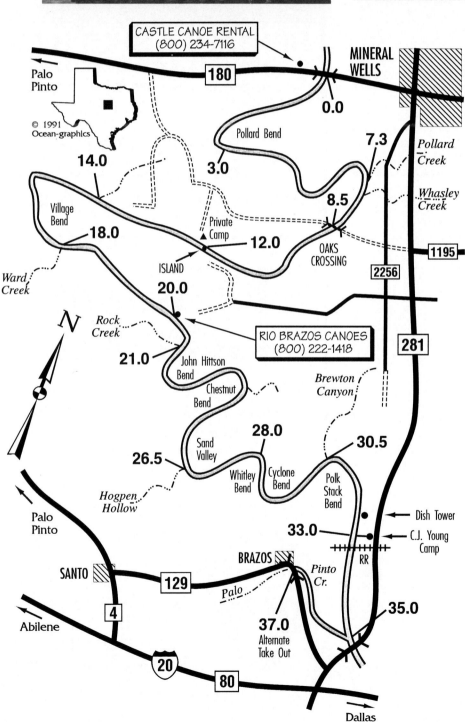

22

CANOE RENTAL & SHUTTLE SERVICE: Castle Canoe Rental, (817) 659-3313 or Rio Brazos Canoes, (800) 222-1418 or (817) 325-9354.

DISTINGUISHING FEATURES: The river and surrounding area is clean and unpolluted. Flow is always adequate for a fun trip when water is being released from Possum Kingdom. Many small islands and large sand/gravel bars offer good camp sites. There are many small, bubbling rapids, but none so severe as to create hazards to health or equipment. The river bed is wide and open.

FISHING: Black and spotted bass are still the primary fishing attractions. This portion of the Brazos does not receive a great amount of fishing pressure. With good water and weather conditions the local bass will hit just about anything. Keep the baits on the small side and stay with low visibility lines. Bait casting, ultra light, spinning or fly tackle will all produce fish. They won't be large, but they'll be fun.

MAPS: The Palo Pinto County Road Map. Topographical maps are Abilene and Lipan, Texas quadrangles.

RIVER FLOW INFORMATION: Castle Canoe Rental, (817) 659-3313; Rio Brazos Canoes, (817) 325-9354; Brazos Cooperative, Waco (817) 752-2501 and Brazos River Authority, Waco (817) 776-1441.

BRAZOS RIVER
C. J. YOUNG CAMP TO FM 1189
27.1 MILES

PHYSICAL LOCATION: Palo Pinto and Parker Counties. Mineral Wells (13 miles - U.S. 281 crossing), Ft. Worth 70 miles, Dallas 100 miles, Austin 170 miles, and Houston 240 miles.

GENERAL COMMENTS: Avoid the hot summer months if possible. The wide river can be extremely tiresome in a high southerly wind. Good trip for the novice or family, but allow some time for the trip. Take time to swim, fish, and enjoy the river. Probable walking in some of the short shoal areas, especially during the dry seasons.

WATER QUALITY: Clear and clean flowing over gravel, rock, and numerous sand shoals.

WATER FLOW: The river will have numerous shallow areas, but walking will be minimal, especially if any water is being released from Possum Kingdom.

PREFERRED SEASONS: Fall and Spring. Water flow is generally better, temperatures are more tolerable, and the scenic beauty is at its best.

HAZARDS: None, other than those presented by the remoteness of the area.

PUT IN: Launch for the top 14.5 mile section at C.J. Young's camp (just past the railroad crossing on Hwy. 281), (817) 325-6052. There is a small fee for leaving a vehicle or to put in/take out. An alternate put in is on Palo Pinto Creek at the Hwy. 129 crossing, south of the small town of Brazos, Texas. The launch site for the lower 12.6 miles is off the west side of the river below the IH-20/Hwy. 80 crossing at 14.5 miles.

Abilene

BRAZOS

Palo Pinto Creek

129

281 → Mineral Wells

0.0

C. J. Young Camp

© 1991 Ocean-graphics

Stephenville

2.2

Dobbs Valley

4.2

6.2

Island

20

80

Gilbert Valley

10.2

Littlefield Bend

8.2

Rock Creek

N

Meeks Bend

14.5

11.7

Hill Creek

Rock Creek

Potato Hill Bend

18.5

113

Millsap

20

Lazy Bend

18.8

Grindstone Creek

Cougar Branch

24.0

Brock Junction

Wash Branch

25.5

DENNIS

1189

BROCK

Lipan

27.1

Weatherford

TAKE OUT: For the upper section, take out at the IH-20/Hwy. 80 crossing. If you float the lower section or take the entire trip take out at the FM 1189 crossing at Dennis.

CAMPING: Although primitive river sites are abundant, there are no public/private camps in this area. When you camp in the river bed stay above the generating high water mark.

CANOE RENTAL & SHUTTLE SERVICE: The closest is Rio Brazos Canoes, off Hwy. 281, south of Mineral Wells, (800) 222-1418 or (817) 325-9354.

DISTINGUISHING FEATURES: The river becomes slower and wider as it meanders through decreasingly rugged country. In many places the craggy bluffs give way to wooded bottom lands. Sand bars are large and abundant offering excellent camping areas or paddling breaks.

FISHING: The same tackle, techniques and fish prevail as on the previous Brazos sections. Count on the main action coming from largemouth and spotted bass. Stay with medium to light tackle with lures to match.

MAPS: Palo Pinto and Parker County Road Maps. The topographical maps are the Lipan and Dennis Texas quadrangles.

RIVER FLOW INFORMATION: Rio Brazos Canoes, (817) 325-9354; Brazos Cooperative, Waco (817) 752-2501 or Brazos River Authority, Waco (817) 776-1441.

BRAZOS RIVER
MITCHELL FORD TO BRAZOS POINT CROSSING
28.5 MILES

PHYSICAL LOCATION: Somervell County in north Central Texas. Cleburne 15 miles, Dallas 75 miles, Waco 100 miles, Austin 170 miles, and Houston 260 miles.

GENERAL COMMENTS: Avoid the hot summer months. The river is wide and unprotected from the sun and wind. With adequate water flow from Lake Granbury, this is a good trip for the novice or family. However, the length of this trip makes good planning essential. This is a good "get-away-from-it-all" trip. It's safe, scenic and accessible.

WATER QUALITY: The water quality is excellent as it comes directly from the bottom of Lake Granbury.

WATER FLOW: The upper section, Mitchell Ford to FM 200, is almost totally dependent on water being released from the reservoir. If there is little or no water release - consider the lower section, FM 200 to the crossing northeast of Brazos Point.

PREFERRED SEASONS: Like the other sections of the Brazos, spring and fall are the best. Much will depend upon the volume of water being released from the lake. A strong southerly wind remains a problem. Avoid hot dry seasons.

PUT IN: To run the upper 15.5 miles - launch at Mitchell Ford, west of FM 2174. For the lower 13 miles, put in below the FM 200 crossing south of Rainbow. It is possible to put in at the Hwy. 67 crossing east of Glen Rose, but not recommended. The east bank is steep and the trail is long.

TAKE OUT: The FM 200 crossing is the best take out for the upper section. The take out for the lower, 13 mile trip, is at Braden's Camp, just below the bridge crossing and on the south bank.

CAMPING: On the river, camp sites are abundant and adequate. Be sure to pitch camp above the generating high water mark. Keller's Camp, (817) 897-2314 and Oakdale's Camp 'N' Fish, (817) 897-2478 are both located on the upper section from Mitchell Ford to FM 200. Dinosaur Valley State Park, located 4 miles west of Glen Rose via U.S. 67 and FM 205 offers primitive camping and facilities. Braden's Camp (817) 797-4561, is at the take out for the lower section, northeast of Brazos Point.

CANOE RENTAL & SHUTTLE SERVICE: The rental agencies in this area offer both canoes and shuttle service. See the map for locations and phone numbers.

DISTINGUISHING FEATURES: This section is very scenic, flowing through heavily vegetated rolling hills covered with cedar, live oak, and post oak. The Paluxy River intersects the Brazos 1.5 miles below the Highway 67 crossing.

FISHING: Black bass and spotted bass are abundant but generally small. Fish the fast water for the spotted bass and concentrate on slow, deep pools with natural cover for the black bass. Tackle can vary from the heavy bass rig to ultra light, however, the clearer the water, the lighter and less visible the line needs to be. Clear water also dictates smaller baits. Productive lures will range from large, noisy top water's to small spinners and jigs. Catfishing is usually good except when the river is extremely low and clear. The camps in this area can supply up-to-date information on who's biting what and where. Consult some of these folks before you make your trip.

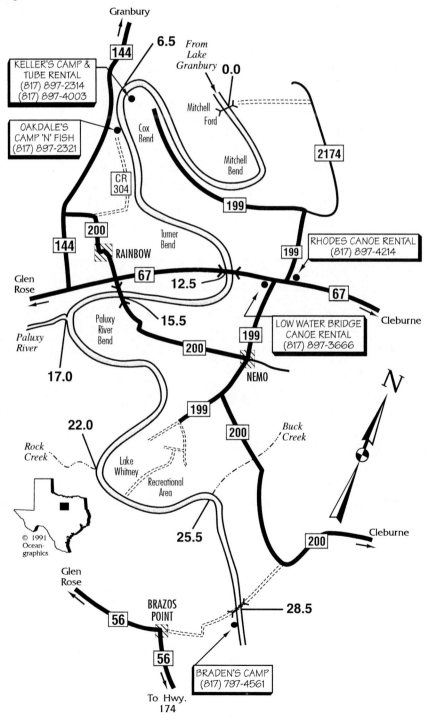

AREA ATTRACTIONS: The Dinosaur Valley State Park off FM 205, west of Glen Rose. Here, the 105 million year-old formations have eroded to expose numerous dinosaur tracks and there is a model exhibit of a 70' Brontosaurus and a 45' Tyrannosaurus Rex. Other attractions include a van tour of the Comanche Peak nuclear power plant, the 5,000 seat Texas Amphitheater in Glen Rose — open with live shows each Friday and Saturday evening from June 1 through November 24, and Fossil Rim Wildlife Center, on Hwy. 67 south. These 2,900 acres are the homes of more than 1,000 free roaming animals. Over 10 miles of paved roads allow visitors to enjoy an African safari without leaving their cars.

MAPS: Somervell and Hood County Road maps. Nemo, Glen Rose and Brazos Point, Texas topographical quadrangles.

RIVER FLOW INFORMATION: Keller's Camp and Tube Rental (817) 897-2314, Rhodes Canoe Rental (817) 897-4214, Low Water Bridge Canoe Rental (817) 897-3666, the Brazos Cooperative, Waco (817) 752-2501 and the Brazos River Authority in Waco (817) 776-1441.

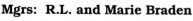

BRAZOS RIVER

LAKE WHITNEY
TO CAMERON PARK (WACO)
36.0 MILES

PHYSICAL LOCATION: McLennan, Hill, and Bosque Counties in Central Texas. Waco 30 miles, Dallas 80 miles, Austin 175 miles, Houston 220 miles, and San Antonio 270 miles.

GENERAL COMMENTS: This section of the Brazos has good access, can easily be broken into three separate trips and offers fun floats for almost everyone. This section can be enjoyed by novices, families or groups. For a little extra, take the 4 mile side trip up or down the Bosque River, downstream from the FM 3051 crossing.

WATER QUALITY: Excellent flowing over sand and gravel. Many clean, clear flowing springs.

WATER FLOW: Upper section totally dependent upon water release from Whitney Dam. Many shallow areas above FM 2114 crossing when water is not being released. Also long stretches of shallow water exist between Reddell's Camp and the headwaters of Lake Brazos. No shallow areas are present at generating levels. Although some walking maybe required, river is negotiable at low water levels.

PREFERRED SEASONS: Like other sections of the Brazos, spring and autumn offer the overall best river and weather conditions. However, the section between the FM 2114 crossing and Reddell's Camp has enough water for enjoyable floats, even when the river is low during the hotter summer months.

HAZARDS: A strong southerly wind will probably be the only hazard encountered on this section of the Brazos at normal water levels.

"It Shrunk"

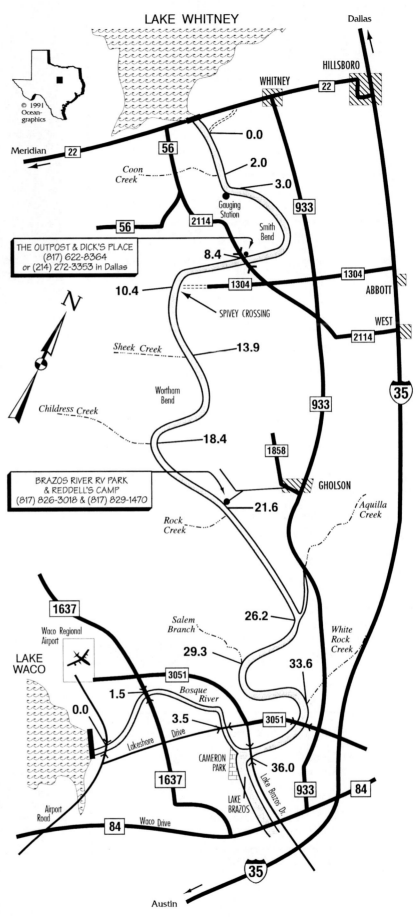

in the summer months. Shallow in many areas and will demand some walking at nongenerating levels.

FISHING: Fishing for largemouth and spotted bass is usually good. It is generally better at low or no generating levels. Fish the spots showing natural cover where shallow water meets deep water, shaded areas and fast flowing water next to undercut banks. Spinners, small topwaters, plastic worms, grubs and shallow running floating/diving baits are all producers. Use light, low visibility line for best results.

AREA ATTRACTIONS: In Waco there are historic Fort Fisher and the Texas Ranger Museum or you might have dinner on the Brazos Queen, a replica of an old paddle boat.

MAPS: The McLennan, Hill, and Bosque County road maps. The topographical maps are the Allen Bend, Whitney, Laguna Park, Smith's Bend, China Springs, Gholson, and Waco West, Texas quadrangles.

RIVER FLOW INFORMATION: The Outpost-Dick's Place, (817) 622-8364; Reddell's Camp, (817) 826-3018 or 829-1470; or the Corps of Engineers in Fort Worth (817) 334-2214, or (817) 334-2196.

PUT IN: Put in for the three trips is immediately below the dam off the east bank; at Dick's Place at the FM 2114 crossing - 8.4 miles or Reddell's Camp west of Gholson, Texas at 21.6 miles. There will be a charge for putting in or taking out at the private camps.

TAKE OUT: Take out for the three sections is Dick's Place at 8.4 miles, Reddell's Camp at 21.6 miles, and at Cameron Park (west side) or along Lake Brazos Drive (east side), both at 36.0 miles.

CAMPING: There is a public camping area with R.V. hookups, restrooms, shelters, and water adjacent to the launch point below the dam. Reddell's offers camping areas with water, electricity, fuel, R.V. hookups, restrooms, pavilion, and fire grates. Many natural camp sites can be found along the river. Be aware of the ever present sand bars and fire ants along the river. They both can make any camp site unpleasant. The Lake Whitney Recreational Area is located on the lake, 4 miles southwest of Whitney on FM 2114. It offers 137 camp sites, water, electricity, screened shelters, restrooms, showers, dump station and screened group shelters - (817) 694-3793.

CANOE RENTAL & SHUTTLE SERVICE: The Outpost-Dick's Place, (817) 622-8364, offers rentals and shuttles only for their own canoes.

DISTINGUISHING FEATURES: A wide, clear and clean river. Many sand and gravel bars, limestone bluffs and springs. Very hot

Launch below Whitney Dam

BRAZOS RIVER
HIDALGO FALLS

PHYSICAL LOCATION: Brazos and Washington Counties in South Central Texas. Navasota 8 miles, Houston 60 miles, Austin 125 miles, and San Antonio 165 miles.

GENERAL COMMENTS: This is not to be considered a "float trip." It is a "run the rapids, turn around and run 'em again" section of river. This is a great place to test skill in whitewater, learn whitewater techniques, test new equipment or just have a great time running and re-running the rapids.

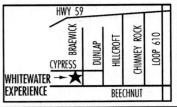
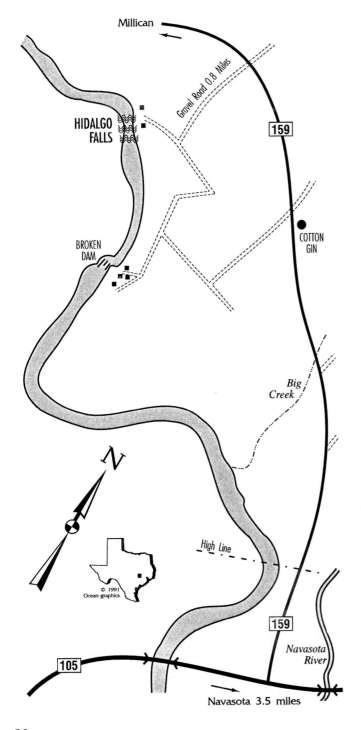

Millican

Gravel Road 0.8 Miles

159

HIDALGO FALLS

BROKEN DAM

COTTON GIN

N

© 1991 Ocean-graphics

Big Creek

High Line

159

Navasota River

105

Navasota 3.5 miles

WATER QUALITY: Ranges from off color to muddy depending on how long it's been since the last rain.

WATER FLOW: Always adequate for running the series of rapids and small falls. Rapids, depending on flow level, will range between Class I and Class IV categories.

PREFERRED SEASONS: Anytime you don't mind getting wet.

HAZARDS: None except the heavy whitewater and large standing waves. Be able to handle yourself and your equipment if capsized in the fast water.

PUT IN: Launch at the private camp immediately above the first falls. Take FM 159 3.2 miles north off Hwy. 105. Take a left on the gravel road at the 3.2 mile mark, go .8 mile down the gravel road to a "T," take the right road to the river. Someone MAY be at the river camp to collect a put in fee. However, it will be wise to pick up a key to the gate at the Shell station on the north side of Hwy. 105/90 just inside the Navasota, Texas city limits.

TAKE OUT: Take out where you put in or take the short 5 mile float trip to the Hwy. 105 crossing.

CAMPING: Washington on the Brazos Park, just south of Hwy. 105, can be used for day camping only. The is a limited primitive camping area adjacent to the put in above Hidalgo Falls.

CANOE RENTAL AND SHUTTLES: You probably won't need a shuttle here. The closest rental agency is Whitewater Experience in Houston.

DISTINGUISHING FEATURES: The wide Brazos tumbles over shallow falls and around massive boulders. The shallow quiet area along the east bank allows an easy route to get your canoe or kayak back upstream to re-run the rapids. High standing waves, souse holes and abundant whitewater churn the Brazos at this point.

FISHING: There is excellent catfishing along this section of the Brazos.

AREA ATTRACTIONS: Just about anything you want to do is in Houston only 60 miles or so down the road.

MAPS: The Washington and Brazos County road maps. The topographical maps are the Washington and Millican County quadrangles.

RIVER FLOW INFORMATION: Whitewater Experience (713) 522-2848.

CADDO LAKE

PHYSICAL LOCATION: Harrison and Marion Counties in North East Texas. Marshall 18 miles, Dallas 150 miles, Lufkin 95 miles, Houston 210 miles and Jefferson 12 miles.

GENERAL COMMENTS: Have maps and compass. It's easy to get lost when everything looks alike. If launching at Hwy. 43 or Caddo Lake State Park, you enter the Carter Lake area through Carter Lake Canal, marked with Boat Channel Marker #3. If putting in at Blair's Landing, you reach Carter Lake via Smith's Slough, marked with name sign and Boat Channel Marker #3-A.

WATER QUALITY: Good to excellent. Dark - characteristic of East Texas streams.

WATER FLOW: None - flat water, back up from Caddo Lake, the largest natural lake in the south.

PUT IN/TAKE OUT: There are three well-defined put in/take out points: The first is at the Hwy. 43 public boat ramp approximately 2 miles north of Hwy. 134. Adequate parking is available. The second is located in the Caddo Lake State Park. There is a small entrance fee to the park. There are restrooms, picnic areas, camping, and showers. The third is at Blair's Landing. Stay on FM 2198 to Uncertain, Texas. Take a left on the Mound Pond Road after passing the Caddo Lake Church (it's on your right).

CAMPING: The best camp sites are the islands between Old House Slough and Carters Chute. The islands in this area are two or three feet above water level and offer good camp sites or picnic areas. It's approximately 6 miles to Blair's Landing and approximately 10 miles from Hwy. 43. Caddo Lake State Park is off Hwy. 43 via FM 2198 and PR 2. This park has 48 campsites, water, electricity, 9 cabins, screened shelters, restrooms, showers, dump station, concessions, recreation hall, boat ramp, and seasonal canoe rental. For more park information, call (903) 679-3351.

CANOE RENTAL & SHUTTLE SERVICE: Available in the area.

DISTINGUISHING FEATURES: Very scenic and totally remote. Extensive lily pads and Spanish moss covered cypress trees. Very popular fishing and bird watching area.

FISHING: Large mouth bass are the primary game fish in this area. Due to the extensive heavy cover, moss, lily pads, cypress roots and downed timber, weed-less lures and heavy lines are recommended. Plastic worms, jig and pig and other weed-less rigged bottom bumping baits take the majority of fish from Caddo. Noisy top waters and shallow running spinning baits generally produce well in spring and early summer.

MAPS: The Harrison and Marion County road map. The topographical maps are the Karnack and Smithland, Texas quadrangles; the Potters Point and Trees, Texas/Louisiana quadrangles. We also recommend using a fishing/navigational map of Caddo Lake.

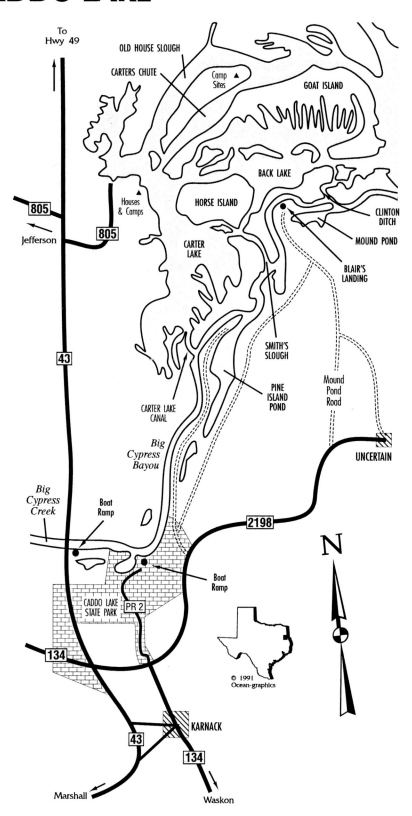

LAKE AND BAYOU INFORMATION: Caddo Lake State Park (903) 679-3351.

COLORADO RIVER
HWY. 190 TO COLORADO BEND STATE PARK
29.8 MILES

Map labels:

To Hwy. 580 · 190 · 190 · Lampasas · 0.0 · Red Bluff · 1.9 · Burnt Branch · Antelope Creek · Lost Branch · 3.3 · 4.9 · N · © 1991 Ocean-graphics · Salt Creek · Rough Creek · Raven Bluff · 7.0 · Lometa · Raven Cliff · Glory Hole · 9.6 · 581 · San Saba · 11.6 · 580 · 580 · 580 · Lampasas · Flat Rock · 16.5 · Mc Anelly Creek · 15 · 17.5 · Lynch Creek · Cherokee Creek · 19.4 · BEND · Cherokee · 501 · Barefoot Falls · Mc Anelly Bend · Brahma Canyon · Windy Canyon · Eagle Draw · Sulphur Springs · 22.2 · Tie Slide Creek · Hughes Hollow · 23.0 · Gorman Falls · 25.4 · Gorman Cr. · Gorman Cave · COLORADO BEND STATE PARK · Hurley Hollow · Post Oak Creek · Yancey Creek · 28.5 · 29.8 · Lake Buchanan - 12 miles · Springs

---

PHYSICAL LOCATION: San Saba, Lampasas Counties in Central Texas. Waco 120 miles, Austin 90 miles, Houston 280 miles, and San Antonio 175 miles.

GENERAL COMMENTS: Many of the private roads are closed during deer season. It's not recommended that the trip be taken during that period. This is generally a remote section with few public access points. Each of the sections can be floated in one day if you really push it. However, it's recommended that you allow at least a day and a half for each section. Be sure to include a good pair of wading/walking shoes if you plan on making the trip in mid to late summer. Everyone can enjoy this trip at almost anytime of the year.

WATER QUALITY: Clear and clean as it flows intermittently over solid rock and gravel.

WATER FLOW: Generally there is adequate flow for an enjoyable trip. However, during extended dry periods there will be many sections with low water.

PREFERRED SEASONS: Spring primarily. Fall is a good second choice. Water and weather conditions are more favorable during these seasons.

HAZARDS: Although many of the small rapids can cause some minor problems, the two major areas to look out for are Barefoot Falls between Lynch Creek and Brahma Canyon and Gorman Falls at 25.4 miles.

PUT IN: Put in at the Highway 190 crossing west of Lampasas, or for the trip on the lower section put in at Flat Rock, west of Bend, Texas.

TAKEOUT: If floating the upper section, the first take out will be Flat Rock at the 15.0 mile point, west of Bend, Texas off of Hwy. 580. The second take out is at Sulphur Springs Camp at 22.2 miles. There is a nominal charge for camping or taking out at the Sulphur Springs Camp and Flat Rock. NOTE: Gorman Falls is now closed to the public and does not allow canoe put in or take out. If you pass Sulphur Springs, plan on taking out in Colorado Bend State Park at 29.8 miles. If you miss this last take out, remember it's another 12 plus miles to Lake Buchanan.

CAMPING: Colorado Bend State Park (915) 628-3240, offers primitive camping only, water and chemical toilets, picnic areas and boat ramp. From Bend, Texas there is approximately 3.6 miles of unpaved road, then 6 miles of rough unpaved road to the Park Headquarters near the river. Sulphur Springs Camp at the 22.2 mile mark offers primitive camping facilities. Natural primitive camp sites along the river are numerous and adequate. When canoe

camping, stay in the river bed and off private property.

CANOE RENTAL & SHUTTLE SERVICE: Sulphur Springs Camp has canoes and tubes Some of the camp operators or the locals will shuttle the vehicle for a fee.

DISTINGUISHING FEATURES: There are many shallow, exciting rapids along the entire trip. Most occur where the creeks intersect the river. The upper section is a twisting, remote scenic stretch of river. There is a small fun rapid immediately above the bridge crossing at Bend. There are others below the intersection of Cherokee Creek. Barefoot Falls, between Lynch Creek and Brahma Canyon, is one of the most photogenic and exciting portions of this trip.

FISHING: White/Sand Bass fishing is tremendous during the spring run up from Lake Buchanan. Small jigs, usually white or yellow, fished in tandem (2 at a time) are proven killers on the white bass. Black bass and spotted bass can be taken any time of the year except the exceptionally cold days of winter. Stay with light weight tackle and light weight, low visibility lines. Concentrate on the shaded areas and spots with medium to slow currents.

AREA ATTRACTIONS: The Vanishing Texas River Cruise up the Colorado from Lake Buchanan offers a close up view of the Bald Eagle, wildlife studies and the scenic beauty of the Colorado River and the Texas Hill Country. For information on the cruise, call (512) 756-6986.

MAPS: San Saba and Lampasas County Road Maps. The topographic maps are the Bend and the Wolf Ridge Texas quadrangles.

RIVER FLOW INFORMATION: Colorado Bend State Park (915) 628-3240.

COLORADO RIVER
HWY. 183 (AUSTIN) TO BASTROP
50.0 MILES

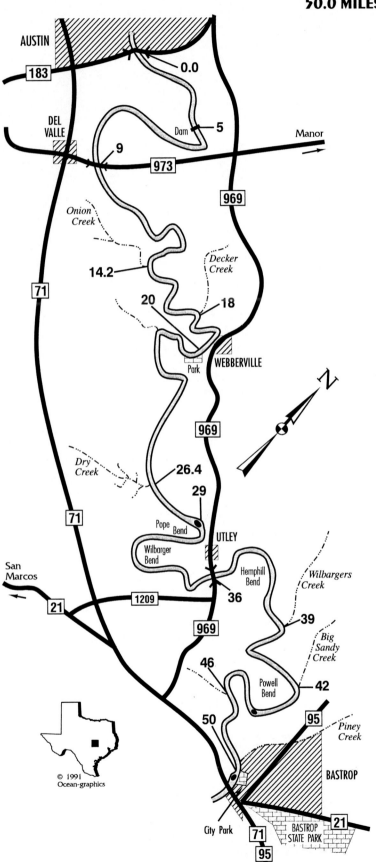

PHYSICAL LOCATION: On the edge of the Texas Hill Country in Travis and Bastrop Counties in South Central Texas. Southern outskirts of Austin, San Antonio 95 miles, Waco 100 miles, Houston 220 miles, and Dallas 200 miles.

GENERAL COMMENTS: The river is wide and slow moving - a strong head wind will cause problems as it will along the entire Colorado River. Although the total trip is long, there are enough put in/take out points to break this section into a series of trips. This is a good family or group trip. Prior to 1984 this section of the Colorado was a "dumping" area for the overtaxed sewage disposal system of Austin. In 1984 The CCC, Clean Clear Colorado River Association was formed to initiate a clean up of the river. With the help of numerous individuals, The Texas Parks and Wildlife Dept. and the Lower Colorado River Authority, the Colorado River had regained most of its clarity, cleanliness and beauty by 1990. On February 1, 1991, the Texas Water Commission initiated a program which gives citizens the opportunity to help in protecting Texas' water resources. If you're interested, call Dave Buzan at (512) 463-8206.

WATER QUALITY: Good and clear as it flows out of Town Lake in Austin. Sand, gravel, and rock bottom.

WATER FLOW: Usually very good and adequate for float or fishing trips. Some shoals and gravel bars will be encountered but will pose no problems except during excessively hot, dry seasons creating below average river conditions.

PREFERRED SEASONS: Any time there is adequate flow. Precautions should be taken during extreme cold weather due to the possibility of having to walk in the shallow areas.

HAZARDS: There is a 3 foot high dam located approximately halfway between Hwy. 183 and FM 973

(5 miles,) the hydraulic current here can be dangerous at normal and high water levels. Overall, the lower Colorado is virtually hazard free.

PUT IN: Put in below the Hwy. 183 crossing (Montopolis Bridge) in East Austin. An alternate put in/take out point would be the county park at Webberville (20 river miles and approximately 10 miles from Austin on FM 969). There is good access and a launching ramp at the park.

TAKE OUT: Take out below the FM 969 bridge at 36 miles or make the total trip and take out at the city park in Bastrop. See the Bastrop to Smithville summary for directions to the park. An emergency put in/take out is in the Pope Bend area. A trail comes down to the river 1.8 miles by road above the FM 969 crossing.

CAMPING: Bastrop State Park (512) 321-2101, located one mile east of Bastrop on SH 21 offers 72 campsites, water, electricity, cabins, lodge, restrooms, showers, dump station, group camp, primitive camping area and park store. Camp sites with picnic tables are available in the county park at Webberville. There is a limited area for camping at the FM 969 crossing and at the city park in Bastrop. Natural camp sites are abundant and adequate.

CANOE RENTAL & SHUTTLE SERVICE: None in the area.

DISTINGUISHING FEATURES: Most of the creeks along this section are picturesque and beautiful, especially Onion Creek. There are many gravel bars and islands offering excellent camp sites.

Accordin' to this map, there's a portage around here somewhere

FISHING: Largemouth and spotted bass are abundant in the Colorado. They will generally average larger sizes than their relatives in the faster flowing streams. Areas with slow to moderate current such as shaded undercut banks, brush piles, drop-offs and creek mouths always seem to hold bass. Small crank baits, plastic worms or grubs, small shallow running spinning baits and small top waters are all good producers.

AREA ATTRACTIONS: Enjoy pari-mutuel horse racing at Manor Downs at Manor, Texas just east of Austin. The bright lights of Austin offer an unending menu of activities, tours and assorted fun things to do, places to go and things to see.

MAPS: The Travis and Bastrop County road maps. The topographical maps are the Bastrop, Austin East, and Montopolis, Texas quadrangles.

RIVER FLOW INFORMATION: Colorado River Longhorn Canoes in Columbus, (409) 732-3723.

COLORADO RIVER
BASTROP TO SMITHVILLE
26.2 MILES

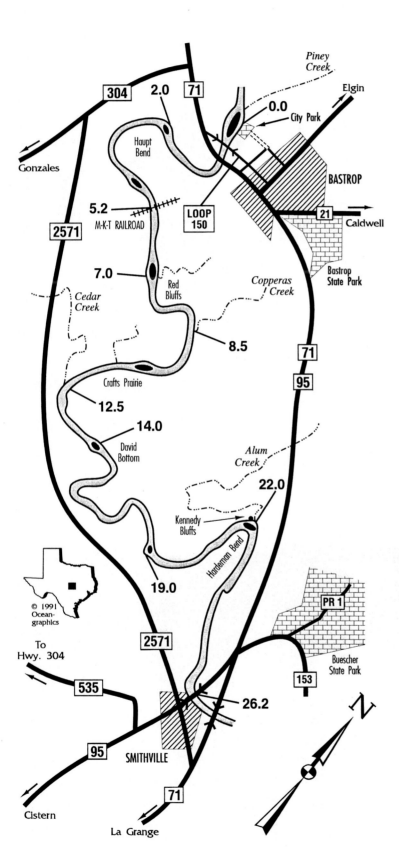

PHYSICAL LOCATION: Bastrop County in South Central Texas. Austin 30 miles, Houston 200 miles, Waco 115 miles, and San Antonio 90 miles.

GENERAL COMMENTS: There are no hazardous areas or rapids on this trip. It is a good group trip, but allow plenty of time. There are no access points from the put in to the take out, except over private property. Due to the river being wide and shallow, a high south wind will make this a tough trip.

WATER QUALITY: Clean and clear as it flows over sand, gravel, and some rock outcroppings. Will be extremely muddy after local rains.

WATER FLOW: Though some shoal areas exist, there is always adequate flow for enjoyable float trips.

PREFERRED SEASONS: Anytime. Spring and fall naturally are the most scenic, and temperatures are more conducive to canoeing.

HAZARDS: There are virtually no water hazards on the river. The trip length can be demanding. Allow enough time to comfortably make the trip. The Colorado like any of the Central and South Texas streams, supports its share of fire ants. Keep these mean little critters in mind when walking the shore lines or pitching camp.

PUT IN: City Park boat ramp, northwest of Bastrop. To reach the put in, go north of Hwy. 71 on Main Street. Stay north on Main until you reach Farm Street. Turn left on Farm Street and go directly to the river.

TAKE OUT: Take out below the Hwy. 71 bridge north of Smithville. There is good access to the river and a launching ramp.

CAMPING: There are public camping areas in Bastrop State Park (512) 321-2101, Bastrop City Park, and Buescher State Park (512) 237-2241. The abundant sand and gravel bars offer a variety of natural camping areas. If camping on the bank, as always, obtain the landowner's permission.

CANOE RENTAL AND SHUTTLE: None in the area.

DISTINGUISHING FEATURES: Slow moving river with wooded banks consisting of pecan, elm, sycamore, and willow trees. The river is generally wide with numerous sand and gravel bars. This area is fairly remote with very few access points.

FISHING: The same general fishing information will apply to this section as to the previous trip.

AREA ATTRACTIONS: Same as the previous section.

MAPS: The Bastrop County road map. The topographical maps are the Bastrop and Smithville, Texas quadrangles.

RIVER FLOW INFORMATION: Colorado River Longhorn Canoes in Columbus, (409) 732-3723.

COLORADO RIVER

SMITHVILLE TO LA GRANGE
36.2 MILES

PHYSICAL LOCATION: Located in Bastrop and Fayette, Counties in south central Texas. Austin 25 miles, Houston 180 miles, San Antonio 90 miles, and Waco 110 miles.

GENERAL COMMENTS: This is a leisurely and scenic trip but it's long. Keep this in mind when planning the trip. Be in fair physical condition and allow plenty of time.

WATER QUALITY: Generally good, with the exception being after local rains. Then the river becomes muddy due to the red sandy soil.

WATER FLOW: Usually adequate for any float trips. No portages. Even the shoal areas are short and should present no problems.

PREFERRED SEASONS: Water flow during most seasons is adequate for enjoyable float trips. Spring and autumn are the most colorful, but this section of the Colorado is a good trip any time of the year.

HAZARDS: The river is virtually hazard free. Be on the look out for the troublesome fire ants.

PUT IN: Put in below the Hwy. 71 crossing on the northwest side. An existing Texas Parks and Wildlife boat ramp offers good access.

TAKE OUT: Take out on the east bank downstream from the Hwy. 71 crossing west of La Grange. There is a small camping area here, good access and a boat ramp.

CAMPING: There is space for camping at both the put in and take out points. Buescher State Park (512) 237-2241, near the put in, offers the most in camping facilities and amenities.

CANOE RENTALS AND SHUTTLES: Colorado River Longhorn Canoes, (409) 732-3723.

DISTINGUISHING FEATURES: Several large cliffs exist along this section, and many springs lined with ferns issue from these formations. Many petrified logs and fossils have been discovered in the cut banks in this area.

FISHING: Basically the same regarding fish and equipment as the previous section.

AREA ATTRACTIONS: Monument Hill in La Grange. It bears a memorial dedicated to Captain Nicholas Dawson and his men, who fought and died at Salado Creek and to the men killed in the "Black Bean Lottery" massacre following the Mier Expedition of 1842. The bodies of these Texas heroes were brought to Monument Hill in 1848 to be reburied. Another attraction in La Grange is the Kreische Brewery. La Grange was home to the infamous "Chicken Ranch," made famous by Burt Reynolds and Dolly Parton in the movie, "The Best Little Whorehouse in Texas." For further information, contact the La Grange Chamber of Commerce, (409) 968-5756.

MAPS: Bastrop and Fayette County road maps. The topographical maps are the Smithville and La Grange West Texas quadrangles.

RIVER FLOW INFORMATION: Colorado River Longhorn Canoes in Columbus, (409) 732-3723.

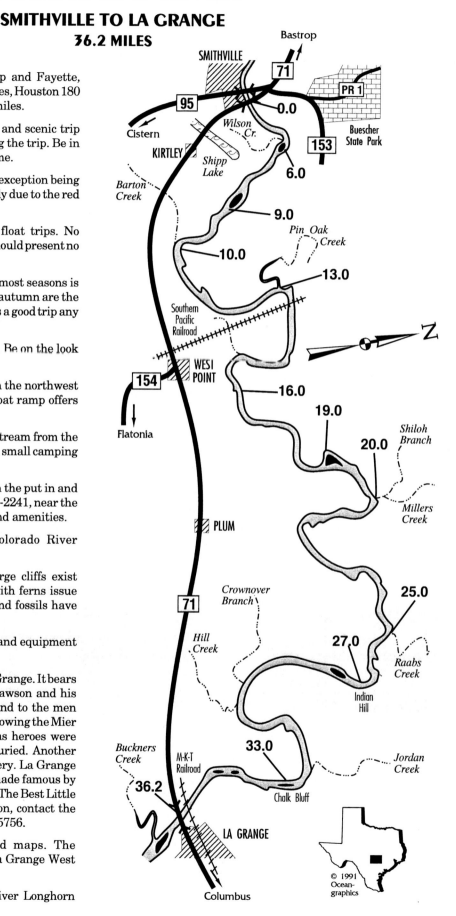

COLORADO RIVER

LA GRANGE TO COLUMBUS
43.0 MILES

PHYSICAL LOCATION: Fayette and Colorado Counties in South Central Texas. Houston 100 miles, Austin 70 miles, Dallas 250 miles, Waco 120 miles.

GENERAL COMMENTS: A scenic trip which everyone can enjoy during almost any season. Its many islands offer gravel "rest areas" or camp sites. If the river is clear, bass fishing is good. When muddy, the catfish take over. Due to the width and shallow areas, this trip is really tough in a strong southerly wind. Also, the trip length should be taken into consideration. There are no public access points between La Grange and Columbus.

WATER QUALITY: Good. Generally clear and clean as it flows over the gravel and sand river bed. Easily muddied after rains, but remains virtually non-polluted.

WATER FLOW: Always adequate for an enjoyable float trip. However, expect some short shallow areas requiring some walking during low water periods.

PREFERRED SEASONS: This portion of the Colorado can be enjoyed during any season although spring and autumn generally offer optimum conditions.

HAZARDS: The river is still virtually hazard free. However, the length of the trip can cause problems if you don't prepare for it. This should be a minimum 3 day trip. Plan and pack accordingly. Keep in mind that a strong southerly wind will make for some difficult paddling.

PUT IN: The east bank of the river immediately downstream from the Hwy. 71 crossing west of La Grange. A good gravel road leads to a launching ramp at the river.

TAKE OUT: Below the Hwy. 71B crossing (36.5 miles,) at the ramp in the Columbus Chamber of Commerce Park. Alternate take out is the Hwy. 90 crossing (43.0 miles,) east of Columbus. If you want a short trip, put in at the Park, Hwy. 71B, and take out at Hwy. 90. This is 6.5 miles. The take out at Hwy 90 is long. Look it over before deciding.

CAMPING: Public camping areas include the Columbus Chamber of Commerce Park or the area adjacent to the launch area east of La Grange. Facilities at both are limited. There are no private camp grounds in this area. Natural camp sites along the river are abundant, but unless the camp is to be pitched on one of the many sand or gravel bars, these camp sites are on private property.

CANOE RENTAL AND SHUTTLE SERVICE: Colorado River Longhorn Canoes in Columbus, (409) 732-3723. Due to the distance, plan to take care of your own shuttle.

DISTINGUISHING FEATURES: Atop the bluffs on the right, as the river makes the first left turn is Monument Hill. The river is wide and bordered by huge cottonwoods, pecan and sycamores.

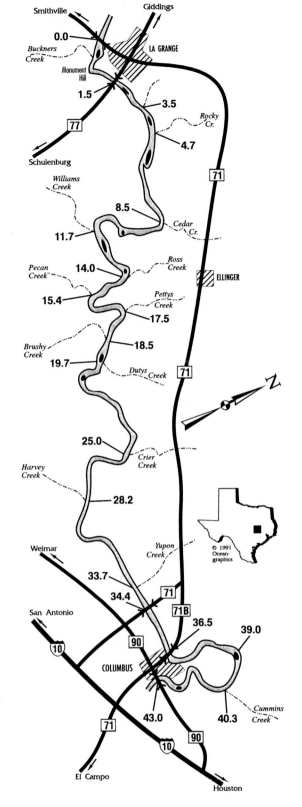

FISHING: Fish and tackle will stay about the same as that of the previous sections.

AREA ATTRACTIONS: Monument Hill and the Kreische Brewery in La Grange.

MAPS: The Colorado and Fayette County road maps. The topographical maps are the La Grange West, La Grange East, Ammannsville, Ellinger, Borden, and Columbus Texas quadrangles.

RIVER FLOW INFORMATION: Colorado River Longhorn Canoes (409) 732-3723.

DENTON CREEK

GRAPEVINE RESERVOIR TO CARROLLTON DAM
11.6 MILES

PHYSICAL CONDITION: Tarrant and Dallas Counties in North Central Texas. Dallas 30 miles, Ft. Worth 25 miles, and Denton 35 miles.

GENERAL COMMENTS: An enjoyable, scenic trip, with enough skill testing turns to keep the trip interesting. A good trip for the novice or family at low levels and a skill testing run for the experienced at high levels.

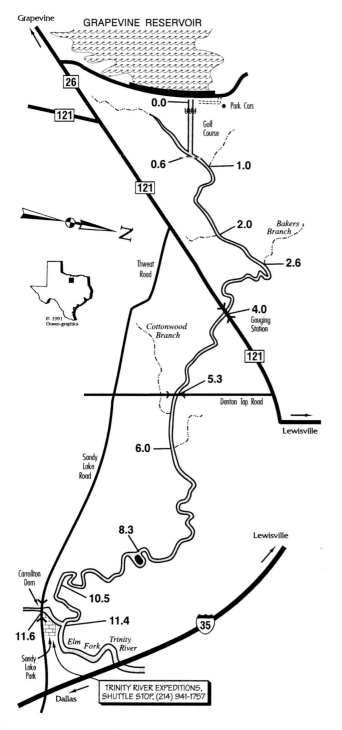

WATER QUALITY: Good when water is being released from Grapevine Dam.

WATER FLOW: Totally dependent upon water being released from Grapevine Dam. Any flow over 60 cfs. is adequate for an enjoyable float trip. At flow rates over 100 cfs. the creek becomes hazardous and caution should be used when negotiating the chutes and quick turns. Be experienced in fast water to attempt this trip at flow levels approaching or exceeding 300 cfs.

PREFERRED SEASON: Spring, early summer, and late fall due to the probability of adequate flow levels.

HAZARDS: If the flow rate is 500 cfs. or better, there is a bad rapid immediately below the put in. At high levels this rapid will have monstrous standing waves and "haystacks." Decked canoes or kayaks are better at the high water levels.

PUT IN: Launch below the dam at the dam control outlet. After getting the canoes and equipment to the water, move the cars to the parking area (see map). DO NOT leave cars parked at the launch point.

TAKE OUT: If you want a short trip, take out at the Denton Tap Road, 5.3 miles. It's another 6.3 miles to the take out at Sandy Lake Park above Carrollton Dam off Sandy Lake Road. You will reach the junction of Denton Creek and the Elm Fork of the Trinity at 11.4 miles. Sandy Lake Road is another 0.2 miles DOWNSTREAM on the Trinity.

CAMPING: Sandy Lake Park offers good camping areas and picnic tables. No overnight camping is allowed.

CANOE RENTAL AND SHUTTLE SERVICE: Doc Baker's Canoe Rental, (214) 371-0434, North Texas Canoe Rental on Whitlock Lane, (214) 245-7475, High Trails, Garland (214) 272-3353, Trinity River Expeditions (214) 941-1757.

DISTINGUISHING FEATURES: Very scenic, twisting, Narrow channels, shrouded and overhung by dense vegetation. A remote area, although close to the Dallas/Ft. Worth metropolitan complex.

FISHING: Denton Creek offers only minimum fishing opportunities. This is considered just a fun float trip.

AREA ATTRACTIONS: Nearly anything you might want to do or see is in the Dallas/Ft. Worth metroplex.

MAPS: The Tarrant and Dallas County road maps. The topographical maps are the Carrollton and Grapevine, Texas quadrangles.

RIVER FLOW INFORMATION: North Texas Canoe Rental (214) 245-7475, Trinity River Expeditions (214) 941-1757. Corps of Engineers, Fort Worth (817) 334-2214 or (817) 334-2196, Dallas Water Utilities (214) 428-4945.

DEVILS RIVER
BAKERS CROSSING (HWY. 163) TO ROUGH CANYON MARINA
47.7 MILES

PHYSICAL LOCATION: Extreme South West Texas in Val Verde County. Del Rio 55 miles, San Antonio 200 miles, Houston 397 miles, and Fort Worth/Dallas 400 miles.

GENERAL COMMENTS: The overall scenic beauty, its remote nature and the whitewater recreational experiences mark the Devils River as one of the few streams in Texas retaining definite "wild characteristics." This river has long been shrouded in controversy concerning stories of unpleasant experiences of "trespassers." From Baker's Crossing to Lake Amistad, the Devils River flows through private property and large ranches ranging up to 20,000 acres. Some of the landowners have been downright hostile to river runners and "trespassers." They claim their property rights, which in some instances date back to the Spanish Land Grants, include all the banks and bottom of the river. Consequently, if you step out of your boat and onto the river bottom, you are trespassing. For what its worth, there is a letter dated January 24, 1973 from Bob Armstrong, Commissioner, Texas General Land Office, to Clayton T. Garrison, Executive Director, Texas Parks and Wildlife Dept., stating that the river bed from Lake Amistad to the Hwy. 163 crossing is publicly owned. On the other hand, however, it also states that the subject of the stream bed ownership is complicated and that land grants in question have been patented under various laws and three separate governments during the course of Texas history. Needless to say, there is no doubt of the outcome if arguing these points out in the middle of nowhere with some irate landowner toting a Winchester. Be VERY COURTEOUS, keep a cool head and stay off private property! Be sure to carry all you'll need, but travel as light as possible. At normal to low levels, expect some walking and pulling through some of the shallow restricted channels. GOOD WADING SHOES are an absolute necessity. The abrasive rocks will wear the soles completely off a second rate pair of shoes. Long pants are great to help protect shins from those same rocks.

WATER QUALITY: Excellent. Believed by many to be the cleanest flowing stream in Texas. At this printing, the water from the springs is safe to drink.

Put in at Baker's Crossing

© 1991 Ocean-graphics

Juno

Baker's Crossing Campground
0.0 (Old Bridge)
Bluff Canyon
4.0
5.0
Grey Canyon
Sycamore Canyon
Miller Canyon
7.3
13.1
DEVILS RIVER STATE PARK
Hwy. 277
9.4
Dolan Creek Road
Dolan Creek
Springs
15.0
Snake Springs
Falls Canyon
Dolan Falls
16.4
19.0
Three Tier Waterfall
Indian Creek
21.0
Rough Canyon
Dry Devils River
163
Blue Sage Subdivision both sides of River
25.1
Dead Mans Creek
Turkey Bluff Canyon
26.0
29.6
Sonora
32.2
277
Little Satan Creek
33.8
Rocksprings
Gauging Station
38.5
377
Satan Canyon
COMSTOCK
277
Langtry
377
90
43.0
Devil Shores Subdivision
N
Boat Ramp
Rough Canyon Marina & Recreational Area
PR 2
Lake Amistad
47.7
Del Rio
To Hwy. 90

WATER FLOW: General adequate for float trips except during extended dry spells. Flow levels are subject to EXTREME fluctuations due to frequent flash flooding. Always camp high and keep your eye on questionable weather. It will be wise to check the flow levels prior to making the trip. Check with Baker's Crossing, (915) 292-4503.

PREFERRED SEASONS: Early spring through mid summer and early to mid autumn are generally considered the optimum seasons. Due to the many long north to south pools, some over a mile long, a high south wind and the scorching summer temperatures make for tough paddling. This is especially true over the last 20 miles which include the headwaters of Lake Amistad.

HAZARDS: Other than the before mentioned landowners, consider the remoteness of the area a hazard. Plan and pack accordingly. The river gradient averages between 15 feet per mile on the upper half and 7 feet per mile on the lower section. Most of the rapids will fall in the Class II to Class III categories, but will upgrade quickly as the river rises and flow rate increases. Most of the rapids are formed by boulder gardens or solid rock shelves, few with defined channels. All rapids are easily scouted prior to running. DO NOT RUN DOLAN FALLS at 16.4 miles. This is a 10 to 12 foot vertical drop with severe hydraulic currents. Take out well above the falls and portage on the left. Almost every long pool will end in a willow/reed jungle. The only passages through will be narrow twisting rock infested finger channels. The challenge here is to pick the correct channel to get you back to open water. Take the time to locate the correct channel or you can be easily lost, high and dry, in the "jungles" for hours. A situation similar to Humphrey Bogart and the "African Queen."

PUT IN: Launch below the old low water highway crossing off the Baker's Crossing campground.

TAKE OUT: The first take out is at the Devils River State Park, at approximately 15.5 miles. NOTE: TO USE THE PARK AS A PUT IN/TAKE OUT YOU ARE REQUIRED TO HAVE A GROUP OF NOT LESS THAN FOUR (4) BOATS. For information regard-ing the Devils River State Park, call the Park Superintendent

(915) 395-2133, or the Texas Parks Service (800) 792-1112. It is mandatory that you contact the Park Superintendent to have the gates to the Park unlocked. Schedules for using the Park must be arranged with the Superintendent. The second and last take out is Rough Canyon Marina on the left bank at 47.7 miles. At this printing arrangements can be made with High Bridge Adventures, in Comstock (915) 292-4495, for them to meet you in the extreme headwaters of Amistad Lake and help you to the marina.

CAMPING: The Rough Canyon Recreation Area is on Recreational Road #2 approximately 7.5 miles off Hwy. 277 north of Del Rio. It offers trailer sites, restrooms, covered camping/picnic areas, boat ramp and restrooms. There are good shaded primitive campsites, some with electricity, at Baker's Crossing. There are numerous excellent river camp sites, but keep in mind what we've said about trespassing. Camp in the river bed whenever possible.

CANOE RENTAL AND SHUTTLE SERVICE: There are no rental agencies in this area. Shuttles are available from High Bridge Adventures, in Comstock, (915) 292-4495, or individuals in Rough Canyon, Texas. Check with the Hughey's at Baker's Crossing (915) 292-4503 or Rough Canyon Marina (512) 775-8779 for current names and phone numbers. Due to the extreme distances and time required, shuttles in this area can be expensive. Have your prices and terms worked out before you make the trip.

DISTINGUISHING FEATURES. This is a very remote and wild area. Nearly everything sticks, bites or stings. Be careful of scorpions and centipedes when setting up camp. Under normal flow conditions, the river will almost double in flow volume past the Dolan Creek junction. This is because of the large influx of spring flow in and around the Dolan Springs area. The river is bordered by craggy wide canyons, some with cliffs ranging up to 400 feet above the river bed. This country is rugged, remote and rocky - but beautiful. Litter and debris along the river is almost non-existent. Keep it that way! If you pack it in, pack it out!

FISHING: One word covers it, FANTATIC! Largemouth bass will be caught consistently, but the smallmouth is by far the most prominent game fish. Although light weight tackle is the recommended equipment, try to stay with an 8 to 10 pound, low visibility line. The rocks along the Devils develop an extremely abrasive surface which wears through the exceptionally light weight lines very quickly. Small baits fished in the swift water at the base of rapids and falls, along weed lines and over drop-offs will produce consistently. Small topwaters, spinning baits, plastic grubs, tube worms, 4 inch plastic worms, crawfish imitations, and the small floating/diving minnows are all good bait choices. Catfishing can also be described as great. Channels, blue and the huge yellow cats are consistently taken on trot lines, drop lines and rod and reel.

AREA ATTRACTIONS: Just miles and miles of beautiful scenery, However, for the real party animals, Villa Acuna, Mexico lies just across the border from Del Rio. Alamo Village, the location of the filming of the movie "The Alamo," is in Bracketville, 32 miles east of Del Rio.

MAPS: The Val Verde County road map and the Baker's Crossing, Telephone Canyon, Dolan Springs, Clark Waterhole, Lechuguilla Creek, Satan Canyon, Gillis Ranch and Rough Canyon, Texas topographical quadrangles. Also, the Amistad National Recreational Area, Texas-Coahuila topographical map published by the U. S. Dept. of the Interior.

RIVER FLOW INFORMATION: High Bridge Adventures, (915) 292-4495, Baker's Crossing (915) 292-4503, and the Devils River State Park Superintendent (915) 395-2133.

FRIO RIVER
FIRST FM 1120 CROSSING TO HWY. 127
20.0 MILES

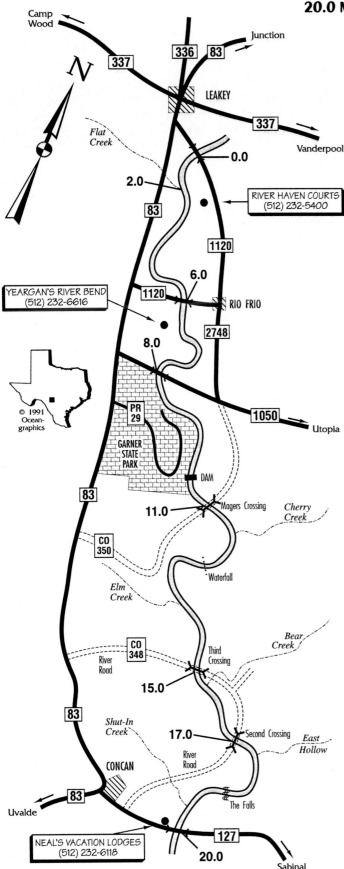

PHYSICAL LOCATION: Located in the heart of the Texas Hill Country, Real and Uvalde Counties in South Central Texas. San Antonio 80 miles, Austin 135 miles, Corpus Christi 210 miles, Houston 320 miles, and San Angelo 125 miles.

GENERAL COMMENTS: The Frio is one of the outstanding waterways, in terms of scenic beauty, in the state. The Frio Valley offers much more than just river fun. Due to the variety and abundance of good accommodations, this area is regarded as a great place for off-season vacations. Approximately 145 species of birds have been observed here. This number includes the rare golden cheeked warbler and the black capped vireo. As the Frio becomes too cold to float in late autumn, the valley explodes into the fantastic colors of fall. Always call ahead to confirm there is enough flow for canoeing. Due to the many rapids, exercise caution. Tie in and waterproof all gear. Give an extra amount of respect to private property and the land owners in this area - especially in that some sections of the Frio are PRIVATE PROPERTY. Have some canoeing experience. Not a novice stream.

WATER QUALITY: Excellent. The Frio is fed by springs and flows over a bed of limestone and gravel. The water is exceptionally clear and clean.

WATER FLOW: The Frio, even at the best of times, is a relatively shallow stream. It is totally dependent upon springs for normal water levels. Under usual seasonal conditions, except mid to late summer, there is generally enough water for enjoyable float trips.

PREFERRED SEASONS: Avoid the extremely hot months of summer or extremely cold weather periods.

HAZARDS: Although there are numerous rapids and chutes (which, if run improperly, could create some problems), the only natural danger points are the water fall located approximately 4 miles below Garner State Park and the "Falls" located less than a mile above the Hwy. 127 crossing. Also, be

FM 1120 Crossing

42

aware of possible barbed wire fences across the river. These fences can be extremely hazardous when stretched across a rapid. NOTE: These fences on the Frio are LEGAL - do not cut them. Due to old Spanish land grants, the river bed, as well as the adjoining land, was deeded to the property owners.

PUT IN: FM 1120 east of Leakey is recommended as the "top" put in point. Also, for auto protection, it is a good idea to launch from one of the private camps off FM 1120. One camp is located approximately one mile south, the second is another mile down FM 1120. Garner State Park is an excellent put in for the float to the Hwy. 127 crossing at Concan.

TAKE OUT: Take out points are numerous. They include the second FM 1120 crossing, west of Rio Frio and Garner State Park, Magers Crossing at 11.0 miles, the "Third" River Road Crossing at 15.0 miles, the "Second" River Road Crossing at 17.0 miles and Neal's Lodge campground immediately above the Hwy. 127 crossing southeast of Concan.

CAMPING: There are numerous private camps which offer excellent facilities. These include River Haven Courts approximately 2½ miles downstream from the FM 1120 put in (512) 232-5400, Rio Frio Bed and Breakfast on the north side of Rio Frio (512) 232-6633, Yeargan's River Bend campground off Hwy. 83 approximately mid-way between FM 1120 and FM 1050 (512) 232-6616 and Neal's Vacation Lodges and Campground located at Hwy. 127 and the Frio (512) 232-6118. Garner State Park has excellent facilities which include 211 campsites with water, 146 with water and electricity, screened shelters, restrooms, showers, dump stations, cabins, group facilities, grocery store, laundromat and various shops. Reservations are almost a necessity during the summer months. For reservations call (512) 232-6132.

CANOE RENTAL AND SHUTTLE SERVICE: There are no rental agencies along the Frio, however some of the private camps will shuttle cars for a fee.

DISTINGUISHING FEATURES: The overall beauty of the Frio is outstanding. The clear water, limestone bluffs, and stately bald cypress trees provide a picturesque setting for a float trip. Numerous rapids and the one waterfall all add another dimension to the character of the Frio.

FISHING: As the locals will tell you, there are a lot of fish in the Frio, but they are very difficult to catch because of the extremely

clear water and the narrow shallow channel. Wade fishing is the recommended method. Use as light a test line as possible and stay with small and ultra light baits. Largemouth, spotted and Guadalupe bass will furnish most of the action. Catfishing in the deep pools along rock ledges and submerged boulders is usually good, especially after a rise while the river is still "off color."

AREA ATTRACTIONS: Just miles and miles of beautiful scenery. Approximately six miles north of Leakey on Hwy. 336, a marker denotes the site of the McLauren Massacres, the last Indian massacre in Texas. Travel seven miles south of Leakey on FM 1120 and see the national champ of Texas live oak tree. In Leakey, visit the Real County Historical Museum. Lost Maples State Park is only 21 miles east via Hwy. 337. Bandera Downs is 49 miles east via FM 1050 and Hwy. 470.

MAPS: The Real and Uvalde County road maps. The topographical maps are Rio Frio, Concan, Magers Crossing, and Leakey Texas quadrangles.

RIVER FLOW INFORMATION: Contact any of the previously mentioned river camps or the park ranger at Garner State Park (512) 232-6132.

GUADALUPE RIVER

BRINKS CROSSING TO SEIDENSTICKER CROSSING
19.5 MILES

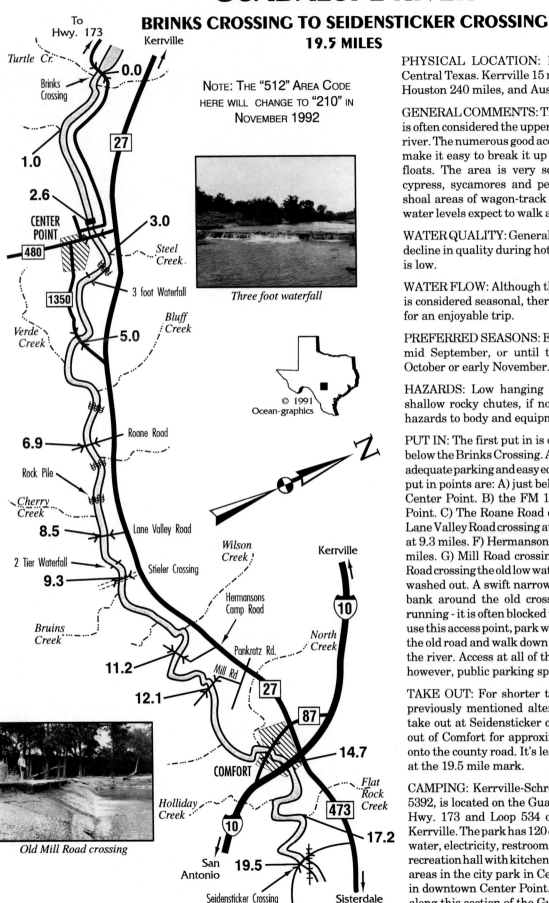

NOTE: THE "512" AREA CODE HERE WILL CHANGE TO "210" IN NOVEMBER 1992

Three foot waterfall

© 1991 Ocean-graphics

Old Mill Road crossing

PHYSICAL LOCATION: Kendall County in South Central Texas. Kerrville 15 miles, San Antonio 60 miles, Houston 240 miles, and Austin 75 miles.

GENERAL COMMENTS: This portion of the Guadalupe is often considered the uppermost floatable section of the river. The numerous good access points along this section make it easy to break it up into a number of short, fun floats. The area is very scenic and shaded by large cypress, sycamores and pecans. There are numerous shoal areas of wagon-track limestone river bed. At low water levels expect to walk and pull some in these areas.

WATER QUALITY: Generally very good but expect some decline in quality during hot, dry seasons when the river is low.

WATER FLOW: Although this section of the Guadalupe is considered seasonal, there is generally adequate flow for an enjoyable trip.

PREFERRED SEASONS: Early Spring to late June and mid September, or until the water gets cold in late October or early November.

HAZARDS: Low hanging limbs, small log jams and shallow rocky chutes, if not taken seriously, can pose hazards to body and equipment.

PUT IN: The first put in is on the left side, immediately below the Brinks Crossing. A large rock shelf here affords adequate parking and easy equipment handling. Alternate put in points are: A) just below the Hwy. 480 crossing in Center Point. B) the FM 1350 crossing east of Center Point. C) The Roane Road crossing at 6.9 miles. D) the Lane Valley Road crossing at 8.5 miles. E) Stieler crossing at 9.3 miles. F) Hermansons camp road crossing at 11.2 miles. G) Mill Road crossing at 12.1 miles. At the Mill Road crossing the old low water crossing has been partially washed out. A swift narrow channel runs along the left bank around the old crossing. Check this out before running - it is often blocked with logs or downed trees. To use this access point, park where the State has blocked off the old road and walk down the old paved road surface to the river. Access at all of these crossings is fair to good, however, public parking space is pretty limited.

TAKE OUT: For shorter trips, take out at any of the previously mentioned alternate put ins. For the final take out at Seidensticker crossing, take Hwy. 473 east out of Comfort for approximately 3.8 miles, turn right onto the county road. It's less than a mile to the take out at the 19.5 mile mark.

CAMPING: Kerrville-Schreiner State Park, (512) 257-5392, is located on the Guadalupe at the intersection of Hwy. 173 and Loop 534 on the southeastern edge of Kerrville. The park has 120 camp sites, screened shelters, water, electricity, restrooms, trailer dump station, and a recreation hall with kitchen. There are primitive camping areas in the city park in Center Point, just off Hwy. 480 in downtown Center Point. There are no private camps along this section of the Guadalupe.

CANOE RENTAL AND SHUTTLE SERVICE: The closest rental agencies are Fred Collins Workshop or Jellystone Park in Bandera.

DISTINGUISHING FEATURES: Huge, age-old cypress trees, and a multitude of springs can be found along this section of the Guadalupe. The upper portion is moderately populated, with homes and cabins along both banks of the river. Even with the proximity to developed areas, few folks will be seen along the river, except a few fisher-people at the crossings.

FISHING: Spotted and Guadalupe bass are the main attractions. They generally won't be large, but there are usually a lot of them. Fish the fast water, especially if it offers cover and shade. For best results, stay with the light test, low visibility lines and small baits. Fishing for yellow cat, and the sporty, channel cat is generally good, except during the extremely hot, low water seasons and the cold winter months.

AREA ATTRACTIONS: Visit the Cowboy Artists of America Museum, the Classic Car Show or the Wax Museum - all in Kerrville. The Point Theatre in Ingram offers dramatic and musical productions staged on the banks of the Guadalupe. You may also like to take a guided tour over the 50 square miles of the Y.O. Ranch. Zebras, giraffes and antelope are among the 58 different species of exotic animals on the ranch, located on Hwy. 41, 32 miles northwest of Kerrville. For additional information call the Kerrville Convention and Visitors Bureau, (800) 221-7958.

MAPS: The Kerr and Kendall County road maps and the Comfort, Center Point, and Waring Texas topographical quadrangles.

RIVER FLOW INFORMATION: Corps of Engineers, Fort Worth (817) 334-2214 or (817) 334-2196, or contact the outfitters on the downriver section.

NOTE: THE "512" AREA CODE HERE WILL CHANGE TO "210" IN NOVEMBER 1992

© 1991
Ocean-graphics

COMFORT
473
1621
Seidensticker Crossing
0.0
2.1
Block Creek
River Bend Road
Lower River Bend Crossing
Haufler Crossing
3.8
Old San Antonio Rd.
WARING
5.9
Coffee Hollow
Joshua Creek
8.2
9.1
Zoeller Lane
10
473
Violet Creek
13.7
87
1376
SISTERDALE
Old Crossing
BOERNE
474
Werner Creek
Bear Creek
24.3
17.8
25.2
San Antonio
Ammans Crossing
Spicewood Canyon
474
Goss Cr.
473
Spring Creek
31.0
Thornton Canyon
Swede Cr.
36.0
Big Spring Canyon
Sultenfuss Crossing
3160
39.3
3160
Bergheim
BERGHEIM CAMPGROUND & R.V. PARK, (512) 336-2235
Kendalia

GUADALUPE RIVER
SEIDENSTICKER CROSSING TO HWY. 3160
39.3 MILES

PHYSICAL LOCATION: Located in the Texas Hill Country, Kendall County in South Central Texas. San Antonio 50 miles, Houston 230 miles, Austin 70 miles and Dallas/Ft. Worth 250 miles.

GENERAL COMMENTS: This is a beautiful and popular portion of the Guadalupe. It is much less populated and commercialized than the previous section. The rapids are more frequent and more demanding, especially on the lower part of this trip. During normal to high water levels, rafting has become quite popular along this section. The variety of good access points allow you to easily plan a trip to fit your time frame and capabilities.

WATER QUALITY: Due to the river being almost totally dependent on free flowing springs, the water quality remains good to excellent.

WATER FLOW: Extremely long dry periods can create a problem of low water, but there is generally adequate flow for an enjoyable trip. During low periods, however, rafting is almost impossible.

PREFERRED SEASONS: Early spring through mid-summer and late fall are generally considered the optimum seasons. Its usually best to avoid the dog days of summer and cold days of mid winter.

HAZARDS: Low hanging limbs, log jams and rocks will pose minor problems. The low water crossings can be especially hazardous at high water levels. The old Hwy. 1376 bridge can be especially hazardous. Run the left channel, or portage. The danger at the crossings is being swept under or being trapped beneath the crossing. If in doubt, ALWAYS scout these before attempting to run any of them.

PUT IN: The first put in for this section is off the gravel bar on the left side of the river immediately downstream from Seidensticker crossing. To reach the crossing, take Hwy. 473 east out of Comfort for 3.8 miles, turn right onto the county road - the crossing is about a mile further on. Alternate put in points are: A) Lower River Bend crossing at 2.1 miles. Here the access to the river is good but the bridge is narrow and the parking area is very limited, B) Haufler crossing at 3.8 miles, C) the old San Antonio road crossing, north of Waring, at 5.9 miles, D) the Zoeller Lane crossing at 8.2 miles or, E) Ammans Crossing at 25.2 miles.

TAKE OUT: Any of the alternate put ins will work well as take outs depending on the length of trip desired. The last take out for this section is the FM 3160 crossing (Sultenfuss crossing,) or immediately downstream from the bridge, on the left bank, at Bergheim Campground. Access to the river at Bergheim Campground is short and easy.

CAMPING: Bergheim Campground has full R.V. hookups, water, electricity and private shaded campsites. Natural river campsites are abundant, but many are on private property. ALWAYS OBTAIN PERMISSION!

CANOE RENTAL AND SHUTTLE SERVICE: Bergheim Campground (512) 336-2235, Bigfoot II (512) 438-4617, Guadalupe Canoe Livery (512) 885-4671 or 964-3189, and Big Foot Canoes (512) 885-7106.

DISTINGUISHING FEATURES: Very typical of the Texas Hill Country. There are numerous clear flowing springs, towering limestone bluffs and rugged rock outcroppings. The river banks are lined with huge cypress, sycamores, pecan and live oaks. Yucca, as well as many other types of cacti flourish on the hilly slopes above the river while moss and ferns abound along the shorelines. The many small fun rapids will keep this trip exciting.

FISHING: The fish along this section will be larger, on the average, than those found further upstream. Spotted bass and Guadalupe bass are still the most prominent, but you'll start to catch more largemouth here. The same rules and recommendations apply to equipment light weight, low visibility lines and small to medium sized baits. Yellow cat and channel cat are abundant and seem to be especially active three days to a week after a rise.

AREA ATTRACTIONS: Subterranean sight-seeing is available at two caves - the beautiful Cave Without a Name and the popular Cascade Caverns. Both are located in Kendall County.

MAPS: The Kendall County road map and the Waring, Sisterdale and Kendalia, Texas topographical quadrangles.

RIVER FLOW INFORMATION: Bergheim Campground, Bigfoot II, Guadalupe Canoe Livery and Bigfoot Canoes.

Travertine waterfall, map page 48

Rust Falls, map page 48

GUADALUPE RIVER
FM 3160 TO REBECCA CREEK ROAD CROSSING
23 MILES

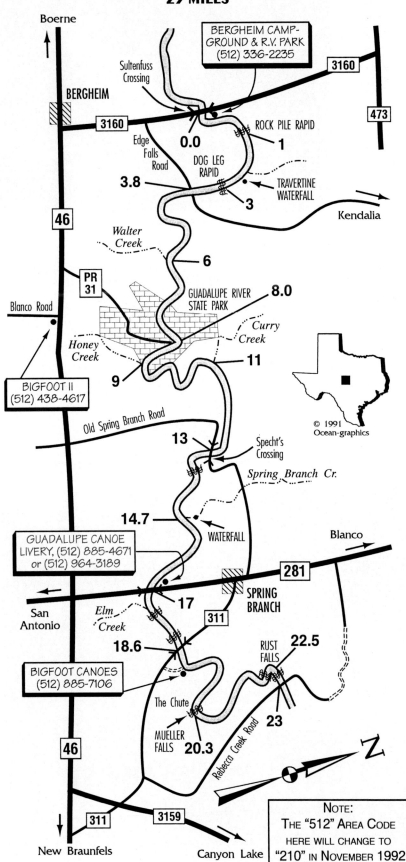

PHYSICAL LOCATION: Kendall and Comal Counties in South Central Texas. San Antonio 50 miles, Austin 75 miles, Waco 160 miles, and Houston 210 miles.

GENERAL COMMENTS: This section requires more paddling skills than the upper trips. The rapids are considerably larger and can be extremely difficult, especially at above normal river levels. This can be an exciting 2 to 3 day trip with numerous Class II rapids. Also, this section can be broken down into 3 or 4 one day floats.

WATER QUALITY: As the Guadalupe still depends primarily on springs for its flow, the water quality remains in the good to excellent categories.

WATER FLOW: River flow volume grows as it continues downstream. Usually adequate flow for float trips, especially for canoes, even during summer low water periods.

PREFERRED SEASONS: Spring and autumn remain the optimum seasons, however, the summer months have continually gained in popularity. Proper precautions should be taken during the winter months due to the numerous rapids which keep paddlers wet.

HAZARDS: As on the previous section, overhanging limbs, rocks and numerous logs will create some problems if not handled properly. There are approximately 55 rapids on this trip. Many of them are hazardous and should be considered dangerous at above normal water levels. The first is "Rock Pile" Rapid, located one mile below the FM 3160 crossing. Two miles further downstream is the tough "Dog Leg" Rapid. There are also some exciting rapids between Walter Creek (6 miles) and Curry Creek (11 miles). Although numerous and exciting, only two of the remaining rapids are generally considered formidable. These are Mueller Falls at 20.3 miles and Rust Falls at 22.5 miles. Both of these are definitely hazardous to paddlers and equipment. They are normally Class II/Class III, but become extremely dangerous at higher flow levels.

PUT IN: The first put in is below the FM 3160 crossing (Sultenfuss crossing,) or immediately downstream from the bridge, on the left bank, at Bergheim Campground. Alternative put ins are: A) The Edge Falls Road access at 3.8 miles (the old low water crossing is no longer there.) B) The Guadalupe River State Park access at 8.0 miles. C) Specht's Crossing at 13 miles. D) Guadalupe Canoe Livery at Hwy. 281 and the Guadalupe, 17 miles. E) Bigfoot Canoes, downstream from the Hwy. 311 crossing, at 18.6 miles. Always remember, there will be a fee charged for putting in, taking out or parking at any of the outfitters. However, they all offer good safe facilities.

TAKE OUT: Any of the alternative put ins can also be considered alternate take outs. If you feel you are not quite up to running Mueller or Rust Falls, take out at the Hwy. 311 crossing or immediately downstream at Bigfoot Canoes. The last take out before getting into the headwaters of Canyon lake is the Rebecca Creek Road crossing at 23 miles.

CAMPING: The Guadalupe River State Park (512) 438-2656, on PR 31, off Hwy. 46 between Boerne and the junction of Hwy. 46 and Hwy. 281 offers 105 campsites, electricity, water, restrooms, showers, and a dump station. Bergheim Campground, adjacent to the FM 3160 crossing, offers full R.V. hook-ups, electricity, water, restrooms and private shaded campsites. Bigfoot Canoes, downstream from the Hwy. 311 crossing, has a number of camping areas with limited facilities. With the exception of old highway crossings and road right-of-ways, there are no other public camping areas along this section of the Guadalupe. Be careful and courteous if camping on private land along the river. ALWAYS OBTAIN PERMISSION. The land owners in this area take a dim view of river runners camping on their land without asking.

CANOE RENTAL AND SHUTTLE SERVICE: Bergheim Campground (512) 336-2235, Bigfoot Canoes (512) 885-7106, Bigfoot II (512) 438-4617, and Guadalupe Canoe Livery (512) 885-4671 or 964-3189.

FISHING: Again fish, fishing techniques and equipment will remain basically the same as the previous sections of the Guadalupe.

AREA ATTRACTIONS: Plan to visit Natural Bridge Caverns and Wildlife Ranch located on FM 3009 due west of New Braunfels or Dinosaur Flats on FM 2673, halfway between Sattler and Startzville, west of Canyon Lake. Other attractions include the Schlitterbahn Water Park, on the Comal River in downtown New Braunfels, or browsing through the quaint shops of historic Gruene, Texas on the west bank of the Guadalupe, just north of New Braunfels.

MAPS: Kendall and Comal County road maps and the Kendalia, Spring Branch, Anhalt and Fisher, Texas topographical quadrangles.

RIVER FLOW INFORMATION: See Canoe Rental & Shuttles.

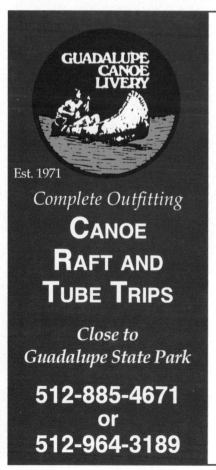

Our *Rivers* Are FANTASTIC!

Pecos River

Mulberry, Hell Roaring Falls

Caddo Lake

Buffalo Winter

San Marcos

Cossatot

Guadalupe

GUADALUPE RIVER

THREE SECTIONS - CANYON DAM TO CYPRESS BEND PARK
22 MILES OVERALL
OVERALL GENERAL RIVER INFORMATION

PHYSICAL LOCATION: Due north of New Braunfels, Comal County in Central Texas. Houston 200 miles, Dallas 240 miles, Austin 45 miles, and San Antonio 65 miles.

GENERAL COMMENTS: This section of the Guadalupe is the most popular and most crowded river in the state. Its whitewater, scenic beauty and proximity to large metropolitan areas make it a favorite with river runners. To avoid some of the crowds, plan your trip during the week. Anyone floating the Guadalupe, especially at above normal water levels, should have some whitewater experience, and should wear life preservers. Although many older people and children enjoy the thrills of the Guadalupe each year, we recommend that they be in good physical shape and be able to handle themselves well in the water. Do not take your valuables on the river. Leave your keys with your outfitter. If it's absolutely necessary to take your glasses, attach one of the floating headstraps so you can find them in the river. Leave jewelry and watches at home. It is illegal to have any glass or styrofoam containers on the river. It is illegal to consume alcohol before noon on any Sunday. The local "federales" are happy to fine anyone they can catch with a beer before noon on Sunday. We have split the river into 3 separate sections which each provide exciting river runs. The first section is from Canyon Dam down to Third crossing on River Road(pages 52 and 53); the second section is from Third crossing on River Road to First Crossing on River Road (pages 54 and 55); the last section is from First crossing on River Road to Cypress Bend park in New Braunfels (pages 56 and 57).

WATER QUALITY: Clear and cold as it comes off the bottom of Canyon Lake. River temperature at the dam is under 60 degrees. It warms about one degree per mile.

WATER FLOW: Below Canyon Lake the Guadalupe's flow is determined totally by water release through the dam. This flow is always measured in cfs.(cubic feet per second). Most campgrounds, outfitters and local stores post a daily update on the current cfs. flow rate. Flows ranging from 100 to 300 cfs. are generally considered a safe level. The river, except for numerous shoal areas, is navigable at these levels. However, there will be some walking as the flow slips below the 250 cfs. mark. As the flow climbs above the 400 cfs. level, rapids become more dangerous. Above 600 cfs. the rapids and hydraulic currents are definitely considered dangerous for river runners and equipment. The optimum level for excitement and uninterrupted flow is between 400 and 900 cfs. Flow above 1,000 cfs. is extremely dangerous. All river runners should have adequate river knowledge, hopefully some whitewater experience, and always wear life preservers at the high cfs. levels. It is wise to consult the outfitters concerning the dangers of the river.

PREFERRED SEASONS: Avoid the cold winter season - you will always get wet on this portion of the Guadalupe. With adequate flow, all other times of the year will be great fun.

HAZARDS: As the flow rate rises the hazards increase proportionately. Each dam, rapid, bridge and rock garden becomes a potential danger spot. Primarily it's the volume of water (cfs.), which determines the severity of each hazard. These will be covered individually in the three sections which follow.

PUT IN/TAKE OUT: With the exception of the public launch site immediately below Canyon Dam, the majority of the others are on private property. There are a number of outfitters who will allow individuals to put in/take out at their facilities. A fee is charged for access to the river as well as for leaving a vehicle on their property. Most outfitters, however, require that you rent river equipment from them in order to have access to the river at their locations. If using your own equipment, you should make arrangements for putting in and taking out prior to trying to get on the river.

CAMPING: Private camping areas are abundant and offer a wide variety of amenities. These amenities will vary greatly from camp to camp. On weekends and especially holidays, overnight camping reservations are mandatory.

CANOE, RAFT, TUBE RENTAL AND SHUTTLE SERVICE: There are numerous outfitters, rental agencies and shuttles covering the entire river front from the first Hwy. 306 crossing below the dam extending the entire length of River Road and onto Loop 337. Over the past few years rafting has become quite popular on the Guadalupe. Rafting offers safer transportation than canoeing, is more convenient for families or groups, doesn't demand the skill necessary for canoeing, and doesn't require as much need to avoid river obstacles. In rafts, more violent waters can be negotiated with less fear of capsizing. Rafts of all sizes are available at the majority of outfitters along the river.

DISTINGUISHING FEATURES: Typical Hill Country terrain with sheer limestone bluffs, rocky shoals, rushing whitewater, and numerous springs. Much more residential and commercial development than the upper Guadalupe. Very scenic, especially along the old River Road running along and crossing the river four times from FM 2673 to Dam 6.

FISHING: Due to its cool waters and swift, oxygenating currents, the Guadalupe below Canyon Dam is stocked with trout every year. The record catch at this printing is a few ounces over 6 pounds. Fly fishing equipment and ultra-light tackle are the recommended methods for taking the trout. Small artificial flies and natural baits such as corn and small spinning baits are good producers. The majority of the better trout fishing is on the first 7 miles below the dam. Fish the rapids below the small dams, along undercut banks and rock outcroppings. This is a cool weather sport after most of the river runners have gone home. There are many areas available for day or season lease. Most of the outfitters can supply the necessary information. Don't forget a trout stamp is required.

MAPS: The Comal County road map and the Sattler, Texas topographical quadrangle.

RIVER FLOW INFORMATION: Check with any of our listed advertisers for up-to-the-minute river flow information.

Gruene Crossing rapids

It is with rivers as it is with people; the greatest are not always the most agreeable nor the best to live with.

— Henry Van Dyke

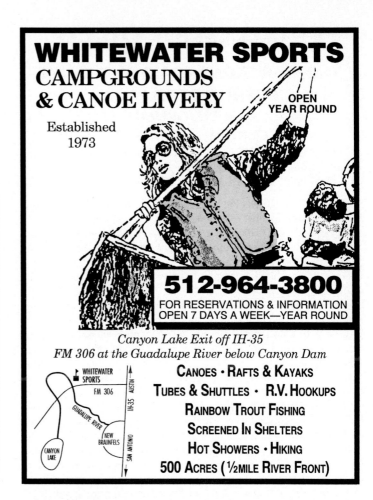

GUADALUPE RIVER

SECTION I
CANYON DAM TO THIRD CROSSING
ON RIVER ROAD
10.5 MILES

GENERAL COMMENTS: This section can easily be broken down into a number of shorter trips. With the exception of Horseshoe Falls, the rapids in this section are exciting but not as wild or turbulent as those further on downstream.

HAZARDS: Horseshoe Falls at 1.5 miles has taken MANY lives over the years. DO NOT attempt to run this one at any water level! The hydraulic current is exceptionally strong and the water below the falls is aerated, offering little support for any craft. Portage on the left over the flat rock shelf. Dam 1, just above the first crossing

on Hwy. 306, is more a nuisance than a danger. It can be portaged or run on the right. There is also a small channel against the left bank which can be used to skirt the dam. The river drops over some rock ledges just above the second Hwy. 306 crossing. Stay in the swift water to the extreme left. Although there will be large standing waves here, it is easy to negotiate. Dam 2 and Dam 3, both immediately below the second crossing on Hwy. 306, can be hazardous, and both have strong hydraulic currents at flow levels above 350 cfs. Run Dam 2 through the "slot" just a little to the left of center. Dam 3 has a narrow cut against the right bank. Dam 4, at 6 miles, is difficult to run, but is not considered dangerous. The water below the dam is very shallow, flowing over solid rock. The danger here is in damaging equipment or getting banged up by the rocks. Run it almost dead center or portage/line over the left side along the shoreline. "S" Turn Rapids, a few hundred yards downstream from Dam 4, require a 90 degree turn to the right down a fast channel of whitewater, then another 90 degree turn to the left. There are large standing waves throughout this rapid. The primary hazard here is swamping the craft in the standing waves. There is a small, but tricky rapid just above the private bridge at 7.2 miles. Stay to the left and out of the trees along the right bank. Devils Playground, at 8.5 miles, is a stair-step rapid, cascading over a number of solid rock shelves. The best route is to the extreme right close to the shoreline. Bad Rock Rapid, at 9.0 miles, is a large boulder sitting dead center in the main current. From upstream, this rock is barely visible at flow levels above 400 cfs. The most direct route is the narrow channel between the rock and the right bank. The greatest danger here is hanging on the rock and the river wrapping your craft around it. Take care not to be pinned between your capsized boat and the rock. Exercise caution with the bridge piers below the private crossing directly below Bad Rock Rapid.

PUT IN: The first launch site is immediately below the dam. Put in off the south (right) bank. This site can only be used by private craft. By law, the outfitters are not permitted to put in here because of the dangers encountered at Horseshoe Falls, located at the 1.5 mile mark downstream. Alternative put ins are at any of the outfitters located along this stretch from Hwy. 306 on down.

TAKE OUT: The first take out is at the first crossing on Hwy. 306. Below this any of outfitters will usually allow take out for a small fee.

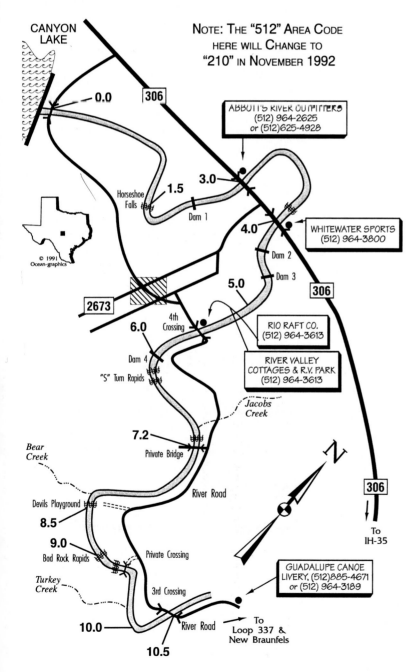

NOTE: THE "512" AREA CODE HERE WILL CHANGE TO "210" IN NOVEMBER 1992

CANYON LAKE

306

0.0

ABBOTT'S RIVER OUTFITTERS
(512) 964-2625
or (512) 625-4928

3.0

1.5

Horseshoe Falls

Dam 1

4.0

WHITEWATER SPORTS
(512) 964-3800

Dam 2

Dam 3

5.0

306

© 1991 Ocean-graphics

2673

4th Crossing

6.0

RIO RAFT CO.
(512) 964-3613

Dam 4

"S" Turn Rapids

RIVER VALLEY COTTAGES & R.V. PARK
(512) 964-3613

Jacobs Creek

Bear Creek

7.2

Private Bridge

River Road

306

To IH-35

Devils Playground

8.5

9.0

Bad Rock Rapids

Private Crossing

Turkey Creek

3rd Crossing

GUADALUPE CANOE LIVERY, (512)885-4671
or (512) 964-3189

10.0

River Road

To Loop 337 & New Braunfels

10.5

53

SECTION II
THIRD CROSSING TO FIRST CROSSING ON RIVER ROAD
5 MILES

GENERAL COMMENTS: This is a relatively short section with many small, fun rapids and quiet shaded pools. This section offers a good environment for the novice or anyone just wanting a quiet, relaxing, but fun float down the river.

HAZARDS: The only true hazard on this section is the "Chute" at 1.8 miles. Here the right portion of the river flows over a small dam (Dam 5). To the left, carved through solid limestone, is a narrow twisting "chute" of whitewater and large standing waves. This offers a roller coaster ride with a quick right turn away from a large rock at the end of the run. Due to the extremely narrow channel, there is little room to maneuver in the "Chute." This is a very popular spot, so crowding can always be a problem. Allow enough space for other river runners. This is a good place to get hurt if there is a jam of bodies in the "Chute."

NOTE: THE "512" AREA CODE HERE WILL CHANGE TO "210" IN NOVEMBER 1992

To Canyon Lake & Hwy. 306

River Road

3rd Crossing

0.0

Deep Creek

GUADALUPE CANOE LIVERY, (512) 885-4671 or (512) 964-3189

TEXAS CANOE TRAILS, INC. (512) 625-3375

The Chute Dam 5

BEZDEK'S RENTALS (512) 964-2244

1.8

ABBOTT'S CAMPGROUND (512) 964-2685 or (512) 625-4928

2.6

N

2nd Crossing

3.5

River Road

ABBOTT'S RIVER OUTFITTERS, (512) 625-4928 or (512) 964-2625

Stairstep Rapids

1st Crossing

5.0

To Loop 337 & New Braunfels

© 1991 Ocean-graphics

Devils Playground, map page 53

Above Dam 8, map page 56

Dam 6, map page 56

SECTION III
FIRST CROSSING ON RIVER ROAD TO CYPRESS BEND PARK
6.5 MILES

NOTE: THE "512" AREA CODE
HERE WILL CHANGE TO
"210" IN NOVEMBER 1992

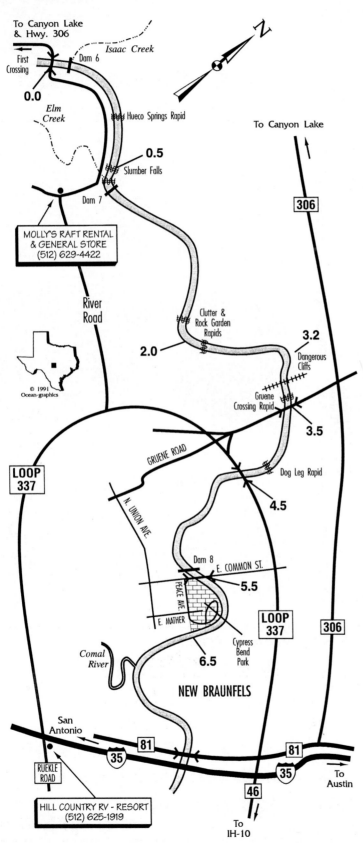

GENERAL COMMENTS: This section of the Guadalupe is the most popular in the State. Its fast flowing rapids offer whitewater thrills for all types of river runners. Rafting, canoeing, tubing and kayaking all share a portion of the river excitement. However, with all this fun goes respect for the river, and responsibility. These waters can be extremely dangerous for anyone who is ill-prepared, has had too much to drink, or fails to exercise good common sense. Adequate skill is necessary to negotiate this section safely. Experience in whitewater is definitely helpful. Have adequate flotation to support an overturned craft. Wear life preservers. Tie in and waterproof all valuable gear.

Although take out is allowed in Cypress Bend Park, no camping of any type is permitted. At this printing, individual take out is free. However, for any company or sponsored groups using the park, there is a fee.

HAZARDS: This is the wildest, most exciting, most crowded, and most hazardous section of the river. Starting immediately below the First Crossing are the remaining concrete piers of an old crossing (Dam 6). The second opening from the left bank is the best place to run this old crossing, especially at normal to low water levels. Less than a quarter mile downstream is Hueco Springs Rapid, the most turbulent and difficult on this lower section. The safest route is as far to the left as possible. The wildest and most exciting is just to the left of the huge boulder in mid stream. This large rock creates some very tricky rapids and currents. This boulder

Gruene Crossing Rapids

56

Lower Slumber Falls

has wrapped a lot of boats and has been responsible for many broken bones. If you capsize above the main rapid stay upstream or away from the overturned craft. Do not allow yourself to be pinned between the rock and an overturned canoe or raft. Life preservers should always be worn at Hueco Springs. Downstream, at 0.5 miles, is the two part rapid, Slumber Falls. The first section of the rapid drops quickly to the right with large erratic standing waves. Just as you clear this first section, the river turns immediately to the left and cascades over a small dam (Dam 7.) This dam creates one of the most dangerous hydraulic currents on the river. Line up with the center of the dam as quickly as possible and shoot it dead center, going as fast as possible. At water levels above 500 cfs. speed and strength are needed to break your craft out of the hydraulic below the dam. At the 2 mile mark, Clutter & Rock Garden Rapids divide the river into narrow twisting channels filled with rock and cypress trees. Usually the best route is the swift channel along the right bank. The cliffs along the left bank at 3.2 miles are EXTREMELY DANGEROUS. Not for river runners, but for the misinformed who think they can SAFELY high dive off them into the river. MANY lives are lost along these cliffs each year. DO NOT DIVE OFF THESE CLIFFS!!! Gruene Crossing Rapid, directly above Gruene Crossing, is a jumble of boulders with no definite channel. Stay mid stream as you make the left turn down the rapids. The rapid, though wild and exciting, is not the true danger here. The low water. Gruene Crossing, bridge can be a boat bender and bone breaker if you allow yourself to be swept under it. At flow rates of 400 cfs. and higher, safe passage under the bridge is impossible. After running the rapid, work yourself into the eddy water along either bank. The easiest portage is on the left. Dam 8, above the Common Street crossing, is large but easily negotiated. Run it dead center, but use caution to avoid the Common Street bridge pilings immediately below the dam. Be prepared to go to the right at the base of the dam.

Hueco (Waco) Springs Rapids

Upper Slumber Falls Rapids

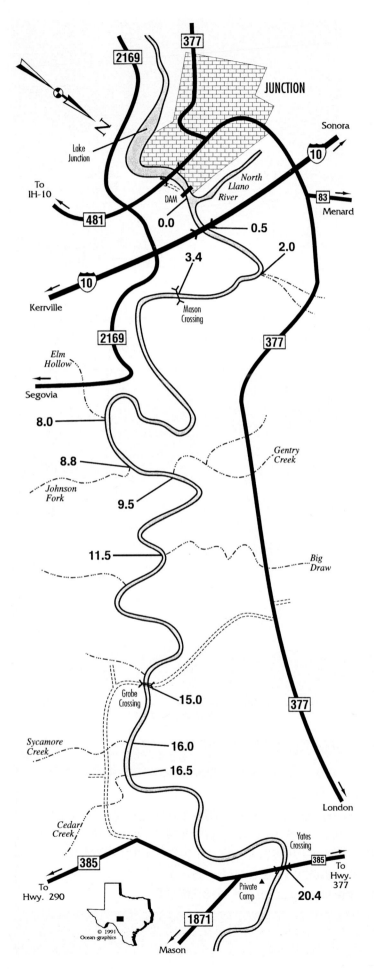

LLANO RIVER
JUNCTION TO HWY. 385
20.4 MILES

LOCATION: Located adjacent to Junction, Texas in Kimble County in Southwest Central Texas. San Antonio 120 miles, Dallas 200 miles, Houston 250 miles, and Austin 145 miles.

GENERAL COMMENTS: A true jewel of the Hill Country. A trip which is scenic and ever changing. Anyone who allows enough time for this trip will thoroughly enjoy it. Expect some walking over some short shoal areas, especially during the summer months.

WATER QUALITY: Good to excellent. The river is spring fed and generally flows over a solid limestone river bed which maintains the high water quality.

WATER FLOW: This upper section usually has sufficient flow for enjoyable float trips. The river will widen out, especially along the lower third of the trip producing more shoal areas and shallower water.

PREFERRED SEASONS: Fall through early summer. Although the summer months are generally considered seasonal, floating during this time can be enjoyable if there has been enough rainfall to maintain a good water level. There is little shade on the Llano so be prepared for a lot of sunshine.

HAZARDS: There are many small rapids and falls, but none which are considered dangerous. The rock bottom and outcroppings can put a few dents in your craft, but pose no great threat to life or limb. From time to time, some of the ranchers stretch barbed wire fences across the river. These are rare, but will pose a hazard to river running, especially in fast water areas.

PUT IN: Launch below the dam on the south bank in the Junction City Park. There are also a number of launch sites between the park and the IH-10 crossing.

TAKE OUT: Take out at the FM 385 crossing at 20.4 miles or the private camp on the right bank, immediately below the bridge. An alternate take out point is Grobe Crossing at 15 miles. This crossing is best reached off Hwy. 377 and can be recognized from the highway by the "High Point Brangus Ranch" sign, the white railing and the entrance over the cattle guard. It is 2.7 miles from Hwy. 377 to the river. DO NOT try to find this crossing off the dirt road which connects FM 2169 and Hwy. 385 on the other side of the crossing. Without an intimate knowledge of the area you will get lost!

CAMPING: Junction City Park offers adequate camping areas, but limited facilities. The camp at 20.4 miles has river access and primitive camp sites, but is limited regarding other facilities. The South Llano State Park, 5 miles west of Junction off Hwy. 377, has 58 electrical camp sites with water, 12 walk-in campsites with only water, primitive camping areas, and restrooms. The river frontage and bottomland of the park is closed to the public from October to April to protect one of the most significant winter roosting areas of the Rio Grande Turkey. Natural camp sites are good and abundant, but on private land. Obtain permission!

CANOE RENTAL AND SHUTTLE SERVICE: Rentals and possibly shuttles from Coleman Canoes (915) 446-3540.

DISTINGUISHING FEATURES: Clear, clean stream flowing over fluted limestone. Small rapids at normal levels, but is extremely hazardous at high water levels. Bank vegetation consists primarily of cedar, live oak, mesquite, pecan, sycamore and yucca.

FISHING: Generally good to excellent. Spotted, largemouth and guadalupe bass are abundant and usually hungry. Many species of perch, including the Rio Grande perch, can be found in the Llano. Concentrate most of your fishing in areas where there is current. Stay with medium to light tackle with low visibility lines. Small crank baits resembling wounded minnows or crawfish usually produce. Small spinning baits, small plastic worms, grubs, jig combinations and small topwaters will all catch fish. Catfishing rates right along with bass fishing in popularity. Channel cat and the giant yellow cats are routinely caught on trot lines and drop lines, as well as rod and reel.

AREA ATTRACTIONS: The Texas Tech Center, Schreiner Park, O. C. Fisher Museum and Library are all in Junction. For more information on area attractions and local events, contact the Kimble County Chamber of Commerce, 402 Main, Junction, Texas 78649, (915) 446-3190.

MAPS: The Kimble County road map. The topographical maps are the Junction, Big Draw, and Yates, Texas quadrangles.

RIVER FLOW INFORMATION: Gene Coleman of Coleman Canoes (915) 446-3540.

SOUTH LLANO RIVER
SECOND HWY. 377 CROSSING TO JUNCTION CITY PARK
16.6 MILES

PHYSICAL LOCATION: Originates just west of Junction, Texas in Kimble County, Southwest Central Texas. Dallas 275 miles, Austin 150 miles, San Antonio 120 miles, and Houston 310 miles.

GENERAL COMMENTS: The South Llano originates in the "Country of 1,100 Springs." The high spring input volume almost guarantees adequate flow month after month. In normal years, the river level will vary only a few inches. In extremely dry years you will have to wade in only a few places, and then not for long. The scenery varies from tall cliffs to flats with large overhanging pecan trees. However, sooner or later, you are going to get just a little bit wet in the small twisting rapids. Just by the way, the north arrow on the map is correct, this river does flow northward.

WATER QUALITY: Excellent. Since the river is totally spring fed, its waters flow, continually clear and clean, over beds of solid limestone, rocks and gravel.

WATER FLOW: Always adequate for an enjoyable float trip.

HAZARDS: Small rapids, falls, and low water crossings make the trip interesting, but normally aren't considered dangerous. There is a steel bridge at Boone Crossing, 3.6 miles. At low to normal water levels, you can float under the bridge. At high water levels it can be quite dangerous. Occasional drift piles under the bridge can also pose some hazards, even at low water levels. The low bridge at Flat Rock Crossing, 14.9 miles, requires that you portage on the right bank. When in doubt, scout these areas.

PUT IN: The first put in is immediately below the 2nd. crossing on Hwy. 377, off the right bank. Alternate put ins are; the first crossing on Hwy. 377, at 1.4 miles or the South Llano State Park Crossing (PR 73) at 11.2 miles.

Second Crossing put in - at low water level

TAKE OUT: The last take out is on the right bank, above the dam in Junction City Park. Any of the prior mentioned alternate put ins could also be used as take outs for shorter trips. An additional take out is the Flat Rock Crossing at 14.9 miles.

CAMPING: South Llano State Park (see Llano River writeup for details) offers good facilities. Primitive camping is available along the river and at the City Park. There are also a couple of private camps along Hwy. 377.

CANOE RENTAL AND SHUTTLE SERVICE: Coleman Canoes (915) 446-3540. Shuttle available for rented canoes. Some campground owners will shuttle for a small fee.

DISTINGUISHING FEATURES: Clear, clean spring water. Numerous small, fun rapids, fast water, and long quiet pools. Can be very hazardous at high water levels. Great variety of flora and fauna. Great for bird watching and photography.

FISHING: Same as the Llano River, but usually better. Same equipment and techniques will apply.

AREA ATTRACTIONS: Same as the Llano River. For more information contact the Kimble County Chamber of Commerce, 402 Main, Junction, Texas 78649, (915) 446-3190.

MAPS: Kimble County road map available from the Chamber of Commerce, 402 Main, Junction, Texas 78649. The topographical maps are the Bailey Creek, Junction and Telegraph, Texas quadrangles.

RIVER FLOW INFORMATION: Gene Coleman of Coleman Canoes, (915) 446-3540.

Because It was There ··· That's Why!

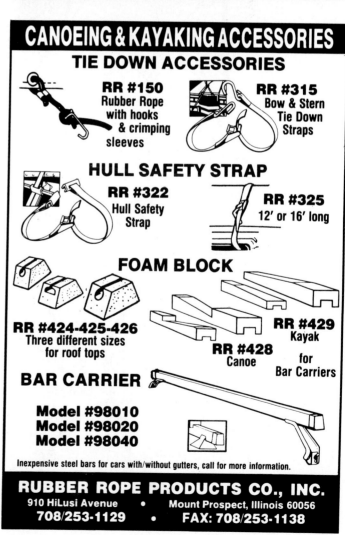

MEDINA RIVER
MEDINA TO BANDERA
19.5 MILES

NOTE: THE "512" AREA CODE HERE WILL CHANGE TO "210" IN NOVEMBER 1992

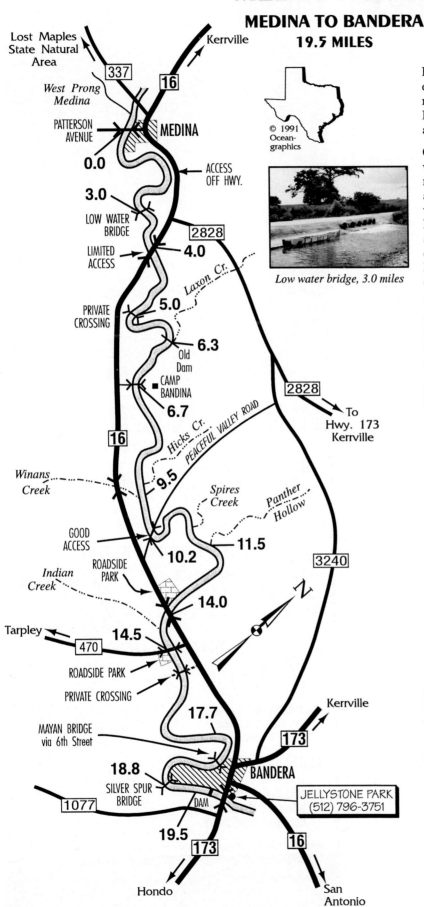

Lost Maples State Natural Area

West Prong Medina

Kerrville

337   16

PATTERSON AVENUE   MEDINA

0.0   ACCESS OFF HWY.

3.0

LOW WATER BRIDGE

LIMITED ACCESS   2828   **4.0**

Laxon Cr.

PRIVATE CROSSING   **5.0**

6.3

Old Dam

CAMP BANDINA   **6.7**

16

Hicks Cr.   PEACEFUL VALLEY ROAD   2828   To Hwy. 173 Kerrville

Winans Creek   **9.5**

Spires Creek   Panther Hollow

GOOD ACCESS   **11.5**

ROADSIDE PARK   **10.2**

Indian Creek   **14.0**   3240

N

Tarpley   **14.5**
470

ROADSIDE PARK

PRIVATE CROSSING

17.7   Kerrville

MAYAN BRIDGE via 6th Street   173

18.8   BANDERA

SILVER SPUR BRIDGE   DAM

1077   JELLYSTONE PARK (512) 796-3751

19.5   16
173

Hondo   San Antonio

© 1991 Ocean-graphics

Low water bridge, 3.0 miles

PHYSICAL LOCATION: Bandera County, south central Texas. San Antonio 45 miles, Austin 120 miles, Dallas 330 miles, Houston 270 miles. Beautiful Texas Hill Country, good roads and river access.

GENERAL COMMENTS: Abundant aquatic life visible in the clear water. The trip is scenic, refreshing and exciting. The sections immediately above and below the Mayan Bridge crossing are very shallow with a river bed of solid, grooved limestone (wagon track) which makes walking almost mandatory, slow and difficult. Under normal conditions, almost everyone can enjoy the Medina. Distance can easily be adjusted to fit your capabilities. Tie in and waterproof all gear.

WATER QUALITY: The Medina flows cool and clean over gravel and solid limestone. Under normal conditions it is exceptionally clear because it is totally spring fed.

WATER FLOW: Will be low during hot, dry periods as springs are depleted. Will be high and dangerous immediately after heavy rains, however, the Medina is generally back to normal in only a few hours.

PREFERRED SEASONS: Spring and Fall offer the best water conditions and best river scenery. However, with normal rainfall, the upper section can be floated in summer, but expect some short walks in the low water areas. Many areas of this upper section are totally canopied by towering cypress trees.

HAZARDS: The primary hazards are narrow, twisting channels, over-hanging limbs and downed trees. All these require a certain amount of control and ability in negotiating the river. High water makes the Medina exceptionally dangerous. The old dam, at 6.3 miles, can be run through the center or to the right. If you're in doubt, portage left.

PUT IN: The first launch site is the Patterson Avenue crossing in Medina which has an adequate parking area, shade and picnic table. Alternate put ins are: 1) the south side of the Hwy. 16 crossing at 4.0 miles - a short walk is necessary from the parking area to the river but it's easy and offers good river access. 2) the Camp Bandina crossing at 6.7 miles is a great put in. However, if parking a vehicle, leave it in the area between the highway and the river - the land on the other side of the river is private. 3) the Peaceful Valley Road crossing at 10.2 miles - offers easy access and a fair amount of shaded parking.

TAKE OUT: The best take outs for this section are either of the roadside parks at 14.0 miles and 14.5 miles. If you want a longer

trip, take out on the left bank in the Bandera City Park anywhere between the Silver Spur bridge and the dam above Hwy. 173.

CAMPING: A small area at the Patterson Avenue put in. Below the Hwy. 16 bridge at 4.0 miles. The roadside parks at 14.0 and 14.5 miles. The City Park, adjacent to the dam, in Bandera. Any camping on the river should ONLY be with the landowners permission.

CANOE RENTAL & SHUTTLE SERVICE: Fred Collins Workshop (512) 796-3553, Bandera Watersports (512) 796-3021/3022, and Jellystone Park (512) 796-3751.

DISTINGUISHING FEATURES: Rugged cedar and live oak covered hills laced with numerous raw outcroppings of limestone and sheer limestone bluffs frame the river. Free-flowing springs are abundant and large bald cypress offer shade to the river runner.

FISHING: Small to medium black bass and spotted bass are abundant. Various perch, including Rio Grande perch, take small, artificial or live bait. Monster yellow cat are best taken in deep water along rock shelves or downed timber a few days after a rise. Channel cat can best be caught just out of the current along undercut banks and deep channels. Due to the clarity of the water, it's best to use light line and small bait. Don't expect big fish, but count on a lot of action.

AREA ATTRACTIONS: Bandera is known as the "Cowboy Capital of the World" - cowboys, rodeos and "western" are the order of the day. Bandera Downs offers year round pari-mutuel horse racing. Lost Maples State Park is home to the Bigtooth Maple tree - fall colors are magnificent. Great Country and Western night life. Medina is the "Apple Capital of Texas" - if you want anything "Apple" you'll find it in Medina. Call the Bandera County Convention & Visitors Bureau for info. (800) 364-3833.

MAPS: The Bandera County road map. The Bandera, Tarpley Pass and Rock Cliff Reservoir Texas topographical quadrangles.

RIVER FLOW INFO: Fred Collins Workshop (512) 796-3553, Bandera Watersports (512) 796-3021/3022, and Jellystone Park (512) 796-3751.

MEDINA RIVER
BANDERA TO RUEDE'S CAMP
13.0 MILES

PHYSICAL LOCATION: Bandera and Medina Counties, South Central Texas. San Antonio 45 miles, Austin 100 miles, Dallas 330 miles, Houston 270 miles.

WATER QUALITY: Remains clear and clean but does not have the clarity of the upper river.

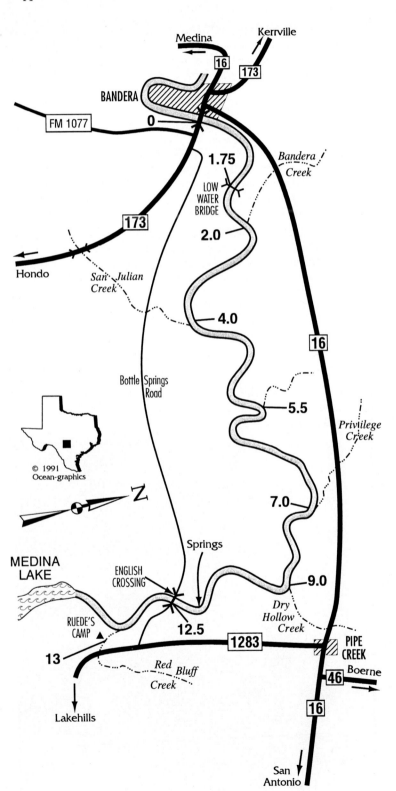

GENERAL COMMENTS: This section has no public access, so be prepared to make the entire trip. However, there are good emergency take out points on the right bank just above the San Julian Creek intersection at 4.0 miles and on the left bank just below the Privilege Creek junction at 7.0 miles. Cool off as you sit neck deep in the two huge springs at the 12.0 mile mark.

WATER FLOW: Generally more volume than the upper river, except during extreme dry periods. During these times the river actually goes "underground" at Privilege Creek, 7.0 miles, and does not have flow until it passes the big springs at 12.0 miles.

PREFERRED SEASONS: Same as the upper section.

HAZARDS: Small falls, rock outcroppings, and trees in the river present the most prominent hazards. These hazards escalate in severity as the river level rises. The Medina should be considered dangerous at above normal water levels. The low water bridge at 1.75 miles is extremely dangerous and a real boat cruncher.

PUT IN: Put in on the south side below the Hwy. 173 crossing on the southern edge of Bandera..

TAKE OUT: Take out at English Crossing, at 12.5 miles or at Ruede's camp at 13.0 miles. NOTE: English Crossing allows very limited parking, and no protection for your vehicle. Ruede's Camp offers a good place to leave the car - for a nominal charge, of course. However, Ruede's is a very long, steep and difficult take out.

CAMPING: There are no public camping areas except at the Park in Bandera or at Ruede's Camp. Although there are abundant camp sites on the river, they are ALL on private property. Obtain permission before driving the tent stakes.

CANOE RENTAL & SHUTTLE SERVICE: Fred Collins Workshop (512) 796-3553, Bandera Watersports (512) 796-3021/3022, and Jellystone Park (512) 796-3751.

DISTINGUISHING FEATURES: Generally the same as the upper section except the river bed is more open, wider and has far less shade. Shoreline bluffs are much higher on this section.

FISHING: Black and spotted bass usually run larger on this lower section, but their numbers drop considerably. The deep holes in the lower river are home for the really big yellow cats. White bass often get in the lower portion of this section during their spring run upriver from Medina Lake. Like the upper section, light line and small lures will be productive.

MAPS: The Bandera and Medina County road maps. The Bandera and Medina Lake, Texas topographical quadrangles.

RIVER FLOW INFORMATION: Fred Collins Workshop, (512) 796-3553; Bandera Watersports (512) 796-3021/3022, and Jellystone Park (512) 796-3751.

NECHES RIVER,

HWY. 21 TO HWY. 7
31 MILES

PHYSICAL LOCATION: Located in Houston County in Southeast Texas, adjacent to the Davy Crockett National Forest. Lufkin 15 miles, Houston 100 miles, Austin 210 miles, and Waco 150 miles.

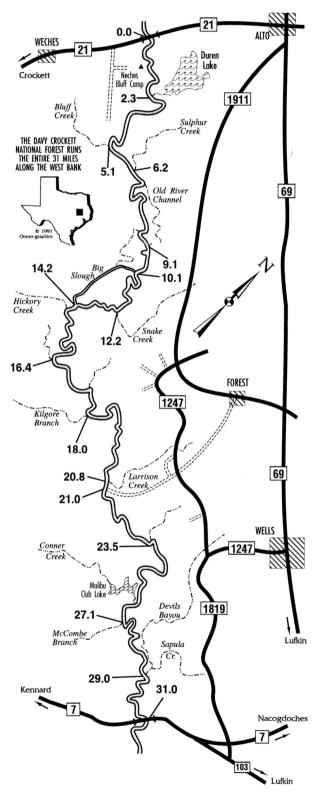

GENERAL COMMENTS: The complete 31 mile float is a good two day trip at adequate to high water levels. If the river is low, plan to take out at the 21 mile point. Consider the upper 21 miles a minimum two day trip. The remaining 10 miles can be handled in one day. However, if you decide to take the trip at low water levels, add an extra day to both sections. This is a very remote trip with very little access. Keep the time and distance in mind when planning the trip. Pack accordingly. Take all drinking water.

WATER QUALITY: Generally on the muddy side due to the slow flow and soil type in this region.

WATER FLOW: Very seasonal. Flow totally dependent on water release from Lake Palestine or run-off. The published flow rate at Alto, Texas (approximately 6 miles from put in) indicates what you can expect on the river. Generally at minimum flow rates (40 cfs), there is adequate water for canoeing.

PREFERRED SEASON: Late fall, spring and winter generally offer the best canoeing conditions.

PUT IN: Launch at State Hwy. 21 bridge southwest of Alto, Texas.

TAKE OUT: Take out at the gravel county road at the 21 mile point on the public access off FM 1247 south of Forest. Only the north side of this road is open. There is no longer access to Hwy. 7 from the west bank. Private property borders the river at the 21 mile point, be careful not to trespass. There is paved access at Hwy. 7 and a parking area.

CAMPING. The Ratcliff Lake Recreation Area, in the Davy Crockett National Forest, is located one mile west of Ratcliff on PR 277C north of Hwy. 7. It has 75 campsites, flush toilets, dump station, group camping area and shelter, cold showers and concessions. For information call the Neches District, (409) 544-2046. Mission Tejas State Historical Park, located just north of Hwy. 21, west of the top put in point, has 15 campsites, water, electricity, restrooms, showers, group camping, picnic pavilion, and dump station. For information call (409) 687-2394. Neches Bluff offers primitive camping close to the put in. Ratcliff Lake has a developed campground area located only a few miles from both the put in/take out points. On the river there are several primitive camping sites on USFS land. The Davy Crockett National Forest covers the right (west) bank for the entire trip.

CANOE RENTALS & SHUTTLE: There is limited canoe rental at Ratcliff Lake, but no shuttle service.

DISTINGUISHING FEATURES: A very remote river wilderness bordered by the Davy Crockett National Forest. The river twists and turns with many false channels, downed trees and dense stands of timber along both banks. Wildlife is varied and abundant. Local development is at a bare minimum.

FISHING: Largemouth bass fishing can be fair to good. Small lures worked on light to medium tackle seem to work best. Due to the large amount of downed timber and overhanging brush, shorter rods and medium to heavy weight lines are recommended. Weed-less baits, worms, grubs, imitation minnows, and small topwaters all work well. Catfishing is usually good on trot lines, drop lines or by bottom fishing with rod and reel.

AREA ATTRACTIONS: Visit the Mission Tejas State Historical Park with its mission replica, the Mission San Francisco De Los Tejas, and the Rice Family log home.

MAPS: USFS Davy Crockett: National Forest Map, Houston County Map. The topographical maps are the Neches, Forest, Kennard N.E., Wells, and Wells S.W. quadrangles.

RIVER FLOW INFORMATION: The Park Ranger, Davy Crockett National Forest, Neches District, (409) 544-2046.

NECHES RIVER
TOWN BLUFF TO HARDIN COUNTY PARK
44.5 MILES

PHYSICAL LOCATION. Extreme East Texas in Tyler, Jasper, and Hardin Counties. Dallas/Ft. Worth 250 miles, Beaumont 30 miles, Lufkin 75 miles, and Houston 100 miles.

GENERAL COMMENTS: A river which anyone, or any group, in fair physical condition, can enjoy during any season. Allow plenty of time for this/these trips. This section is long and the current is slow. Keep the distances in mind when planning and outfitting for this trip. A very remote area, this entire trip runs through the Big Thicket National Preserve. There is little to no access to the river other than the few spots mentioned.

WATER QUALITY: Good, as it comes from Steinhagen Lake but gradually takes on the "tea" color (tannic acid) characteristic of all East Texas streams.

WATER FLOW: Always adequate for float trips.

PREFERRED SEASONS: Offers good float conditions during all seasons. Excessive dry periods pose only minor problems in the upper sections.

HAZARDS: Very few hazards at normal flow levels. There will be numerous logs and downed trees. Prepare for the East Texas mosquitoes. Keep the remote nature and length of this trip in mind. BE SURE TO CARRY ALL DRINKING WATER.

PUT IN: Launch off the concrete ramp, at Eason Bait and Fish Market, on the west bank east of Town Bluff. There is a nominal fee for camping, parking or launching.

TAKE OUT: The first take out is at Sheffield Ferry Boat ramp, on the east bank below FM 1013. It's 28 miles to the next take out at Hardin County Park or John's Lake Slough camp, just up river from the park. To reach the park, driving from the south on Hwy. 92, the turn is approximately 1.8 miles from the FM 1122/Hwy. 92 intersection. Turn right at Camp Craven Road. Cross a paved road after 1.1 miles and continue straight ahead. After another 2.5 miles the road will fork, take the right fork. Hardin County Park is another 1.4 miles. Caution: The last mile requires a four wheel drive vehicle in wet weather. Alternate take out: take the left hand fork, an all weather road (before reaching Hardin County Park) which leads to John's Lake Slough, the camp and launching ramp. A fee is charged for parking/launching.

CAMPING: Hardin County Park has a good area for camping and some tables, but very limited facilities. There is also a small campground on the south east corner of the FM 1013 crossing. Natural camp sites are numerous at normal or low water levels, but are under water when the river is high. Campers Cove offers limited facilities (2 miles north of Town Bluff on Hwy. 92). Magnolia Ridge Bluff Park is 6.5 miles north of Town Bluff on Hwy. 92. The Big Thicket National Preserve extends along both banks for the entire 44.5 miles. A 1 to 5 day camping permit is required for camping in the Preserve. Permits are available from the Big Thicket National Preserve, 3785 Milam, Beaumont, Texas 77701, (409) 839-2689. They also offer an excellent map of this area.

CANOE RENTAL AND SHUTTLES: Piney Woods Canoe Rental (409) 274-5892.

DISTINGUISHING FEATURES: Solitude. Heavily wooded banks. Slow moving current. Trees and stumps in the river. A twisting, turning channel bordered by true wilderness.

FISHING: Largemouth bass are predominant, primarily in the upper section. Ultra light to medium bass tackle is appropriate. Floating/diving baits work well in spring and early autumn. Medium to deep running crank baits, plastic worms, spinning baits, and topwater baits will all produce. Due to the "tea" color of the water, heavier lines and tackle can be used successfully without spooking the fish. Catfishing is considered good to excellent all along the Neches.

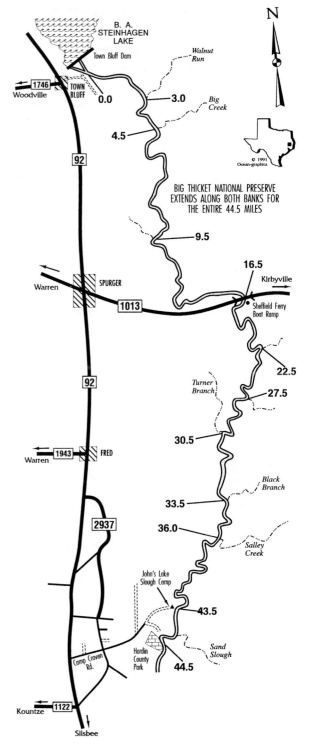

AREA ATTRACTIONS: The Alabama and Coushata Indian Reservation between Livingston and Woodville on Hwy. 190, and the Big Thicket Visitors Station on PR 420 north of Kountze, Texas.

MAPS: The Tyler, Jasper and Hardin County road maps. The topographical maps are the Curtis, Spurger, and Silsbee, Texas quadrangles, also, the Big Thicket National Preserve map.

RIVER FLOW INFORMATION: Piney Woods Canoe Rental (409) 274-5892 or the Corps of Engineers at Steinhagen Lake (409) 429-3491.

NECHES RIVER

HARDIN COUNTY PARK TO HWY. 96
10.5 MILES

PHYSICAL LOCATION: Located in Hardin and Jasper Counties in Southeast Texas. Beaumont 30 miles, Lufkin 90 miles, Houston 100 miles, and Dallas/Ft. Worth 260 miles.

GENERAL COMMENTS: A short trip which everyone can enjoy. Good scenic beauty, especially during spring and autumn seasons. A good one day trip, but can easily be stretched into two days.

WATER QUALITY: More murky than the upper section because of the dirt river bed and issuance from numerous creeks.

WATER FLOW: Always adequate flow for float trips. Current slows as the river widens and approaches the Coastal Plain.

PREFERRED SEASONS: The Neches can be enjoyed anytime of the year. Just prepare for existing or possible changes in weather conditions during winter months.

HAZARDS: River hazards are almost nonexistent, however man-made hazards such as trot and drop lines sometimes snag an unwary river runner. Mosquitoes and other insects will definitely present a problem for the unprepared.

PUT IN: Launch at Hardin County Park or John's Lake Slough. See the trip summary, Town Bluff to Hardin County Park for directions to the park or the slough launch sites.

TAKE OUT: The Hwy. 96 crossing west of Evadale, Texas.

CAMPING: Other than the camping area in Hardin County Park and the primitive camping at John's Lake Slough, there are no public camping facilities on this section of the Neches. Adequate and numerous sand bars offer excellent camping areas along the river. The better areas can usually be found on the inside of a bend just downstream from a steep outside bank. These banks are easily recognizable, reaching vertically upward 10 to 20 feet from the river. Remember, a permit is required from the National Park Service to camp on the river banks.

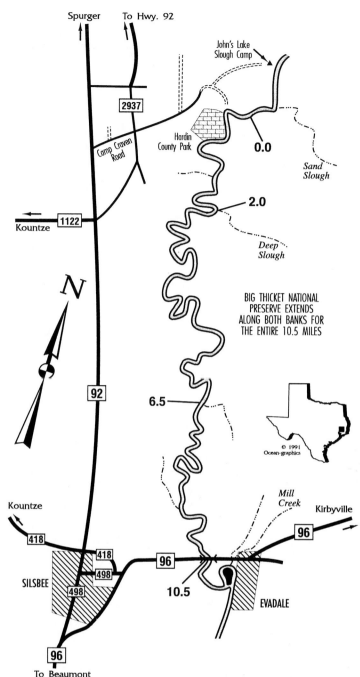

CANOE RENTAL AND SHUTTLE: Piney Woods Canoe Rental, Kountze, Texas (409) 274-5892.

DISTINGUISHING FEATURES: Twisting channel, slow current, cut banks, and numerous sand bars bordered by the towering pines native to East Texas. An "away from it all" type of river. No road crossings or public access other than the put ins and take out.

FISHING: Same as the previous section.

AREA ATTRACTIONS: Same as the previous section,

MAPS: The Hardin and Jasper County road maps. The topographical map is the Silsbee, Texas quadrangle. The Big Thicket National Preserve map is excellent. It can be obtained by writing or calling the Big Thicket National Preserve, 3785 Milam, Beaumont, Texas 77701, (409) 839-2689.

RIVER FLOW INFORMATION: Piney Woods Canoe Rental (409) 274-5892 or the Corps of Engineers (409) 429-3491.

PECOS
PANDALE TO PECOS RIVER MARINA
61.3 MILES

Map labels:

PANDALE — 1024
Bed Rock Ford
Tardy Spring & Canyon
0.0
Spring Canyon
2.6
4.5
7.9
Oppenheimer Canyon
11.2
Live Oak Canyon
Ford
12.2
Cedar Canyon
18.5
Goat Canyon
Evert Canyon
19.7
Moose Canyon
19.0
Boyd Canyon
Pat Rose Canyon
Zixto Canyon
23.4
25.7
27.0
Still Canyon
Hurkul Canyon
29.0
Camp Canyon
Lewis Canyon
30.9
34.6
37.0
LANGTRY
Painted Canyon
Power Line
39.6
Alpine — 90
41.7
45.5
Shackelford Canyon
47.5
Gauging Station & Wier Dam
54.8
49.4
Dead Mans Canyon
Railroad
Rio Grande River
56.7
Pecos River Marina, Boat Ramp & Ranger Station
1024
61.3
PR 67
90
COMSTOCK
Del Rio
LAKE AMISTAD
SEMINOLE CANYON STATE PARK
N
© 1991 Ocean-graphics

Gauging Station & Weir Dam, 47.5 miles

PHYSICAL LOCATION: Southwest Texas, Val Verde County. San Antonio 200 miles, Austin 250 miles, Midland-Odessa 150 miles, Houston 400 miles, and Del Rio 10 miles, (from take out).

GENERAL COMMENTS: Be in good physical condition and properly equipped. This is not to be considered a family outing. This is a extremely remote, rough, unforgiving area. Due to the length of the trip and the remoteness, careful planning is mandatory. It should be considered a 4 day trip, MINIMUM. To make the trip comfortably, plan on five or six days. Be sure to take a GOOD pair of wading/walking shoes. Be experienced in whitewater and wilderness area canoe/camping. Treat the landowners and camp operators with courtesy. Plan your trip/shuttle so that you reach the camp site at the Pandale crossing, before dark. This is a hard place to find, even during daylight plus it seems that all the deer in West Texas use the road at night. There have been numerous accounts of trespassing, especially of visitors to the many caves along the Pecos. Many trespassers have taken artifacts, arrowheads, etc. from these areas. As of this printing, trespassers are being arrested and prosecuted. Please leave private property alone. If you see anyone pirating or destroying these historical areas, please report it to the Park Rangers at the Pecos River Marina (915) 292-4544.

WATER QUALITY: Generally clear and clean, flowing over rock and gravel.

WATER FLOW: Low during extremely hot periods, but flow usually adequate for float trips. There is an island in the river at the put in point; if there is flow around both sides of the island ,expect good water level conditions. If there is flow only through the left channel, the shallow areas are going to present some real problems.

PREFERRED SEASONS: Late spring, early summer, and autumn afford the best climate and water flow. If weather permits, the winter months offer more stable water conditions, but be prepared to get wet . . . pack accordingly.

HAZARDS: The fluted or "wagon track" limestone river bed can be extremely hazardous, especially at low water levels. To clarify this, the limestone is grooved parallel to the current flow. These groves, if not negotiated carefully, can easily cause you to sprain or break an ankle. At normal to high levels, expect some problems from the fluted limestone between the 19.0 mile point and the 23.4 mile point. At low levels, expand the area to reach from 17.0 miles to 24.0 miles. Although there are many small rapids on this trip, the major rapids are: Oppenheimer Canyon Rapid (Class II) at 7.9 miles, Harkell Canyon Rapid (Class I+) at 29.0 miles, Bluff Rapid (Class II) at 30.9 miles, Still Canyon Rapid (Class II) at 37.0 miles, Lewis Canyon Rapid (Class II-III) at 39.6 miles, Shackleford Canyon Rapid (Class II-III) at 41.7 miles, Shumla Bend Rapid (Class II) at 41.8 miles, and the

Painted Canyon Rapid (Class III-IV) at 45.6 miles. This is the most dangerous and is an extremely long rapid, 100 to 125 yards. It's a boulder garden with no definitely defined channels and has a series of three drops. Run ONLY if decked and you have the experience to handle this type of rapid. There is NO PORTAGE here. You can line on the left, but you'll still get wet. Other rapids include the Weir Dam Rapid (Class II) immediately below the Weir Dam at 47.5 miles and Big Rock Rapid (Class II), the last rapid, at 49.4 miles. The Weir Dam is located at approximately 47.5 miles. This will require a short portage. A short distance downstream, Lake Amistad stops the flow of the Pecos. From this point on, approximately 14 miles, it is flat, dead water paddling. A southerly head wind is tough here. The best idea is to have someone with a power boat waiting below the Weir and have them tow the canoe to the take out. Just lay back and take in the scenery for those last hard miles. Note of Warning: Dead cane is sometimes washed up Lake Amistad by high south winds. This can form natural barriers which are almost impassable. You can't go over or through the cane. The best workable method is to get as close to the bank as possible. Have the bowman pry the cane away from the boat while the stern man slowly pushes the boat through the opening. The length and solitude of this trip could prove critical for the unprepared or the inexperienced. Be ready - it's a long, hard trip! Flash floods occur frequently during unsettled weather.

PUT IN: Put in on the east bank at Bed Rock Ford crossing, southwest of Pandale. Note: These are gravel roads and poorly marked. Also, Pandale, Texas is very small and almost impossible to find at night, so have some daylight when you reach the put in.

TAKE OUT: Plan on taking out at the Pecos River Marina at the 61.3 mile mark. It is on the east bank, just downstream from the Hwy. 90 crossing. If at all possible, have someone meet you with a power boat and tow you to the marina.

CAMPING: There is a good primitive camping area immediately below the put in at Bed Rock Ford. Seminole Canyon State Historical Park is located just off Hwy. 90, approximately 45 miles west of Del Rio, a short distance downstream from the confluence of the Rio Grande with the Pecos. It offers 31 campsites, water, electricity, restrooms, showers and a dump station, The Visitor Center has exhibits, and a guided tour to Indian pictographs. There are no public or private camp sites located along the Pecos, however a bank has been formed between the river and the sheer cliffs of the canyon. This high bank offers excellent natural camp sites. Some of the coves along the river offer almost "waterproof" shelters. However, the majority of these are on private property. PLEASE RESPECT THE PROPERTY OWNERS. Keep your river camps clean and pack out what you pack in. There are some fishing camps, but these are PRIVATE.

CANOE RENTAL AND SHUTTLE SERVICE: There are no rental agencies in this area. Shuttles may be arranged with Manuel and Inez Hardwick, High Bridge Adventures, (915) 292-4462 or 292-4495 in Comstock, Texas.

DISTINGUISHING FEATURES: Sheer rocky cliffs getting progressively higher as the river winds southward. Remote primitive environment. Numerous skill testing rapids, coves, and exciting side canyons for the hiker and photographer. After reaching the headwaters of Lake Amistad, the cliffs rise vertically, and offer no access from the river.

FISHING: Generally good to excellent. Smallmouth are the dominant game fish, but black bass and a variety of perch are abundant. The best fishing is in the swift water at the end of rapids, around rocks, over drop-offs or immediately downstream from waterfalls. Due to the clarity of the water, small lures and low visibility light weight lines are necessary. Stay with the smaller plugs for best results. Topwaters, floating/diving crank baits, small plastic worms, plastic grubs and spinner combinations will all catch fish. Catfishing also falls in the "great" category.

AREA ATTRACTIONS: The historic re-creation of Judge Roy Bean's saloon "courthouse" in Langtry, and the fun nightlife of the Mexican border town of Ciudad Acuna, just across the border from Del Rio. Visit the Fate Bell Shelter in Seminole Canyon State Historical Park. It contains some of North America's oldest pictographs - believed to have been painted as long as 8,000 years ago. There are river tours to the caves and canyons of both the Pecos and Rio Grande.

MAPS: The topographical maps are the Pandale, Little Fielder Draw, Everett Canyon, Harkell Canyon, Seminole Canyon, Still Canyon, Pecos High Bridge and the Shumla, Texas quadrangles. Also, the U. S. Geological Survey topographical map of Lake Amistad is very useful. High Bridge Adventures, P. O. Box 816, Comstock, Texas 78837 offers a very accurate set of laminated Pecos River maps for $10.00 plus $2.00 postage.

RIVER FLOW INFORMATION: High Bridge Adventures, (915) 292-4495, or the Pecos River Ranger Station will furnish up-to-date flow information, (915) 292-4544.

RED RIVER

HWY. 81 TO BULCHER
47.0 MILES

PHYSICAL LOCATION: Located in Montague and Cooke Counties, along the North Central Texas/Oklahoma border. Gainesville 25 miles, Dallas/Ft. Worth 100 miles, Wichita Falls 60 miles, Oklahoma City 135 miles, and Tulsa 250 miles.

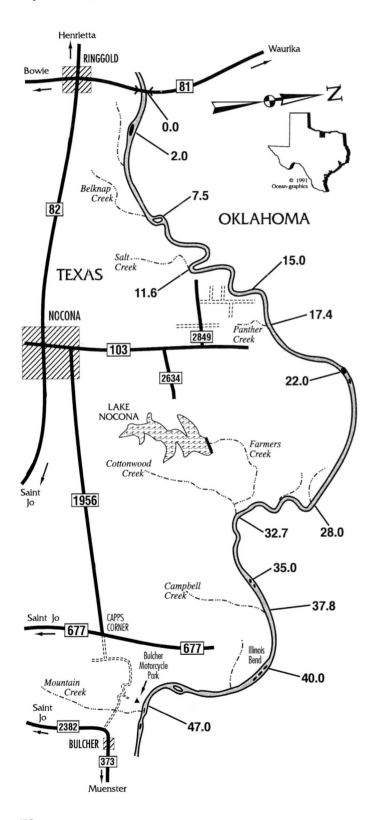

GENERAL COMMENTS: This portion of the Red River above Lake Texoma offers a variety of leisurely trips which anyone can enjoy. Depending on the put in and take out, trips can stretch from a quick, one day float to a trip which can last a couple of weeks. The river is wide for the majority of it's total length, 155 miles, from Hwy. 81, north of Ringgold, Texas to the headwaters of Lake Texoma. Be sure to plan and pack accordingly.

WATER QUALITY: Very red and muddy after rain, to green and murky during dry spells.

WATER FLOW: Low during hot, dry periods - expect to walk through sand bar areas, but flow is usually adequate for float trips.

PREFERRED SEASONS: Generally spring and late autumn or when there is an adequate flow rate to insure water levels appropriate for an enjoyable trip. The river offers very little shade and will be extremely hot during the "dog days" of summer. The Red River lies down the center of "Tornado Alley." Most of the extremely bad weather experienced in North Texas and Southern Oklahoma has a habit of coming straight down the river.

HAZARDS: This river is dangerous, and awesome, at high water levels after very long, heavy rains. It can swell from 100 yds. wide to 300-400 yds., and taking an unplanned swim can mean being in the water for 3-6 miles before reaching shore. Be prepared for sunburn. Poison ivy, snakes and biting insects are plentiful. At low levels, be wary of soft "quicksand" type mud pits, both above water on sand bars and below water in shallow standing water. The mud and water can be deeper than you are tall, making extraction of legs and torso difficult at best.

PUT IN: The initial put in is the Hwy. 81 bridge, 4 miles north of Ringgold, Texas. An alternate put in is the access at the 15.0 mile point.

TAKE OUT: The first take out (15 miles), is 10 miles by road, north of Nocona, Texas. Take Hwy. 103 north to Hwy. 2849, then west for 2 miles, then north on a gravel road until it borders the river at mile 15. The second take out is in the Bulcher Motorcycle Park, at Mountain Creek, 47 miles. Both take outs are on private property and a small fee may be necessary. Access to the second take out is difficult at times. Use caution and common sense.

CAMPING: Numerous natural camp sites are available, but no private or public camp sites. Be sure to camp above the high water mark during rainy weather. Beyond the fences it's all private property. Get permission before setting up camp.

CANOE RENTAL AND SHUTTLE SERVICE: The nearest rental agency is J. W. Canoe Rental in Denison, Texas. Although no commercial shuttle services are available, a shuttle can usually be arranged by calling David Claunch in Gainesville, Texas at (817) 668-6207.

FISHING: Same as the next section.

AREA ATTRACTIONS: In Gainesville, visit the Morton Museum, the historic Victorian style homes on Church, Denton and Lindsey Streets, and the Frank Buck Zoo.

MAPS: Montague and Cooke County Road Maps. The topos are the Ringgold, Belcherville, Fleetwood, Prairie Valley School, Spanish Fort, and Leon North quadrangles.

RIVER FLOW INFORMATION: David Claunch (817) 668-6207, 621 S. Morris, Gainesville, Texas 76240, or the Tulsa C.O.E (918) 581-7811.

RED RIVER
BULCHER TO LAKE TEXOMA
68.0 MILES

PUT IN: The previously described motorcycle park at Mountain Creek, northwest of Bulcher, Texas.

TAKE OUT: The first take out is at 13.0 miles at Warren's Bend, 21.0 miles north of Gainesville off Hwy. 1201. This take out is on private property and may require a small fee and permission. This take out can easily be overlooked if you're not familiar with the river. The second and best take out, on the Texas side, is under the IH-35 bridge, 6 miles north of Gainesville, 40.2 miles. This is one of the few spots where the banks are not steep, it is public access, has plenty of parking area and can be spotted at night by both shuttle drivers and canoeists. The third take out is Dripping Springs at the 60.0 mile point. It's 8.0 miles further to the next take out, the headwaters of Lake Texoma north of Dexter, Texas.

CAMPING: Numerous natural camp sites are available, but no private or public camp sites. Be sure to camp above the high water mark during rainy weather. Beyond the fences it's all private property. Get permission before setting up camp.

CANOE RENTAL AND SHUTTLE SERVICE: The nearest rental agency is J. W. Canoe Rental in Denison, Texas. Although no commercial shuttle services are available, a shuttle can usually be arranged by calling David Claunch in Gainesville, Texas at (817) 668-6207.

DISTINGUISHING FEATURES: The river is wide with large sand bars. It remains unpolluted but very muddy for the duration of this trip. Rugged wooded hills with tall bluffs, to low, flat farm lands border the river.

FISHING: Catfish hold the spotlight, on this section of the Red River, with fish weighing up to 148 pounds being reported. Flat head, channel and blue cat are all caught in the Red River. Trot and jug lines (3 feet of line with a hook tied to a Purex jug and floated along in the current), are the most common ways to catch the catfish. Black bass, spotted bass and stripers are also routinely taken on the upper Red River, but due to the general "red muddy" condition of the river, bass rank far behind the catfish.

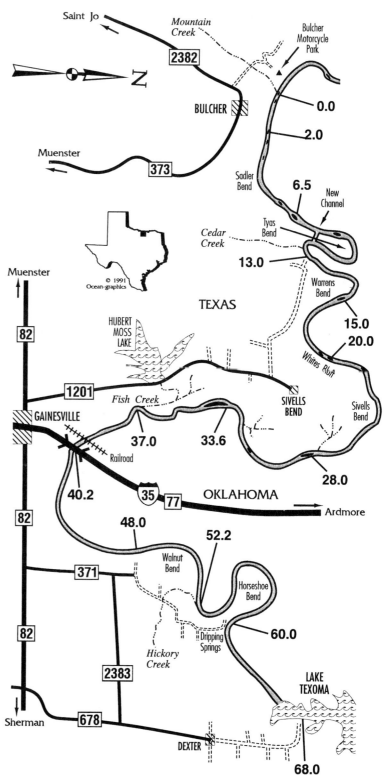

AREA ATTRACTIONS: Same as the previous section.

MAPS: Montague and Cooke, County Road Maps. The topos are the Leon North, Leon South, Marysville, Burneyville, Marietta East, Thackerville, Gainsville North, Callinsburg, Horseshoe Bend, Dexter and Lebanon Texas quadrangles.

RIVER FLOW INFORMATION: David Claunch (817) 668-6207, 621 S. Morris, Gainesville, Texas 76240, or Tulsa C.O.E. (918) 581-7811.

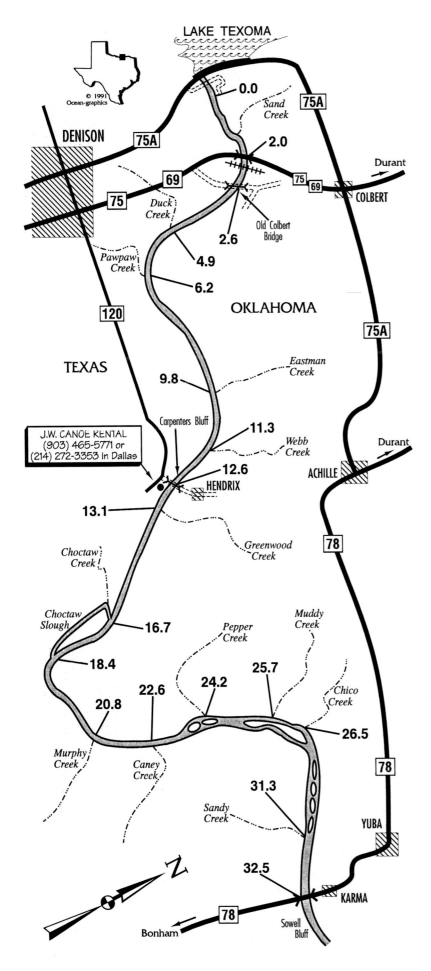

LAKE TEXOMA

© 1991
Ocean-graphics

DENISON

75A

75

69

Duck
Creek

Pawpaw
Creek

120

TEXAS

OKLAHOMA

75A

0.0

Sand
Creek

2.0

75 69

COLBERT

Durant

Old Colbert
Bridge

2.6

4.9

6.2

Eastman
Creek

9.8

Carpenters Bluff

J.W. CANOE RENTAL
(903) 465-5771 or
(214) 272-3353 in Dallas

11.3

Webb
Creek

12.6

HENDRIX

13.1

Choctaw
Creek

Choctaw
Slough

16.7

18.4

20.8

22.6

Murphy
Creek

Caney
Creek

ACHILLE

Durant

78

Greenwood
Creek

Pepper
Creek

24.2

25.7

Muddy
Creek

Chico
Creek

26.5

31.3

Sandy
Creek

78

YUBA

78

32.5

N

78

KARMA

Bonham

Sowell
Bluff

RED RIVER
LAKE TEXOMA DAM TO HWY. 78
32.5 MILES

PHYSICAL LOCATION: Located in Grayson and Fannin Counties, along the North Central Texas/Oklahoma border. Sherman 15 miles, Dallas 55 miles, Ft. Worth 125 miles, Waco 210 miles, Oklahoma City 165 miles, and Tulsa 180 miles.

GENERAL COMMENTS: A leisurely section of river which can be broken up into three or more trips. Non-hazardous and can be enjoyed by everyone. Will be a tough trip in a strong southerly wind, or at extreme low water levels.

WATER QUALITY: Clear and clean when being released from Lake Texoma.

WATER FLOW: Totally dependent upon release from Lake Texoma. At low water levels expect to walk through some of the shallows and shoal areas. At generating levels there will be no problem with shallow water. Good to ideal flow is 5,000 to 10,000 cfs.

PREFERRED SEASONS: Generally spring and late autumn or anytime there is an adequate flow rate to insure water levels appropriate for an enjoyable trip.

PUT IN: The launch point is immediately below the dam on the Oklahoma side. There are campgrounds here. Enter the Corps of Engineers campground at Texoma Dam, Southeast corner, Texas side. Keep to the left on entering the campground and take the lower road on the dam across the river to the campground. Put in on the Oklahoma side.

TAKEOUT: Take out on the right side of the river under the bridge at 12.6 miles. The path here is steep but good. At Hwy. 78, take out on the right above the bridge.

CAMPING: Numerous natural camp sites are available. Be sure to camp above the high water

generating level. Limited camping areas are available below the Lake Texoma Dam. Parking at the Hwy. 78 crossing is permitted, but no camping.

CANOE RENTAL AND SHUTTLE SERVICE: J. W. Canoe Rental, (903) 465-5771, located 6 miles east of Denison, at Carpenters Bluff Bridge, on Hwy. 120.

DISTINGUISHING FEATURES: The river is wide with large sand bars. It remains clear and unpolluted for the duration of this trip.

FISHING: Be sure to have both a Texas and an Oklahoma fishing license. Here, the Red River offers a wide variety of fish, including white bass, spotted bass, hybrid bass, striped bass and largemouth. Huge stripers are regularly taken immediately below Texoma dam and deep holes around structures. The record at this printing is 43 pounds. Small jigs and spinners work best for the white bass. Floating/diving plugs, topwaters and spinning baits will all be productive on the largemouth and spotted bass. The strippers hit a variety of lures ranging from medium running crank baits, topwaters and jigs. Fish the spots with medium to slow currents, especially in shaded areas. On all the game fish except the giant strippers, use light to medium action equipment and low visibility lines. Don't be surprised if you hook a monster alligator gar every once in a while. Fishing for catfish, channel, blues and flat head, is generally great. Blue cat up to 50 pounds, channels weighing in at 2 to 12 pounds and flat head ranging up to 90 pounds are not uncommon.

AREA ATTRACTIONS: Texas: In Bonham visit the Fort Inglish Museum and Park, the Fannin County Museum of History, the Sam Rayburn House Museum, and the Sam Rayburn Library. In Denison, The President Dwight D. Eisenhower Birthplace, the restored Katy Railroad Depot, and the T. V. Munson Vineyard are

points of interest. Gainesville offers the Schmitz Museum, The Morton Museum of Cooke County and the Frank Buck Zoo. Sherman has the Red River Historical Museum, the C. S. Roberts House, and historic Kelly Square. Oklahoma: In Ardmore you might want to drop by The Charles B. Goddard Center for Visual and Performing Arts, the Tucker Tower Museum, or The Carter County Museum. Durant offers the Fairchilds Gallery, and the Three Valley Museum.

MAPS: Grayson and Fannin County road maps. The topographical maps are the Denison Dam, Oklahoma-Texas; the Durant, Oklahoma-Texas, and the Whitewright, Texas-Oklahoma quadrangles.

RIVER FLOW INFORMATION: J. W. Canoe Rental (903) 465-5771, Corps of Engineers; Tulsa (918) 581-7811.

At Least It's All Downhill!

RIO GRANDE RIVER

BIG BEND NATIONAL PARK

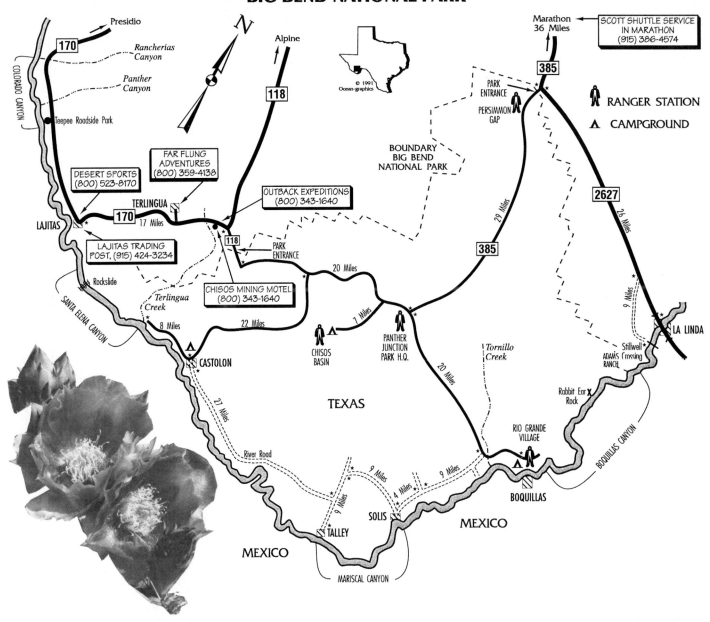

PHYSICAL LOCATION: Extreme West Texas along the Texas Mexico Border. Presidio, Brewster, and Terrell Counties. The most isolated river in Texas. El Paso 250 miles, San Antonio 406 miles, Houston 603 miles, Midland, and Odessa 220 miles.

WATER QUALITY: Generally good except during high water periods when it becomes extremely muddy.

WATER FLOW: The river flow is generally adequate for an enjoyable float trip, with the possible exception of the extreme dry and hot seasons. This area is very susceptible to flash flooding. Take every precaution during unstable weather situations.

PREFERRED SEASONS: November through the first couple of weeks in March is usually the optimum time for floating any section of the Rio Grande. Flash floods are numerous and dangerous during the spring and fall. Summer is exceptionally hot - temperatures exceeding 110° at the river level and the water is

usually low. Try to avoid holidays due to the crowds and shortage of camping areas.

CAMPING: There are public camping areas with facilities in Big Bend National Park at the Chisos Basin, Cottonwood campground at Castolon, and the Rio Grande Village campground. There is a restaurant and motel in the basin if you don't care to rough it all the time. There are limited camping areas at the initial launch point at Lajitas, at Terlingua Creek, at Talley and at Solis. There are many excellent natural camp sites along all of the float trips mentioned later.

CANOE RENTAL AND SHUTTLE SERVICE: Most of the outfitters in the area offer shuttle services for a minimal fee. Check the ads. for addresses and phone numbers. Keep in mind that if you are making your own shuttles, they are long and its quite a distance between service stations.

DISTINGUISHING FEATURES: Sheer canyon walls rising from the river, some over 1500 feet - straight up. Numerous caves, countless springs - both hot and cold, serenity, solitude, wild rapids, friendly and not-so-friendly Mexicans, Indian pictographs, wax works, and best of all - nature as God made it!

MAPS: The Emory Peak, 1:250,000, is the overall topographical map. The topo maps for Colorado Canyon are the Santana Mesa and the Lajitas quadrangles. Topographical maps for Santa Elena Canyon are the Castolon, Mesa de Anguilla, and Lajitas, Texas quadrangles. For Mariscal, the Solis and Mariscal Canyon 1:100,000 topos and for Boquillas, the Solis, Stillwell Crossing, Boquillas 1:100,000 and Dove Mountain; Texas 1:100,000. The county road maps are Presidio, Brewster, and Terrell Counties. The Big Bend National Park Map is also available at Big Bend National History Association.

RIVER FLOW INFORMATION: Call the Park Service (915) 477-2251 or any of the outfitters (see ads.) and ask for the river flow at the gauging station. Anything above 1.7 feet is canoeable. 2.3 to 4.0 are optimum levels. Above 4.5 feet the river becomes extremely swift and dangerous, especially for canoes. Above 7.5 all fresh water springs are covered, and most camp sites are flooded. CAUTION: Only very experienced canoeists (decked) and kayakists should attempt any of these trips at levels between 5.0 and 7.5 feet. For experienced river runners in large rafts, the best level is considered to be between 4.0 and 7.0 feet. NOTE: I said EXPERIENCED, and LARGE rafts.

COLORADO CANYON
1 MILE ABOVE CANYON, OFF HWY. 170 TO LAJITAS
22 MILES

GENERAL COMMENTS: The walls of Colorado Canyon are not as sheer or towering as those of Santa Elena or Mariscal. The Canyon length is approximately 8 miles. This is an exciting and beautiful canyon. The trip is long enough to be fun and demanding, but short enough to allow easy and early take out.

PUT IN: Any point 1 to 1½ miles above the canyon entrance. FM 170 runs very close to the river in this area. Vehicles can be driven almost to the rivers edge at many points.

TAKE OUT: For the short 11 mile trip, take out at the Teepee

Roadside Park. At the roadside park, the shelters are shaped like Tepees and can be seen from approximately a mile up river, It's a tough climb up the bank at the R.S. Park, but it's short. There are picnic tables and grills in the park. The take out for the total 22 miles is Lajitas.

CAMPING: During bad weather, the Tepees Camp offers some shelter from the elements. The best river camp is about half a mile below the Tepees located just above a good rapid. The best site is on the Mexican bank, offering a good view of the rapid and allowing the camp to catch the first rays of the warm morning sun.

RAPIDS AND HAZARDS: Colorado Canyon offers several "rock garden" type rapids which generally fall into the Class II range. These can quickly change to Class III, or better, at high water levels. When in doubt, it's always best to scout them out to be sure.

SANTA ELENA CANYON
LAJITAS TO TERLINGUA CREEK
17 MILES

GENERAL COMMENTS: Be sure all gear is waterproofed and tied in securely. Life preservers are mandatory inside the Canyon. Below the "Rockslide," Santa Elena is beautiful; with coves and majestic side canyons offering exciting places to explore or photograph. Remember, leave them as beautiful as you found them.

PUT IN: The small channel running behind the trading post at Lajitas. This is not the main body of the Rio Grande, but only a narrow channel running along the northern edge of a large island. If the rocks at the ford are covered and the water is fast and muddy, the river will be high and dangerous, especially in the confines of the canyon. Consider ANOTHER TRIP!

TAKE OUT: Take out where Terlingua Creek intersects the Rio Grande.

CAMPING: On the Texas side immediately outside the canyon and below the "Rockslide" on the Mexican bank. The site below the "Rockslide" is covered with ankle deep bermuda grass. Fire wood may be a problem at either site. There is a campsite and picnic area at the take out point (Terlingua Creek intersection).

RAPIDS AND HAZARDS: The only major rapid above the canyon is approximately a mile below the point where the launching channel reconnects with the main river. It has big standing waves and a large souse hole. It is a great place for photos. The dangerous section of Santa Elena is the "Rockslide." It lies around the first major bend to the left, and is less than a mile inside the canyon. When first approaching the 'Slide, large, room sized boulders with small channels between them will be scattered across the channel. This is the FIRST barrier. Immediately behind these first boulders is a clear area, and a place to beach on the Mexican shore. Running the 'Slide is dangerous in high water, and tricky no matter what the water level. There are many blind alleys and suck holes. DO NOT run the 'Slide in high water, and in low water ONLY if you are an experienced fast water canoeist. The boulders are larger than a small house. You will not be able to see over or around them once inside the 'Slide. If you plan to run the 'Slide, beach your boat above it on the Mexican side and scout your route carefully. The first seventy-five yards of the 'Slide are the most dangerous, but none of it is easy. If you decide not to take your chances running the 'Slide, either (1) line and portage along the Texas wall, or (2) portage over the top against the Mexican shore. The Texas side

portage is best and is safe at all but exceptionally high water levels. Even though there is water along part of the Texas side, it is usually slack or eddy water, and can be safely lined or paddled under most conditions. The portage over the top of the "Rockslide" on the Mexican side is to be avoided if possible. It's a man killer. When running the 'Slide, station a couple of "safety" men with lines on the boulders downstream. DO NOT try to go through the 'Slide area, either running it or lining, without wearing an adequate life jacket. Also keep in mind that in winter months the water is cold and that a swimmer becomes quickly chilled and weak in cold water. If someone becomes stranded, assist him as soon as possible before he is too cold to help himself.

MARISCAL CANYON
TALLEY TO SOLIS
10 MILES

GENERAL COMMENTS: This is the shortest canyon trip on the Rio Grande in Big Bend. It is also the most scenic. For the adventuresome, there is a slanting rock shelf which starts a few feet above water level on the Mexican wall upstream from the "Rock Pile." It ends at a cave approximately 100 feet above the river and offers unlimited photographic opportunities. Some of the canyon walls in Mariscal exceed 1,500 feet and offer panoramic beauty unequalled along the Rio Grande.

PUT IN: Where the Talley Ranch Road dead-ends at the river. There is adequate camping space here along the river for a restful overnight before the trip. To reach Mariscal Canyon, take a right turn off the main park road between Panther Junction Park Headquarters and the Rio Grande Village campground. This turn is just before the Tornillo Creek Bridge. This is the road to San Vincente, Solis (your take out point,) Talley (your put in point,) and finally, Castolon. It is approximately 13 miles from the main road to where you must leave a car at Solis. By car from Solis to the put in point at Talley there is another 18 miles of improved dirt road.

TAKE OUT: Solis, as stated above, is approximately two miles on the left after exiting from the canyon. There are no outstanding landmarks at Solis and it would be wise to mark the take out in order not to miss it. There is an old Mexican shack high up on the right bank, but it is difficult to see from water level.

RAPIDS AND HAZARDS: The "Rock Pile" is the first obstacle inside the canyon. The "Rock Pile" is easy to recognize by the large, room size boulder standing solidly in the center of the river. Stay to the Texas side of this boulder and away from the logs and debris usually packed against it and its a breeze. The "Tight Squeeze" is the true challenge of the Mariscal trip. It is approximately one half

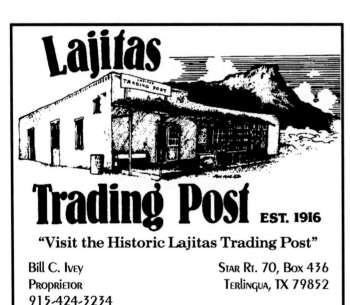

Shooting the "Tight Squeeze" in Mariscal Canyon

mile below the "Rock Pile." Here a huge, flat-topped block of stone fills most of the river channel. There is a narrow shallow gap on the left and a 15 foot wide twisting chute of white water on the right. No matter what the water level, you can beach your boat fifty yards above the "Squeeze" and give it a good long look before you decide to run it. Don't try to go through the left hand gap unless the water is low and you decide to walk through it. The right hand chute is tricky even for an experienced river runner, especially if the water level is high. The river roars through the narrow channel, dropping approximately four feet and piles headlong into a half submerged boulder. You have to make a quick left hand turn as you hit the bottom of the chute to miss the boulder. If the water is running over the top of the flat slab of rock, this is a good indication that the river is at a high and dangerous level. Below the "Tight Squeeze" lies the majority of the canyon. There are no other difficult sections, but you have miles of beautiful scenic canyon.

BOQUILLAS CANYON
RIO GRANDE VILLAGE TO STILLWELL CROSSING
23 MILES

GENERAL COMMENTS: Boquillas is more open and eroded than Santa Elena or Mariscal, but has plenty of deep, sheer canyon walls, and picturesque rock formations. Good camp sites are plentiful and there is usually an adequate supply of fire wood. Camp high enough above the river to avoid a sudden rise which could endanger the campsite. Pull boats above water level and secure them well. After leaving Boquillas, there is a four mile stretch of open country before reaching the take out point at Stillwell. At low water levels, this four mile section is shallow and may require some pulling.

PUT IN: Launch where Rio Grande Village borders the river. This area offers good campsites and a good place to leave vehicles.

TAKE OUT: Immediately below the high footbridge crossing (Stillwell Crossing) on the Adams Ranch. This is approximately 150 miles round trip (BY ROAD) from the Rio Grande Village campground to Adams Ranch and back. The only service station in route is at Panther Junction - and it closes early. Emergency gasoline could be picked up at the ranch. There is a charge per person to take out at the ranch and also a charge to leave the cars there. It's worth it though - the vehicle will be in a safe place and your gasoline and tires will still be there when you get out of the river. For additional information, phone the ranch at 915-386-4355.

CAMPING: There are numerous excellent natural camp sites inside the canyon. Boquillas is well known for its hard, high winds. These come with no warning, and go the same way. Because of the wind, pitch the tent parallel with the canyon, and stake it well. Cover or tie down any items which could easily blow away. This includes canoes, and especially rafts. Keep this wind in mind when selecting a camp site.

RAPIDS AND HAZARDS: There are no rapids or other areas which should be considered exceptionally hazardous in Boquillas. The length of the trip could a problem if adequate precautions are not taken. Allow two or three days for whatever the elements may throw at you.

Colorado Canyon

RIO GRANDE LOWER CANYONS
LA LINDA TO JOHN'S MARINA
83.5 MILES

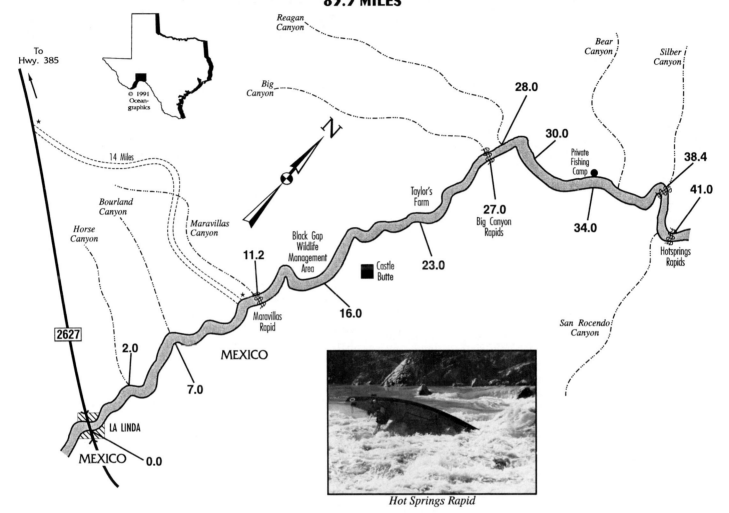

Hot Springs Rapid

GENERAL COMMENTS: Be prepared! Be experienced! Be in good shape! Be careful! This trip ranks at the top in terms of raw beauty, exciting adventure and almost total isolation. It is only for properly prepared and experienced river runners. It can be very arduous and miserable for the careless or ignorant adventurer. Be continually aware of the problems this remote environment creates. You will be miles, and possibly days, away from assistance or medical help. Experience in whitewater, conditioning to paddle 20 miles plus per day and being at home and comfortable in the wilderness are necessary personal ingredients for a safe float on the Lower Canyons. An enjoyable trip is totally dependent upon good planning, good judgement and capabilities equal to the job at hand. Allow a week for the trip and run on a predetermined paddling schedule. The river and weather conditions may determine a change in your schedule. Stay flexible! Remember, low flow levels will dictate shorter daily mileage and can easily eliminate "layover" days.

FLOAT PERMIT: You are required to have a permit to float the Lower Canyons. Gear and equipment regulations are diligently enforced by the Park Rangers. The following regulations are mandatory:

A. Each vessel will carry a U. S. C. G. approved life jacket for each person on board.

B. There will be an extra paddle/oar in each vessel, except that kayaks must have an extra paddle per person.

C. Anyone using inflatable vessels will have an operable pump and a patch kit capable of making major repairs.

D. No vessel will be permitted to carry more than a safe load capacity in person and/or total weight.

E. When the river flow level exceeds 2 meters (approximately 6 ½ feet) permits will be limited to the following: Inflatable rafts with a minimum of 4 compartments and minimum dimensions of 6 feet by 12 feet, decked canoes or canoes at least 50% filled with flotation, or canoes at least 25% filled with flotation and with a full length spray cover, rigid kayaks or dories.

PUT IN: Take U.S. 385 south to PR 2627. Follow PR 2627 to the river. Cross the Gerstacker Bridge at La Linda and stop at the customs office on the Mexican side. Obtain permission at the customs office to launch upstream from the bridge. After leaving the customs office, take the rough dirt road to the right for approximately a quarter mile to the "sand bar" put in. Be careful of getting stuck in the soft sand.

TRIP ITINERARY, MILEAGE, RAPIDS AND ADDITIONAL INFORMATION: For your information, we have included mileages and points of interest other than those shown on the maps. Be careful of the rocks and old reinforcing steel at Heath Crossing, located immediately downstream from the put in.

1.0 Miles - Heath Canyon (Texas)

2.0 Miles - Horse Canyon (Texas)

5.0 Miles - Canyon de Ceferino (Mexico) and Driftwood Canyon (Texas)

6.0 Miles - Scenic Bluff (Mexico) and Bourland Canyon (Texas). Petroglyph site at the base of the mountain 0.2 miles below the canyon.

7.0 Miles - El Caracol Creek (Mexico)

8.0 Miles - Cerro El Barco (Mexico), elevation 3,055 feet above the river. Petroglyph site in the northwest facing "shelter" high up in the cliffs.

10.0 Miles - Las Mulas Creek (Mexico)

11.2 Miles - Maravillas Creek/Canyon (Texas) and Maravillas Rapid. Note the prominent limestone ledges on the Texas side. Maravillas Rapid (Class I to Class II) has large standing waves and strong cross currents. A second rapid, with large standing waves (Class I to Class II) is approximately 100 yards below Maravillas Creek, (an unimproved road, at 11 miles, leads back 14 miles to the Black Gap Headquarters. There are good camp sites on the Mexican side).

13.0 Miles - Small springs (Texas)

14.0 Miles - Black Gap Shelters #12 and #13 (Texas). Small springs (Mexico)

15.0 Miles - Black Gap Shelters #15 and #16 (Texas). La Piedra Parada Creek (Mexico). Small spring (Mexico)

16.0 Miles - Black Gap Shelters #17 and #18 (Texas). Cerro El Zapato (Mexico) Elevation 2,600 feet. Los Burros Creek (Mexico). Good "gravel bar" campsite (Mexico).

17.0 Miles - Cerro El Sombrero, also called Castle Butte or Ship Hill (Mexico) and La Vegas de los Ladrones, Outlaw Flats (Mexico and Texas)

19.0 Miles - Large island. The left channel usually offers best route. Black Gap Shelters #19 and #20 (Texas).

20.0 Miles - Black Gap Shelters #21 and #22 (Texas). Small springs (Mexico).

23.0 Miles - Taylor's Farm (Texas) has expansive grassy flats offering fair to good camp sites. Sierrita de Guadalupe (Mexico), a range of high ridges reaching over 3,400 feet in elevation.

27.0 Miles - Big Canyon, small spring and old rock ruins of candelilla works overlooking the river (Texas). Big Canyon Rapids (Class II) includes medium to large standing waves. Best route is usually just left of center. Currents increase in this area due to river being restricted between closer canyon walls. Good camp site (Mexico).

28.0 Miles - Reagan Canyon (Texas) is characterized by a spectacular rise in the canyon wall. A small rapid.

30.0 Miles - River enters deep canyon with walls reaching up to over 1,500 feet.

31.0 Miles - El Recodo Creek (Mexico)

32.0 Miles - El Reliz Creek (Mexico)

Putting in at La Linda

34.0 Miles - Private fishing camp and Bear Canyon, also called Oso Canyon (Texas).

35.0 Miles - La Yegua Creek (Mexico)

36.0 Miles - Cave, "Cueva de la Puerta Grande" (Mexico) continues over 100 feet into the bluff leading to a large level living area.

37.0 Miles - Las Yeguas Canyon (Texas)

38.4 Miles - Silber Canyon (Texas) and small Class I rapid. Asa Jones pump house (Texas). Hot springs (Mexico). Water is good. There are also some small springs located on the Texas side.

40.0 Miles - Dagger Mountain (Texas), elevation 2,865 feet. San Rocendo Canyon (Mexico) is the largest Mexican drainage along the Lower Canyons. There are numerous springs in the canyon. Hot Springs Rapid (Class III to Class IV) has been created by the outwash of boulders from San Rocendo Creek. Beach above the mouth of the canyon and scout the rapid. This is a tough mean rapid. Be sure you and your equipment are up to the task. When running this rapid, be sure to keep enough space between vessels. Crowding can become quite dangerous in this rapid. If in doubt, line your boat along the Mexican shoreline. There is a good camp site above the mouth of the canyon and below the rapid. Numerous hot springs (Mexico) at the base of the rapids. DO NOT USE SOAP IN ANY OF THE SPRINGS!

41.0 Miles - Hotsprings Rapid (Class III), created by the outwash from San Rocendo Canyon. Use all caution and safety procedures if running this rapid.

Lower Canyons, Class III-IV

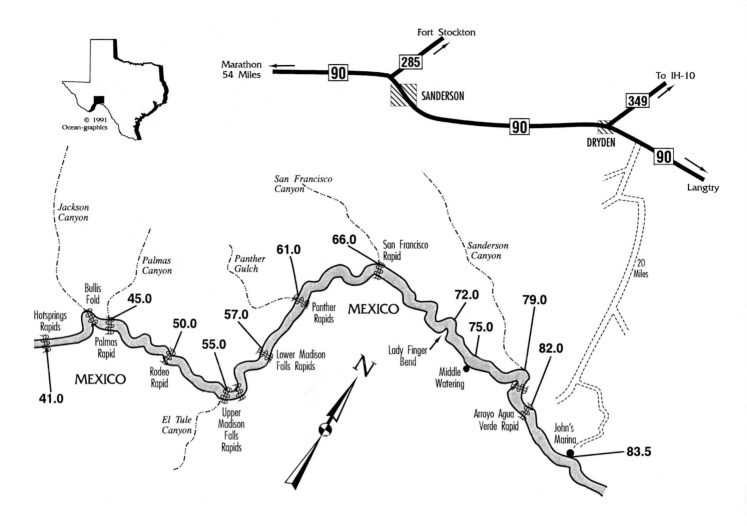

43.0 Miles - Canyon Caballo Blanco (Mexico)

44.0 Miles - Private orange roofed cabin, Dean and Haack Canyons confluence and Bullis Fold (Texas). Bullis Fold derives the name from the horizontal layers of limestone which have been "folded" to a near 90 degree bend. Bullis Fold Rapids (Class II to Class III) has high standing waves, strong cross currents and whirlpools.

45.0 Miles - Palmas Canyon (Texas) exhibits the first Berlander ash trees to be seen. Palmas Rapid (Class II) is primarily a boulder garden. Scout it carefully from the rock slab on the Texas side at the mouth of the canyon.

46.0 Miles - Natural arches high above the river on the Texas side.

50.0 Miles - Canyon Complejo del Caballo (Mexico) and Rodeo Rapids (Class II). The major characteristics of this rapid are the huge standing waves. Due to the outwash from the canyon, the river is extremely narrow here. Right of center usually offers the best channel. The craggy cliffs along this section of the Lower Canyons have long been recognized as prime nesting sites for the Peregrine Falcon.

52.0 Miles - Mal Paso Creek (Mexico)

54.0 Miles - Burro Bluff (Texas). Here the Rio Grande flows directly into the sheer face of the bluff. Stay to the right and be ready to beach on the Mexican side. You are immediately above Upper Madison Falls Rapids and you definitely need to look it over before going one paddle stroke further.

55.0 Miles - Upper Madison Falls Rapid (Class III to Class IV) is a "bad dude" at any level! A generally accepted guideline is to

portage on the Mexican shore at levels of less than 3 feet and more than 4 feet. If the flow is between 3 and 4 feet, the Texas channel can be negotiated, with EXTREME CAUTION, only if SKILLS ARE SUFFICIENT to warrant the attempt. There is a good "rock slab" campsite on the Mexican side below the rapid. An alternate site is just across the river at the base of the Texas bluff BEHIND the river cane. There is a small opening in the cane affording access to the Texas site.

57.0 Miles - Lower Madison Falls Rapids, also known as Horseshoe Falls (Class III) is negotiated best by lining down the Texas side. The Texas channel can be run, with caution, at above normal

Upper Madison Falls Rapid

levels. Springs (Texas) offer good water immediately below the rapid.

60.0 Miles - Panther Gulch (Texas) and Rapid (Class II to Class III). Scout this rapid carefully from the Texas shore before running.

61.0 Miles - Spring (Texas). This is the last dependable drinking water. Remember, you still have over 22 miles to go and you don't want to run out of water.

66.0 Miles - San Francisco Canyon (Texas). A good landmark here is the trailer house on top of the bluff. There is a fair to good campsite on the rocky ledge at the creek mouth. San Francisco Rapid (Class II to Class III) can be run best at above normal flow levels. If in doubt, it's best to line down the Mexican side.

71.0 Miles - Small island. Las Pompas Creek (Mexico).

72.0 Miles - Bone Watering (Texas) offers a large grassy beach affording good camping area. Lady Finger Bend where the Rio Grande makes a complete 180 degree bend.

75.0 Miles - Middle Watering (Mexico) is a long grassy beach with excellent access. This is a great place for the "last night" on the river.

77.0 Miles - Paso Colorado (Texas) where a jeep trail from Texas meets a jeep trail from Mexico.

78.0 Miles - Sanderson Canyon (Texas) forms an extensive drainage area extending beyond Sanderson, Texas. A cable stretches from the fishing camp on top of the bluff to the river for transporting a cable car down to the river. Sanderson Rapid (Class II) runs directly into the Texas wall. Huge boulders crowd the channel along the Texas shore. Check this one out very carefully before running. Line down the right side at low water levels.

81.0 Miles - Taylor Canyon (Texas)

82.0 Miles - Arroyo Agua Verde (Mexico) and Rapid (Class II to Class III) is a rock garden outwash which can be hazardous. The best channel is usually just left of center, but stay clear of the large rock jutting out from the Texas shore. It creates a tricky cross current, especially at high water levels. After the rock, the currents flows directly into the face of the bluff on the Mexican shore.

83.0 Miles - Jabalina Canyon and river gauge (Texas).

83.5 Miles- Take out on the concrete ramp at John's Marina (Texas).

TAKE OUT: It is 20 miles, plus or minus, from US 90 to John's Marina on the Rio Grande. The turn off is one mile east of Dryden, Texas. You will cross 2 cattle guards and reach a "Y" with a rock sign in the fork. Turn left at the sign. You will cross 3 more cattle guards before reaching another "Y". Take the right hand road, go

through a wooden gate and past a windmill and water storage tank on the hill immediately to your left. Take the next left through a pipe gate in the fence line. You will then pass through a second gate, past stock pens on the left, through another gate, past a windmill on your right and then through a fourth gate. John's Marina is just a short distance down the road.

CANOE RENTAL AND SHUTTLE SERVICE: Mike and Sharan Scott, Scott's Shuttle Service, located in Marathon, Texas. They can handle all the shuttles and parking fees for the Lower Canyon river runners. Call them at (915) 386-4574 or write to P. O. Box 477, Marathon, Texas 79842 for the most current rates and fees for a total shuttle package.

MAPS: The topographical maps for this section are the Stillwell Crossing, Bourland Canyon, Las Vegas de Los Ladrones SW, Las Vegas de Los Ladrones, San Rocendo, Bullis Gap, Panther Gulch East, Panther Gulch West, Candilla Canyon East and Taylor Canyon, Texas quadrangles. An excellent source for marked maps and a trip summary is "The Lower Canyons of the Rio Grande," Louis F. Aulbach and Joe Butler, 214 West Troy Road, Houston, Texas 77076. At this printing the cost of the publication is $14.95 . . . and well worth it!

RIVER FLOW INFORMATION: Park Ranger Station (915) 477-2393 or Scott Shuttle Service (915) 386-4574.

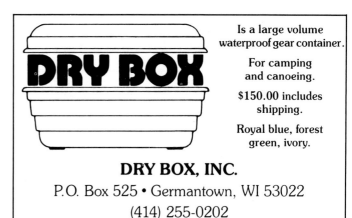

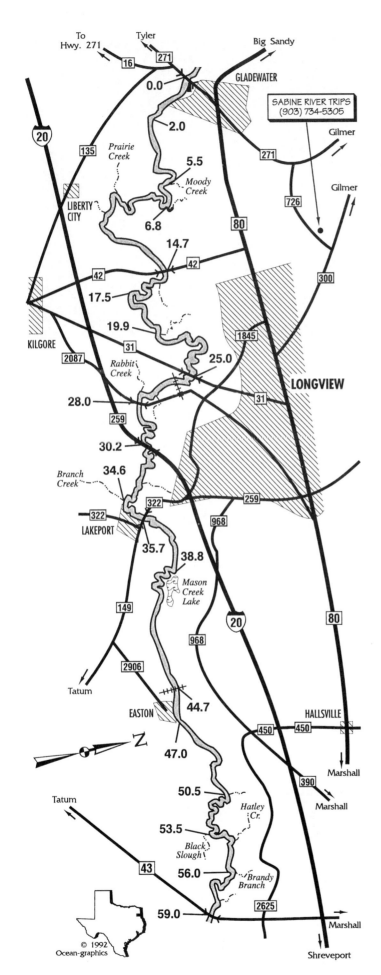

SABINE RIVER
HWY. 271 TO HWY. 43
59 MILES

PHYSICAL LOCATION: In deep northeast Texas, adjacent to Gladewater, Longview, Kilgore, and Marshall in Gregg, Harrison, Rusk and Panola Counties. Dallas 130 miles, Shreveport 60 miles, Austin 260 miles, and Texarkana 65 miles.

GENERAL COMMENTS: Due to the many road crossings, this section of the Sabine can easily be divided into trip lengths which suit your specific time frame and conditioning. The Sabine, in this area, is very scenic as it flows slowly between its pine shrouded banks. Note: Over the past few years the highway numbers of the roads coming into Longview from the south have changed. An up-to-date highway map is necessary to be sure of the correct numbers.

WATER QUALITY: Good but off color due to the tannic acid prevalent in all the East Texas streams.

WATER FLOW: Generally adequate for a good float trip.

PREFERRED SEASONS: Due to the adequate flow levels, the Sabine can be enjoyed year round. The trees offer good shade during the summer months, but the river channel can be extremely hot due to the humidity and lack of breezes.

HAZARDS: Under normal conditions, the Sabine is relatively hazard free. At low water levels expect some problems with long jams. Due to the trees, high water levels should be regarded as dangerous. The drop at the outlet dam downstream from the Hwy. 42 crossing could be hazardous. Check it out before running.

PUT IN: The first put in is at the boat ramp on the northeast corner of the Hwy. 271 crossing. Alternate launch points are the Hwy. 42 crossing (dry weather only), and the boat ramp at the Hwy. 149/Hwy. 322 crossing.

TAKE OUT: Take out at the alternate put ins. The last take out is at the southeast corner of the Hwy. 43 crossing. At Hwy. 43 there is only a beaten path to the river. The access here is poor and can be tough in wet weather.

CAMPING: There are no public or private parks/camping facilities in this immediate area. Occasional sandbars in the river bed offer primitive campsites. The river banks are all private property. Don't camp above the shoreline without permission.

CANOE RENTAL AND SHUTTLE SERVICE: Sabine River Trips in Gilmer, Texas (903) 734-5305.

DISTINGUISHING FEATURES: Lots of pine trees border the slow moving "tea" colored river. Many of the old oil fields still exist along the river. Very scenic, offers a multitude of wildlife.

FISHING: Trot lining for the huge flat head catfish, many going over 70 pounds, ranks at the top of the list. White bass, up to 2 pounds, are consistently caught during the spring spawning season. Various perch, including crappie, can be taken on light tackle. Huge alligator gar offer fishing excitement for those so inclined.

AREA ATTRACTIONS: Gladewater is touted as the "Antique Capital of Texas" and hosts a number of "Antique Show" extravaganzas each year. In Kilgore visit the East Texas Oil Museum and the Kilgore Rangerette Showcase, both on campus at Kilgore College. For more information on the area, contact the Gladewater Chamber of Commerce (214) 845-2626.

MAPS: The Gregg, Harrison, Rusk, and Panola County road maps. The topographical maps are the Gladewater, Kilgore N.W., Lakeport, Easton, Darco and Harris Chapel Texas quadrangles.

RIVER FLOW INFORMATION: Sabine River Trips (903) 734-5305.

Everyone Has To Be Somewhere

SABINE RIVER

HWY. 59 TO HWY. 79

18.5 MILES

PHYSICAL LOCATION: Panola County in East Texas. Longview 25 miles, Marshall 13 miles, Dallas 165 miles, Houston 210 miles, and Shreveport, Louisiana 30 miles.

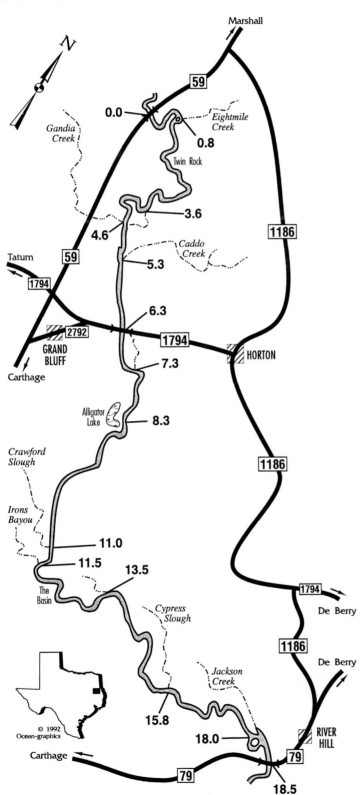

GENERAL COMMENTS: This is a very scenic trip, boasting fantastic natural beauty and an abundance of wildlife. It is a trip which, generally, everyone can enjoy.

WATER QUALITY: Characteristic color of all East Texas streams, due to the tannic acid. Other than the "tea" color, the quality is good.

WATER FLOW: Generally adequate for float trips at any time of the year. Due to the twisting channel and heavy tree cover, the river can be extremely dangerous at high water levels. Be prepared for a lot of floating brush and trees, as well as large whirlpools at high water levels. Expect some log jams and downed trees at normal levels.

PREFERRED SEASONS: The Sabine is an all season river. Like most, spring and autumn are the prime scenic seasons, and generally offer the most tolerable weather conditions.

PUT IN: Launch at the Hwy. 59 crossing approximately halfway between 1-20 and Carthage, Texas.

TAKE OUT: Take out at the Hwy. 79 crossing approximately 12 miles northeast of Carthage.

CAMPING: There are no public or private camps in this area, but there are numerous sand bars which offer excellent camp sites. However, there are many very independent people living in these Sabine bottom lands and many don't want company. So stay close to the river and always get permission to camp on private property.

CANOE RENTAL AND SHUTTLE SERVICE: None in this area. Bring your equipment and plan accordingly.

DISTINGUISHING FEATURES: Slow moving current as the river flows between densely forested banks of willow, towering pines, pecan, black walnut, dogwood, and many other species of trees and flowers native to East Texas.

FISHING: The catfish is "king" on the upper Sabine. Huge flatheads, channel and blue cat are the "finny fare" of this area. Trot line, floating jug line, limb lines, and bottom fishing all produce catfish. Live baits, such as perch, suckers and crawfish work well on the flatheads. Man made baits and "stinkey stuff" consistently catch blues and channels. Black bass and perch can be taken on artificials. For best results, fish the areas with some current and natural cover. Topwaters, shallow running crank baits, and spinning baits all work well. Yellow and orange are usually the preferred colors.

AREA ATTRACTIONS: Other than the remote beauty, this area is short on attractions.

MAPS: The Panola County map and the Grand Bluff, Carthage, and River Hill topographical quadrangles.

RIVER FLOW INFORMATION: National Weather Service Forecast Center, Ft. Worth (817) 429-2631.

SABINE RIVER
TOLEDO BEND RESERVOIR TO HWY. 190
50.3 MILES

PHYSICAL LOCATION: Located in Newton County in southeast Texas. Beaumont 50 miles, Houston 150 miles, Waco 220 miles, Lake Charles, Louisiana 80 miles.

GENERAL COMMENTS: This section of the Sabine is considered one of the most scenic trips in the state. Do not try to rush this trip. Due to the extreme isolation and length of the trip, allow plenty of time, especially on the section from Hwy. 63 to Hwy. 190. Allow three to four days for this lower section.

WATER QUALITY: Good, but "tea" colored (tannic acid), characteristic of East Texas streams.

WATER FLOW: Always adequate for float trips, even at non-generating periods below Toledo Bend Reservoir.

PREFERRED SEASONS: The Sabine is an all season river. Like most, spring and autumn are the prime scenic seasons.

HAZARDS: Few other than downed trees, small log jams and stumps in the river. Don't forget the insect repellent and keep a watchful eye out for snakes. This trip is extremely long and isolated, plan and pack accordingly.

PUT IN: Launch at the man-made channel immediately below the Toledo Bend Reservoir dam. The bank is steep, but will prove no great problem, except during wet weather. An alternate put in is the Hwy. 63 crossing east of Burkeville.

TAKE OUT: The first take out is at the Hwy. 63 crossing. The bank is steep and sandy, but adequate. The drive along the old Hwy. 63 bridge span can be hazardous in wet weather. Use caution: it is almost 40 miles to the next take out at the Hwy. 190 crossing, between Bon Wier, Texas and Merryville, Louisiana.

CAMPING: There are no public or private camps on this section of the Sabine. Abundant and beautiful white sand bars offer numerous natural camp sites, at low or normal water levels.

CANOE RENTAL AND SHUTTLE SERVICE: None in this area. Bring your equipment and plan for needed shuttles.

DISTINGUISHING FEATURES: Slow moving current, clean white sand bars, undeveloped, and very remote. Stately and majestic cypress trees are a dominant feature of the landscape.

FISHING: Fishing for largemouth bass can be rewarding, especially in the upper section. Ultra light to medium bass tackle will work. Shallow to deep running crank baits, plastic worms, grubs, crawfish, medium spinning baits, and topwaters will all produce fish. White bass fishing, immediately below the dam, during generating periods, can be excellent. White or yellow jigs, small spoons and small spinning baits are consistent producers for whites. Catfishing for channel and yellow cat is generally good to excellent especially if the water is just a little off color.

AREA ATTRACTIONS: Just a lot of beautiful scenery characteristic of East Texas and West Louisiana.

MAPS: The Newton County road map. The topographical maps are the Haddens, Wiergate S.E., Merryville, and Bon Wier Texas/Louisiana quadrangles.

RIVER FLOW INFORMATION: National Weather Service Forecast Center, Ft. Worth (817) 429-2631, or San Antonio (512) 826-4679.

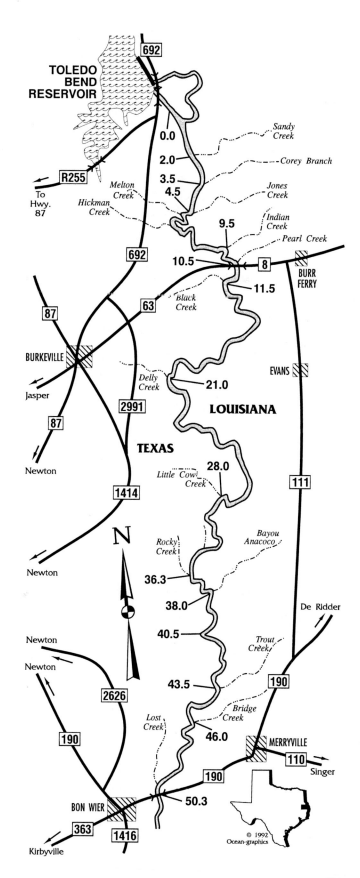

SAN MARCOS RIVER

SAN MARCOS TO STAPLES DAM (FM 1977)
16.5 MILES

PHYSICAL LOCATION: Starting in downtown San Marcos, Texas and running through Hays, Guadalupe and Caldwell Counties in South Central Texas. Austin 40 miles, San Antonio 60 miles, Dallas 230 miles, and Houston 200 miles.

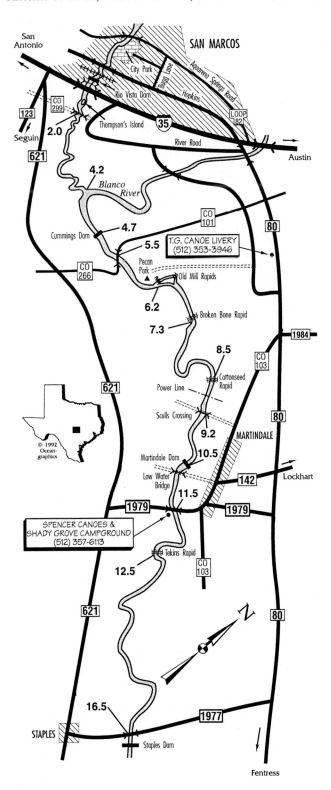

GENERAL COMMENTS: Load canoe as lightly as possible for easy portaging. Tie in and waterproof all gear. This is a good family trip, however, some canoeing experience is desirable. Some of the landowners along the upper sections have been seriously mistreated by a few disrespectful river runners. These folks can be downright hostile if provoked. DO NOT trespass, and quietly paddle away from any confrontation. River access is good, offering put ins/take outs for trips ranging from 5.5 to 16.5 miles.

WATER QUALITY: Good to excellent, flowing directly from Aquarena Springs.

WATER FLOW: This upper portion of the river is fed, almost totally, from the springs. There is constant flow year round, affording adequate water for enjoyable canoeing. The water comes from the springs at a comfortable 72 degrees.

PREFERRED SEASONS: Due to the constant flow, adequate shade and the cool water, this portion of the San Marcos is fun anytime of the year. However, remember, you're going to get wet sooner or later. Keep this in mind when planning a cold weather trip.

HAZARDS: The primary hazards are created by the swift narrow channels shrouded by low overhanging limbs, downed trees and small long jams. The low water bridges, at above normal flow levels, can be dangerous. To be on the safe side, check out the following potential hazard area: The Rio Vista Dam at 1 mile, which can be run through a slot, located approximately one third the distance out from the left bank. This is not dangerous, but it can be rough on equipment and you will definitely get wet. You'll have to duck down to get under the Houston Street bridge immediately downstream from Rio Vista. A pipeline crosses below IH-35 and requires a portage to the left, at all but extremely low water levels. Cummings Dam, at 4.7 miles, should be portaged on the right. Take out ON THE DAM and slide the canoe down one of the concrete supports. Cottonseed Rapid, at 8.5 miles, can get you wet and bang up your equipment. Run it along the left side or portage on the right along the washed out concrete dam. At 10.5 miles, take out and portage Martindale Dam on the right. At high water levels, the low water bridge below Martindale Dam does not offer enough clearance for safe passage. If it's necessary to portage, beach well above the bridge on the right.

PUT IN: The concrete ramp at the San Marcos City Park. Alternate launch points are the CO 101/CO 266 crossing at 5.5 miles, Pecan Park at 6.2 miles, Sculls Crossing at 9.2 miles, the low water crossing below Martindale Dam, and Spencer Canoes/Shady Grove at 11.5 miles.

TAKE OUT: The last take out for this section is immediately below the FM 1977 crossing, east of Staples. Any of the alternate put ins are also good take outs.

CAMPING: The private camps, Pecan Park at 6 miles, and Shady Grove Campground at 11.5 miles, both offer river front camping, water, showers, and electricity. Camping, parking, and launch fees are charged at these campgrounds.

CANOE RENTAL AND SHUTTLE: T. G. Canoe Livery (512) 353-3946, and Spencer Canoes (512) 357-6113.

DISTINGUISHING FEATURES: Consistent water flow and temperature, lush, almost tropical vegetation, including elephant ears, water hyacinths and cannas. A twisting, clean flowing river channel.

FISHING: Due to the speed and constriction of the river, it is very difficult to fish from a boat, except in the backwater above the dams. The best way to fish the flowing sections is to beach your boat and wade. With patience and a quiet approach, largemouth, spotted and Guadalupe bass can be taken consistently. Fly fishing equipment or light weight spinning gear seems to produce best. The clarity of the water demands

light, low visibility lines and small baits. Live baits always seem to get good results. Catfishing is usually good in the slow deep water around brush piles and submerged trees.

AREA ATTRACTIONS: Aquarena Springs, the birthplace of the San Marcos, features Ralph the swimming pig, glass bottom boat cruises, Hillside Gardens, the Alpine Sky Ride and the Submarine Theatre. Visit Wonder World Cave, formed 30 million years ago by a massive earthquake. Take the train ride through the Wildlife Park at Wonderworld. For more information call the San Marcos Convention and Visitors Bureau (800) 782-7653, ext. 177.

MAPS: Hays, Caldwell and Guadalupe County road maps. The topographical maps are the San Marcos North, San Marcos South and the Martindale Texas quadrangles.

RIVER FLOW INFORMATION: T.G. Canoes (512) 353-3946, Spencer Canoes (512) 357-6113, or Pecan Park (512) 392-6171.

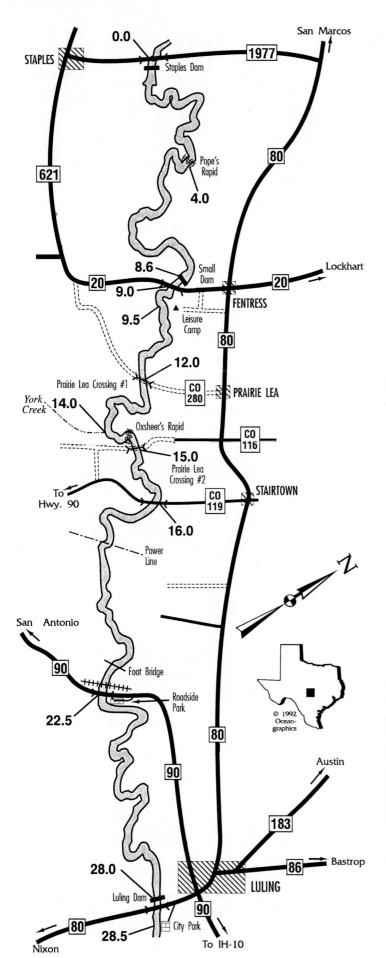

SAN MARCOS RIVER

STAPLES DAM
TO LULING CITY PARK
28.5 MILES

PHYSICAL LOCATION: Caldwell and Guadalupe Counties in South Central Texas. San Antonio 60 miles, Austin 60 miles, Houston 150 miles, and Dallas 240 miles.

GENERAL COMMENTS: Some canoeing experience is desirable. Floating the entire trip could prove over-taxing for small children, but it's considered a good family trip due to the many access points which can shorten the trip if necessary. Trips along this section can vary in length from 1 to 28.5 miles.

WATER QUALITY: Generally clean, but not as clear as upper section due to earthen banks and influx from adjoining creeks.

WATER FLOW: Same as upper section. However, some flow volume will be added from creeks and additional springs. This section will show more of a decrease in flow during the hot summer months. There will be some short shoal areas and gravel bars.

PREFERRED SEASONS: Same as upper section, but water temperatures will vary more due to the distance from originating springs. Large amount of shade on the river lends this section to enjoyable trips, even during the hot summer months.

HAZARDS: Low water bridge crossings at 9 miles, 12 miles, and 15 miles. These low water crossings can be extremely dangerous at above normal flow levels. Luling Dam, at 28 miles, cannot be run. Portage right. Sharp turns, numerous stumps, and downed trees can be extremely hazardous in this area. Take special care to avoid the numerous fishing "drop" lines hung from many of the overhanging limbs.

Cottonseed Rapid, map page 86

88

PUT IN: Right bank immediately below Staples Dam, off FM 1977. Alternate put ins for shorter trips are the Hwy. 20 crossing, west of Fentress at 9.0 miles, the Prairie Lea #1 crossing at 12.0 miles, the Prairie Lea #2 crossing at 15.0 miles, the Stairtown crossing at 16.0 miles, and the Hwy. 90 crossing at 22.5 miles.

TAKE OUT: Any of the alternate put in points work well as alternate take outs. The last take out for this trip is the Luling City Park at 28.5 miles. Portage the Luling Dam on the right, put back into the river and take out in the Park on the left bank, downstream from the Hwy. 80 crossing.

Cummings Dam Portage, map page 86

CAMPING: Because the majority of the property along the river is private, we do not recommend canoe camping. Many of the landowners in this area have been excessively mistreated by a handful of river runners. Some are downright hostile - and usually with good reason. A private camp at 9.5 miles offers cabins, showers and restrooms. Also, Shady Grove Campground and Pecan Park Retreat, only a few miles up the road, cater to river runners. Fees for take out, put in, and camping. The City Park in Luling is public; no fees are required but facilities are limited.

CANOE RENTALS AND SHUTTLES: Spencer Canoes (512) 357-6113, and T. G. Canoe Livery (512) 353-3946.

DISTINGUISHING FEATURES: The river is slower and murkier than the upper section, but still bordered by scenic vegetation. Below the Hwy. 20 crossing the river is increasingly twisting, and contains more fallen trees and stumps. Generally more isolated than the upper section.

FISHING: Here the river has lost much of its clarity, so the quiet slow approach isn't as important. Largemouth, Guadalupe and spotted bass, plus a variety of sunfish, are plentiful in the river. As in most fast flowing streams they are not very big, but they're very aggressive. Fishing for catfish, channels, and yellow cats is very popular on this section.

AREA ATTRACTIONS: Same as the previous section.

MAPS: Guadalupe and Caldwell County road maps. Topographical maps are the Martindale, Kingsbury, and Luling Texas quadrangles.

RIVER FLOW INFORMATION: Pecan Park Retreat (512) 392-6171, Spencer Canoes (512) 357-6113, and T. G. Canoe Livery (512) 353-3946.

Rio Vista Dam, map page 86

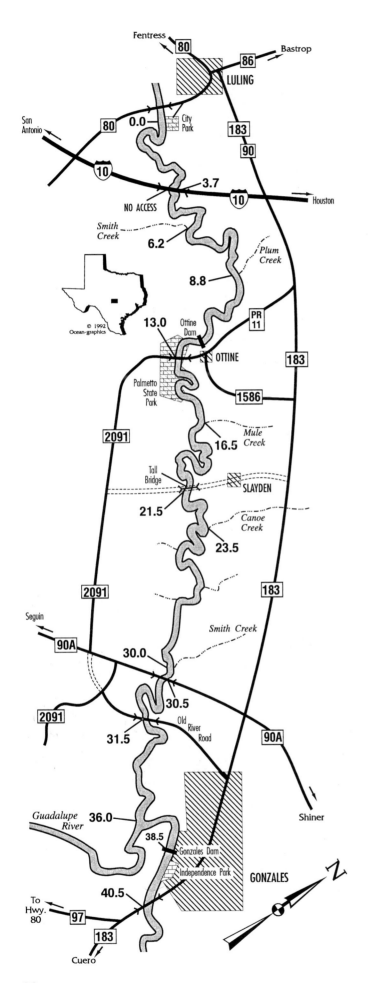

SAN MARCOS RIVER
LULING CITY PARK TO HWY. 183
40.5 MILES

PHYSICAL LOCATION: Located in Caldwell, Guadalupe and Gonzales Counties, South Central Texas. San Antonio 60 miles, Austin 70 miles, Houston 160 miles, and Dallas 250 miles.

GENERAL COMMENTS: Definitely a "get away from it all" trip. Remote and infrequently canoed. Some canoe experience is desirable. Tie in and waterproof all gear. Most of the banks are steep, and extremely slick and muddy after a rain. This "total" trip can be extremely long, but is easily broken into many short enjoyable trips.

WATER QUALITY: Water has gradually become more murky, but is still unpolluted.

WATER FLOW: Continues to slow as river becomes generally deeper. Due to commercial and irrigation use of river water, the river flow will decrease considerably during extremely hot, dry periods. Gravel shoals are more numerous in shallow sections.

PREFERRED SEASONS: Early spring through early summer, and again during the autumn months. This section will require a minimum of walking during the hot summer months.

HAZARDS: Ottine Dam cannot be run. Portage left at normal and low water levels. Portage on the right bank at above normal flow levels. Low water crossing 21.5 miles. Gonzales Dam at 38.5 miles, extremely dangerous - especially at high water levels. Do not run. Beach well above dam and portage right.

PUT IN: Luling City Park, west of Luling on the south side of Hwy. 80. Alternate put ins are Palmetto State Park at 13.0 miles, below the tall bridge at 21.5 miles, and the Hwy. 90-A crossing at 30.5 miles. There is a small roadside park at the Hwy. 90-A crossing.

TAKE OUT: Any of the alternate put ins, plus the old River Road Crossing, west of Gonzales at 31.5 miles, numerous points in Independence Park, south of Gonzales, on west side of Hwy. 183, or on the gravel bar immediately below the Hwy. 183 crossing. There is excellent access in Independence Park, and a fair weather road leading directly to a large gravel bar and the river, below the Hwy. 183 crossing.

CAMPING: Luling City Park at the put in, and Independence Park in Gonzales. The Palmetto State Park (adjacent to the river on Park Road 11, west of Hwy. 183), has 37 campsites, water, electricity, restrooms, showers, dining hall with kitchen, dump station, and picnic areas.

CANOE RENTAL AND SHUTTLE SERVICE: Spencer Canoes (512) 357-6113 and T.G. Canoe Livery (512) 353-3946.

DISTINGUISHING FEATURES: This area is generally remote with continually changing river channel conditions. Many log jams and fallen trees along the undercut banks.

FISHING: Almost identical to the previous section.

AREA ATTRACTIONS: Same as the upper San Marcos, plus the historic sites of the Texas Revolution in Gonzales.

MAPS: Guadalupe, Gonzales and Caldwell county road maps. Topographical maps are the Luling, Harwood, Ottine, Gonzales North and Gonzales South, Texas quadrangles.

RIVER FLOW INFORMATION: Same as previous section.

TRINITY RIVER ⁃ CLEAR FORK
GAUGING STATION TO LOOP 820
3.1 MILES

PHYSICAL LOCATION: Located in Tarrant County in North Central Texas. Ft. Worth 15 miles, Dallas 40 miles, Waco 115 miles, and Austin 205 miles.

GENERAL COMMENTS: A good short leisurely trip to get away from the rat race for a few hours. Skill testing at high water levels. Very scenic in spite of its close proximity to Ft. Worth and Dallas. Travel as light as possible, and tie in and waterproof all gear.

WATER QUALITY: The water quality is good as it is being released from Lake Benbrook, but will be murky because of the earthen channel.

WATER FLOW: Flow is totally dependent upon the release from the lake. At low water levels this trip can be a leisurely fun float, but at higher levels the narrow, twisting channel will prove quite challenging. An enjoyable flow level is 140-160 cfs.

PREFERRED SEASONS: Spring and fall generally when there has been adequate rainfall to allow water release from the dam.

HAZARDS: High water should be considered dangerous on this section of the Clear Fork. Overhanging limbs and trees in the river can easily demolish a canoe during high water. Raul's Dam, and a cable a few hundred yards below the dam are other hazards. Raul's Dam is approximately ten feet high, and should not be run. Portage on the right bank, adjacent to the dam, at low water levels. At high water levels, the portage must be started some distance above the dam on the left bank. Use the left bank portage only when necessary because the path is on private property, behind a residence.

PUT IN: Put in at the man made inlet just below the gauging station. DO NOT launch above the gauging station.

TAKE OUT: Take out at the Loop 820 crossing at the 3.1 mile point.

CAMPING: There are no camp sites along this section.

CANOE RENTAL AND SHUTTLE SERVICE: Due to the brevity of this trip, there is little need of shuttle service. However, canoes may be rented from Double "M" Canoe in Hurst (817) 282-3135.

DISTINGUISHING FEATURES: The Clear Fork is narrow, twisting, and scenic. In many areas it is completely canopied by large pecan, cottonwood, sycamore, and elm trees. It can be low and slow, or fast and fantastic, depending upon the water release.

FISHING: This is not generally considered a fishing stream.

AREA ATTRACTIONS: All the fun things of Ft. Worth including the night life of the "Stock Yards," and the Ft. Worth Zoo.

MAPS: Tarrant County road map and the Benbrook, Texas topographical quadrangle.

RIVER FLOW INFORMATION: Corps of Engineers, Fort Worth (817) 334-2214 or 334-2196. Double "M" Canoe in Hurst, (817) 282-3135.

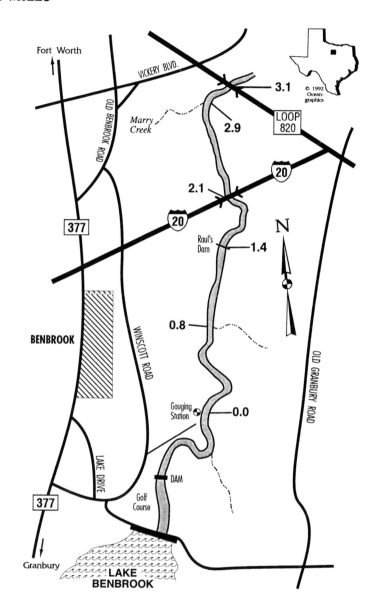

TRINITY RIVER
LIVINGSTON DAM TO LIBERTY
80.0 MILES

PHYSICAL LOCATION: Located in Liberty, San Jacinto and Polk Counties in southeast Texas. Houston 75 miles, Beaumont 70 miles, and Lufkin 55 miles.

GENERAL COMMENTS: Other than a few scattered subdivisions along the upper section, the river retains its natural state. Keep the long distance in mind. Other than the initial short section between the dam and Hwy. 59, the distances are extremely long between road crossings. Plan accordingly. Take adequate food and water. Allow plenty of time and be in good enough physical condition to make the trip.

WATER QUALITY: Excellent as it comes through the Livingston Dam. Although murky, it continues good for the remainder of this section.

WATER FLOW: No current unless water is being released from Lake Livingston. Expect a 2-4 mile per hour current when water is being released. The volume is always adequate for float trips, even during hot, dry periods, or times when no water is being released.

HAZARDS: Trees and stumps in the river are the only potential natural hazards on the Trinity. A section located approximately 3 miles below the dam, has an abundance of large trees and stumps scattered across the river. Drop and trot lines should be regarded as man-made hazards.

PUT IN: The initial put in is off Recreational Road #5 (R5) just below Lake Livingston dam. There is a fee for launching and parking. Alternate put ins are right bank below the Hwy. 59 bridge (there is a boat ramp), the northeast corner of the junction of Menard Creek and Hwy. 146, and the northwest corner of the junction of FM 2610 and Menard Creek. To launch on Menard

Creek at Hwy. 146 adds approximately 9 miles. The creek is usually navigable any time of the year. A fee is required at the Hwy. 146 crossing.

TAKE OUT: The first take out is on the right bank below the Hwy. 59 bridge. The take out here is excellent. There is a boat ramp adjacent to the crossing. A launching and parking fee is required. This take out would be the termination point for a one day trip. The FM 787 crossing at 32 miles, and the TX 105 crossing, at 51 miles, are the next take out points. The take out at the 32 mile mark is up a steep bank at the southeast corner of the crossing. Parking here is limited, but vehicles can be left at the service station approximately a mile northeast of the crossing. Both crossings can also be considered alternate launch points. The Hwy. 90 crossing, west of Liberty, Texas should be the last take out. There is a good road to the river leading to a campground and a Texas Parks and Wildlife boat ramp.

CAMPING: Lake Livingston State Recreation Area is located on the east shore of the lake, ½ mile north of Livingston, on FM 3126. It offers 163 campsites, water, electricity, group trailer area, screened shelters, restrooms, showers, dump station, and group shelter, (409) 365-2201. There is a seasonal campground at the southwest corner of the Hwy. 59/Trinity River junction. An excellent U. S. Forestry campground is located on FM 3126 just north of FM 1988, (409) 592-6462. Natural camp sites are abundant and good. Limited sections of either bank, or the numerous white sand bars offer good camp sites. When sand bar camping, stay above the generating level. If you choose to camp on the banks, remember it's private property. Obtain permission. Don't cut living trees for fire wood. There is an abundance of dead-fall.

CANOE RENTAL AND SHUTTLE SERVICE: Piney Woods Canoe Company in Kountze (409) 274-5892.

DISTINGUISHING FEATURES: A wide river meandering between sloping banks generally dense with hard woods, pine, and underbrush. The lower sections have some marshy areas with large stands of cypress. Schools of mullet ripple the surface and monstrous alligator gar, some exceeding 200 pounds, rise and submerge in the lazy current.

FISHING: Fishing for white bass immediately below the dam during generating periods, is regarded as one of the best locations in the state. Small jigs, small spinning baits, and small spoons are always good producers. White and yellow are usually the best colors. Black bass can be caught in some of the slower waters downstream, but fishing is usually slow, with only minimum numbers of bass caught. Catfishing is generally very good, and sport fishing for the giant alligator gar has become quite popular. Gear for gar fishing usually includes a medium to heavy salt water rod and reel, line in the 30 pound plus class, and wire leaders. Bottom fishing with large, live or cut bait is the most popular method. Because the gar's mouth is solid bone, the gar will pick the bait up and swim off with it. When it stops to swallow the bait, wait a moment and then set the hook. Gar on the Trinity can easily reach weights of over 100 pounds.

AREA ATTRACTIONS: The Alabama Coushatta Indian Reservation on Hwy. 190, just west of Livingston, and the Big Thicket National Preserve, due south of the Reservation. All the fun things of Houston, only 75 miles southeast.

MAPS: The Polk, Liberty, and San Jacinto county road maps. The topographical maps for this section of the Trinity are the Camilla, Livingston, Liberty and Rayburn, Texas quadrangles.

RIVER FLOW INFORMATION: Piney Woods Canoe Company (409) 274-5892, and Canoesport in Houston, (713) 660-7000.

Map

LEWISVILLE LAKE

Denton

McKinney

LEWISVILLE

121

121

35

Grapevine

0.0

© 1992
Ocean-graphics

N

5.3

6.3

TRINITY RIVER
EXPEDITIONS, SHUTTLE
STOP, (214) 941-1757

NORTH TEXAS CANOES
(214) 245-7475

SANDY LAKE ROAD

PARK

9.4

Carrollton
Dam

WHITLOCK
LANE

BELTLINE ROAD

10.5

11.9

CARROLLTON

*Hutton
Branch*

13.3

*Cooks
Creek*

14.2

VALLEY VIEW ROAD

FARMERS
BRANCH

635

14.7

LBJ FREEWAY

ROYAL LANE

Grapevine   16.5

348

ROYAL LANE

18.5

Dam and
Park

35

CALIFORNIA
CROSSING ROAD

19.4

LOOP
12

NORTHWEST
HIGHWAY

IRVING

Downtown Dallas

DALLAS

94

ELM FORK TRINITY RIVER
HWY. 121 TO CALIFORNIA CROSSING
19.4 MILES

PHYSICAL LOCATION: Located just north of Dallas in Denton and Dallas Counties. Dallas 20 miles, Ft. Worth 40 miles, Waco 135 miles, Austin 220 miles, and Houston 240 miles.

GENERAL COMMENTS: A section of river which everyone can enjoy. Easy and frequent good access facilitates adjustment of trip lengths to fit specific schedules and expertise. Close to metropolitan areas, yet remote enough to promote a natural environment.

WATER QUALITY: Good at the put in but begins to muddy quickly. Nonpolluted to Carrollton dam, but "clean pollution" enters from the left a short distance downriver.

WATER FLOW: Minimum to no current. The river is deep and slow, except for the area immediately below Carrollton Dam.

PREFERRED SEASONS: Due to the deep water, and a fair amount of shade, the Elm Fork can be enjoyed almost any time of the year.

HAZARDS: Take care to avoid the numerous drop lines hanging from tree limbs. The Carrollton Dam is extremely dangerous at above normal flow levels. Portage left.

PUT IN: The first put in is off either bank at the Hwy. 121 crossing east of Lewisville. Alternate put ins are the IH-35 crossing, at 6.3 miles, and below the Carrollton Dam, at 9.4 miles. The crossings at Beltline Road, 10.5 miles, Valley View Road, 14.2 miles, and Royal Lane, 16.5 miles, can also be used, but the access points are not as good, and these are not choice locations to leave a vehicle.

Fun is where you find it!

You've dumped several times?
How fortunate!
You ought to know by now
Some of the things
Not to Do!

TAKE OUT: The last take out for this trip is in the park, off California Crossing Road, 19.4 miles, above the dam. Any of the prior mentioned put ins can also be used as alternate take outs.

CAMPING: Sandy Lake Park, immediately above Carrollton Dam, and California Crossing Park both offer excellent primitive camping/picnic areas. However, facilities are limited and no overnight camping is permitted.

CANOE RENTAL AND SHUTTLE: High Trails in Garland (214) 272-3353, Trinity River Expeditions in Dallas (214) 941-1757, and North Texas Canoes on Whitlock Lane, (214)245-7475.

DISTINGUISHING FEATURES: Dirt banks and a slow moving current characterize this section of the Trinity. The banks are densely timbered with oak, willow, cottonwood, and elm. Many beaver cuttings will be seen in stands of young willow.

FISHING: Catfishing with trot or drop lines is just about the limit to fishing on the Trinity.

AREA ATTRACTIONS: The Dallas/Ft. Worth metroplex area offers just about anything you might want to see or do.

MAPS: The Denton and Dallas County road maps. The topographical maps are the Lewisville East, Lewisville West and Carrollton, Texas quadrangles.

RIVER FLOW INFORMATIONS: Corps of Engineers, Fort Worth (817) 334-2214 or (817) 334-2196, North Texas Canoes (214) 245-7475, Trinity River Expeditions (214) 941-1757, and High Trails in Garland (214) 272-3353.

VILLAGE CREEK

HWY. 69 TO VILLAGE CREEK STATE PARK
41.7 MILES

Map labels:

THE ENTIRE 41.7 MILES RUNS THROUGH THE BIG THICKET NATIONAL PRESERVE

Woodville

0.0

Hickory Creek

BIG THICKET VISITORS HEADQUATERS

Turkey Creek

3.9

420

4.5

6.1

69

287

Hestler Creek

8.3

N

Beech Creek

Beaumont Creek

13.8

17.8

KOUNTZE

418

PINEY WOODS CANOE COMPANY, ACCESS POINT (409) 274-5892

18.7

20.4

418

69

287

27.2

327

Spurger

SILSBEE

92

96

Brushy Creek

31.7

69

287

96

© 1992 Ocean-graphics

37.7

PINEY WOODS CANOE COMPANY, ACCESS POINT (409) 274-5892

41.7

LUMBERTON

VILLAGE CREEK STATE PARK

Beaumont

PHYSICAL LOCATION: Big Thicket National Preserve, deep southeast Texas, Hardin County. Beaumont 40 miles, Houston 120 miles, Lufkin 55 miles, and Tyler 130 miles.

GENERAL COMMENTS: This is a serene and scenic trip which anyone can enjoy - novice to expert, groups or individuals, especially if they really appreciate what nature has to offer. The Roy E. Larsen Sandyland Sanctuary controls both sides of the creek from Hwy. 418 to Hwy. 327. This sanctuary has 8 miles of nature trails and is open to the public. To reach the sanctuary from the creek, the entrance is on the left, less than half a mile above the Hwy. 327 bridge. The gate will usually be open and the pedestrian entrance is always open. For more information call (713) 385-1135.

WATER QUALITY: Clean and non-polluted. Tannic acid brown tint due to the run off around the pine trees of East Texas.

WATER FLOW: Generally adequate for an enjoyable float trip. During dry periods the stream will become narrower, and sometimes may be blocked by fallen trees. These are usually more an aggravation than a problem.

PREFERRED SEASONS: Under normal conditions, anytime of the year. The dense bank vegetation protects the stream bed from the intense summer heat, and much of winter's cold wind.

HAZARDS: High water is dangerous because of the narrow, twisting channel, and the heavy growth of timber along the banks. Under normal flow conditions, small log jams and downed trees will pose minor problems.

PUT IN: The Hwy. 69 - Hwy. 287 crossing, north of Kountze. Alternate put ins are: the Hwy. 420 crossing, at the 6.1 mile point, the FM 418 crossing, 18.7 miles, between Kountze and Silsbee (good access, small primitive camping area and adequate parking space), and the access off Hwy. 327, 27.2 miles, west of Silsbee.

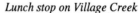

Lunch stop on Village Creek

You too can canoe!

TAKE OUT: For shorter trips, any of the alternate put ins can be utilized as take outs. The next to last take out is a boat ramp, adjacent to the Hwy. 96 crossing, south of Silsbee at 37.7 miles. The final take out will be at Village Creek State Park, 41.7 miles, SCHEDULED TO OPEN, SEPTEMBER 1992.

CAMPING: There are good natural camping areas at the FM 418, and the Hwy. 96 crossings, but no facilities are available. Natural camp sites along the creek are numerous, but permission should be obtained before camping on private land. Permits are required to camp on Big Thicket National Preserve land. The beautiful and abundant white sand bars, especially below the Hwy. 327 crossing, offer excellent natural camp sites. Always leave your camp sites cleaner than you found them. The new Village Creek State Park, just off Hwy. 96, east of Lumberton, will feature a canoe ramp, one acre parking lot, 24 full camping hook ups, 24 camp sites with water, cabin for groups and a mini museum, (409) 755-7322.

CANOE RENTAL AND SHUTTLE SERVICE: Piney Woods Canoe Company in Kountze (409) 274-5892.

DISTINGUISHING FEATURES: The Big Thicket surrounding Village Creek is a wonderland of plants and wildlife. Some plants are considered rare, and are not found anywhere else in the world. The numerous white sand bars offer excellent camp sites and lunch stops. An excellent setting for the outdoor photographer.

FISHING: Only average for largemouth bass, perch and catfish.

AREA ATTRACTIONS: Limited entertainment, restaurants and accommodations in Beaumont, 20-40 miles south.

MAPS: The Hardin County road map, and the Kountze and Silsbee, Texas topographical quadrangles. Big Thicket National Preserve Map, 3785 Milam, Beaumont, Texas 77701, (409) 839-2689.

FLOW INFORMATION: Piney Woods Canoe Company in Kountze (409) 274-5892.

VILLAGE CREEK
ARLINGTON, TEXAS
EVERMAN - KENNEDALE RD. TO IH-20
3.2 MILES
Headwaters of Lake Arlington

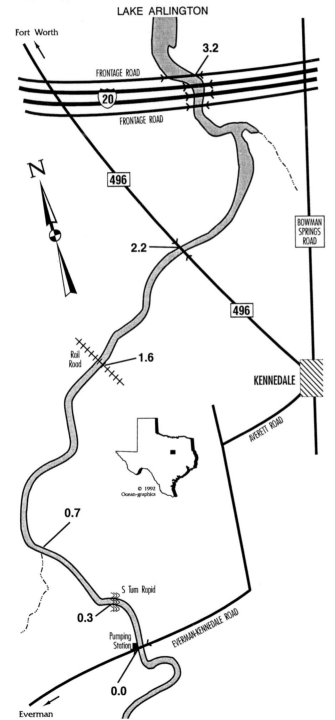

PHYSICAL LOCATION: Between Arlington, Texas and Fort Worth, Texas. Dallas 35 miles.

GENERAL COMMENTS: This is a short afternoon run, a scenic and comfortable "get away from it all" outing. Be careful of fallen trees across the creek and take the time to scout the small rapids.

WATER QUALITY: During hot, dry spells when Lake Arlington is low, water is pumped from Cedar Creek Lake to Village Creek, where it flows into Lake Arlington. During the pumping season, the water is clear and cool.

WATER FLOW: Variable, depending upon pump station output and/or natural flow from Village Creek.

PREFERRED SEASONS: Water flow is usually adequate in dry seasons. In rainy seasons the creek floods, creating hazardous river running due to the narrow, restricted channel, and downed trees.

HAZARDS: The restricted, narrow channel, downed trees, and high water levels are all considered hazardous on Village Creek. This is especially true of the "S" Turn rapids, 0.3 miles from the put in. As the creek makes the left turn into these rapids, downed trees pile up in the turn making it an exceptionally hazardous area.

PUT IN: The bridge on Everman-Kennedale Road. Please note: the northwest corner is posted. Stay off private property. To avoid the probability of getting a ticket, park at least 100 yards from the bridge.

TAKE OUT: The preferred take out is under the IH-20 bridge. Take the Frontage Road, east of the bridge, to get under it. An alternate take out is the northeast corner of the Village Creek bridge on Highway 496, 2.2 miles.

CAMPING: There are no camping areas.

CANOE RENTAL AND SHUTTLE SERVICE: Double "M" Canoe in Hurst (817) 282-3135.

DISTINGUISHING FEATURES: A winding, small stream with gravel bottom; several small rapids and shoals. The creek, in this area, runs south to north.

FISHING: Small bass and a variety of perch/sunfish can be caught along the creek. Ultra light tackle and fly fishing equipment is preferred.

AREA ATTRACTIONS: All the fun the Ft. Worth/Dallas metroplex has to offer, Six Flags, etc.

MAPS: City of Arlington, and Tarrant County road map. The Kennedale, Texas topographical quadrangle.

RIVER FLOW INFORMATION: Double "M" Canoe in Hurst (817) 282-3135.

WHITE ROCK CREEK

DALLAS, TEXAS
WHITE ROCK LAKE TO FAIR OAKS DR. AND BACK
8.0 MILES

PHYSICAL LOCATION: Located in Dallas County, only 5 to 6 miles from downtown Dallas.

GENERAL COMMENTS: A fun outing in a metroplex environment. A good place to spend a few hours on any busy weekend.

WATER QUALITY: Clean but murky colored water characteristic of the Dallas area.

WATER FLOW: Always adequate water for float trips up to the 2.3 mile point, (Skillman Street), during all seasons.

HAZARDS: At high water levels this creek is considered dangerous due to the narrow, twisting channel, and the abundance of overhanging limbs and brush. A good rule of thumb is: if it's hard to paddle upstream, against the current, then don't make the trip. After rains there may be a small log jam or two, but these can usually be easily portaged.

PUT IN: The put in point is off East Lawther Drive, just south of Mockingbird Lane, on the east bank of White Rock Lake. About 50 yards below Mockingbird Lane is a grass bank, extending to the edge of the lake. Put in and take out along this bank.

TAKE OUT: The take out is the put in point. Paddle upstream for 4 miles, and back 4 miles. You won't need a car shuttle, and you can plan your trip for whatever time you have. White Rock Lake offers good picnic areas with tables, but no overnight camping is allowed.

CANOE RENTAL AND SHUTTLE: High Trails, (214) 272-3353, is located in Garland at 3610 Marquis Drive. No shuttle service is needed.

DISTINGUISHING FEATURES: This is a very scenic trip with twisting, narrow channels, surrounded by dense vegetation on both banks. A remote area which makes it hard to believe you are still in Dallas. Just before the railroad crossing, at 1.7 miles, Jackson Branch is on the right. At normal creek levels, it is possible to paddle up the Branch a few hundred yards. The turn around is tough because the water is usually not as wide as the canoe is long. In the summer months, White Rock Creek, beyond the 2.3 mile point, is also very narrow.

FISHING: Don't bother.

AREA ATTRACTIONS: Dallas Cowboys, Six Flags, etc., etc., etc..

MAPS: Topographical maps are White Rock Lake, and Garland, Texas quadrangles. A good Dallas City Map will show the streets and access points.

RIVER FLOW INFORMATION: High Trails (214) 272-3353.

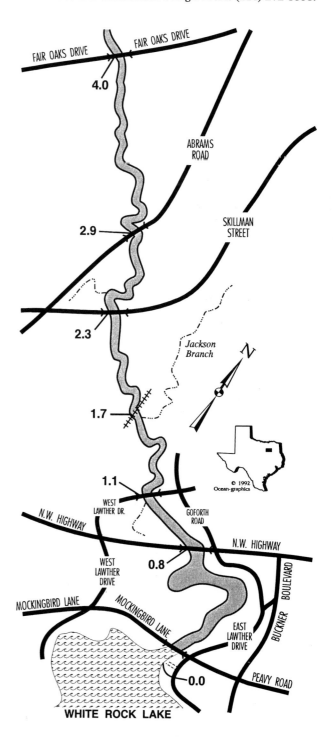

ARKANSAS

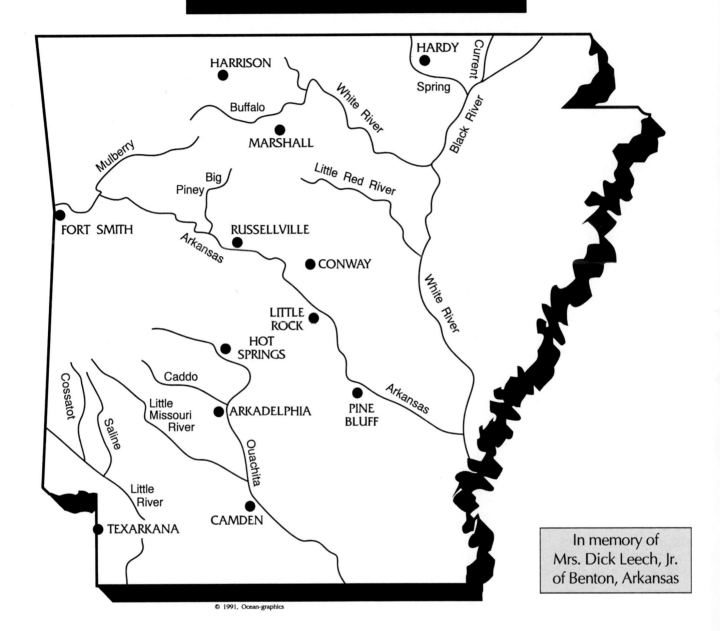

HARDY
HARRISON
Current
Spring
White River
Buffalo
Black River
MARSHALL
Little Red River
Big
Piney
Mulberry
FORT SMITH
RUSSELLVILLE
Arkansas
CONWAY
White River
LITTLE ROCK
HOT SPRINGS
Caddo
Cossatot
Little Missouri River
ARKADELPHIA
Arkansas
PINE BLUFF
Saline
Ouachita
Little River
CAMDEN
TEXARKANA

In memory of
Mrs. Dick Leech, Jr.
of Benton, Arkansas

© 1991, Ocean-graphics

Arkansas has over 9,000 miles of streams, and a good deal of this mileage is great for river running. The variety of enjoyable experiences provided by this assortment of rivers and streams is remarkable; from matchless trout fishing streams, to exhilarating whitewater, to tranquil floats ideal for families, groups, or the first timer.

In this printing, we have mentioned only a few of the unique Arkansas rivers. Rather than go into descriptive detail on the few we've covered, we suggest that you write for the "Arkansas Floaters Kit." The Kit covers 17 of the most popular, scenic and exciting streams in Arkansas, plus it supplies valuable information on parks, governmental agencies, fishing, recreation and other good stuff. Write, requesting the Kit, from: Arkansas Department of Parks and Tourism, #1 Capitol Mall, Little Rock, Arkansas 72201.

Arkansas folks are very proud of their rivers and streams. They sincerely cater to river runners and know that Arkansas really has something special to offer.

COSSATOT RIVER

HWY. 246 TO HWY. 4
9.7 MILES

PHYSICAL LOCATION: Howard and Polk Counties in extreme southwestern Arkansas. Smithville, Oklahoma 35 miles, Arkadelphia 70 miles, Texarkana 60 miles, Dallas 240 miles, Waco 330 miles, and Austin 450 miles.

GENERAL COMMENTS: Have experience in heavy white water. The Cossatot is wild and woolly. It's regarded as one of the most difficult whitewater streams in Arkansas. Use only decked craft, or carry as much extra flotation as possible. Not a family trip, or one for anyone in poor physical condition. During cold weather use wet suits. Tie in and waterproof all gear. Cossatot is an Indian word for "skull crusher" which will give you some idea of what to expect from the river.

WATER QUALITY: Excellent.

WATER FLOW: Borders on being a seasonal stream. Good to excellent flow during wet seasons. Flow levels, measured at the Hwy. 246 bridge: optimum level is 3.5' to 4.5'. At levels above 5.25' Cossatot Falls changes into one long rapid and should be avoided by all except expert paddlers who have taken all available precautions.

PREFERRED SEASONS: Early spring through early summer. Late fall is another good season. Optimum time for water in the river is between November and late May.

HAZARDS: The toughest rapid on the upper 3.5 miles is "5 Step Rapids," a Class III. If you have ANY trouble with this rapid, do not attempt the lower section. When running the lower section, there will be continual rock dodging and tricky cross currents. Thoroughly scout all rapids and have adequate safety precautions in place before running. Zig-Zag, (Class III), is approximately a quarter mile below Ed Banks Rd. It's a quick 90 degree turn ending in a 4 foot drop. Esses is next - this rapid stretches over 200 yards, with a 3 foot drop about mid way. There are a couple more Class III's, and a Class II upstream from the Weyerhaeuser #52600 road crossing. Cossatot Falls, just downstream from this crossing, is a series of six falls which cause the Cossatot to drop over 40 feet in less than half a mile. In sequence these are: Cossatosser - Class III-IV, Eye Opener - Class III, B.M.F. - Class III, Washing Machine - Class IV-V, Whiplash - Class III and Last One - Class III. There are several Class III-IV rapids, including Deer Camp Rapid, Devil's Hollow (most technical drop on the river), and Devil's Hollow Falls, a 6 - 8 foot ledge (portage on extreme right). The last couple of miles will let you relax and get your pulse rate down.

PUT IN: The first put in is the Hwy. 246 crossing between Vandervoort and Athens. Alternate put ins are Ed Banks Road (Weyerhaeuser #52000), at 3.5 miles, or Weyerhaeuser #52600.

TAKE OUT: Take out at either of the alternate put ins, or at the Hwy. 4 crossing, at 9.7 miles. Caution: all the Forest roads will be extremely slick in wet weather.

CAMPING: There are limited primitive camping areas at the Hwy. 246 crossing, the Ed Banks Crossing, the #52600 crossing and the Hwy. 4 crossing. Also, the Shady Lake National Forest Campground offers campsites, restrooms, showers and drinking water. It's located just off Hwy. 246, northwest of Athens, Arkansas.

CANOE RENTAL AND SHUTTLE SERVICE: Available in the area.

DISTINGUISHING FEATURES: Heavy whitewater rapids, boulder gardens, falls, and a very steep gradient. Low during dry seasons, but fast, high, and furious during average or high flow levels.

FISHING: Leave the fishing tackle at home.

AREA ATTRACTIONS: Just enjoy the wild, remote beauty of the river and the area.

MAPS: Polk and Howard county road maps. The topographical map is the Umpire, Arkansas quadrangle.

RIVER FLOW INFORMATION: Up to the minute flow data is available by calling (501) 387-3141. Listen carefully! You will hear a recording say: "Input zero data, then it gives four numbers. These numbers represent the gauge reading. An example might be: zero - three - five - zero. This translates into a reading of 03.50 feet. The recording will go on to say "Input one data, 0001, battery status normal." Everything will then be repeated. Cossatot Weather Observer (501) 394-2321. Little Rock C.O.E. (501) 378-5150.

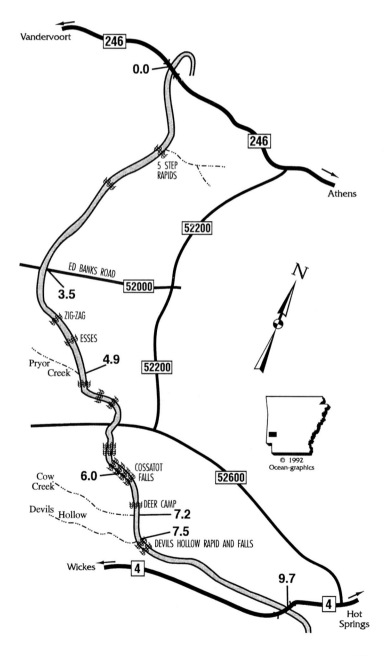

BIG PINEY CREEK
HWY. 123 TO HWY. 164
24.2 MILES

PHYSICAL LOCATION: Pope and Johnson Counties in Northwest Arkansas. Russellville 35 miles, Little Rock 105 miles, Oklahoma City 215 miles, Dallas 350 miles, and Austin 500 miles.

GENERAL COMMENTS: Big Piney Creek is best floated between 2.0 and 4.0 feet. Whitewater canoeing experience is definitely helpful, and even mandatory at flow levels above 4 feet. When running the Big Piney at high levels, boats should be totally decked, or have extra styrofoam or air-bag flotation. The upper section, ending at Long Pool Campground, has an abundance of Class II and Class III rapids, and is definitely not recommended for beginners. The lower section has numerous Class I and Class II rapids, and is generally ideal for the less experienced paddler. Tie in and waterproof all gear. A good deal of the stream is bordered by private property. River runners should take extra precautions to avoid trespassing problems.

WATER QUALITY: Excellent.

WATER FLOW: Should be considered seasonal with good whitewater starting in late November, extending through mid May. Beginning in late May and extending through mid July, the Big Piney is usually low. Expect to walk, and drag, some during this time, however the conditions are excellent for fishing and swimming.

PREFERRED SEASONS: Big Piney Creek is generally considered canoeable from late November until late May. The weather and the water will be cold at this time of year. Plan and dress accordingly.

HAZARDS: There is a multiplicity of twisting, whitewater rapids which challenge even the experienced river runner. Huge boulders, willow "strainers," and rock gardens pose constant threats to you, your canoe, and equipment. The river gradient drops 16 feet per mile in the 6 mile section below the launch point, and 25 feet per mile in the section between Helton's Farm and Long Pool Campground. The Class III rapids you'll run into are Surprise 1-2-3, at 11.5 miles, Surfing Rapid, and Cascades of Extinction at 17.6 miles. There are other skill testing rapids, which if run improperly, can be extremely hazardous.

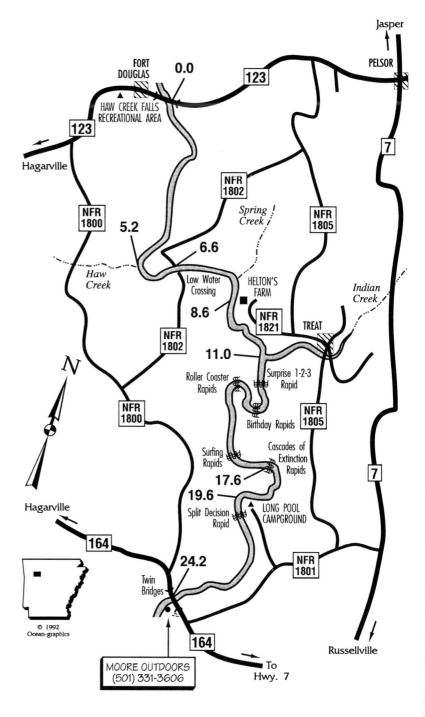

MOORE OUTDOORS
(501) 331-3606

You thought I said what?

with some falling into the Class III category. Many rock outcroppings, boulder gardens and rock shelves create minor, but fun rapids. The numerous creek-side waterfalls add to the scenic beauty of one of the best whitewater streams in Arkansas.

FISHING: Fishing is generally quite good, but difficult due to the fast currents and turbulent rapids. Smallmouth bass rank at the top of the list of game fish. Spotted and largemouth bass, rock bass, longear, and green sunfish are all consistently caught. Fishing is best at the lower flow levels. Although fishing can be a twelve month pastime, it is generally best in the late spring/early summer months. For best results, stay with the lighter tackle and small baits.

AREA ATTRACTIONS: Nearby attractions include the Ozark Hiking Trail, Alum Cove Natural Bridge Area, Pedestal Rocks, and the Moccasin Gap Horse Trail. Many craft shops are located nearby on Scenic Highway 7. On shuttle road NFR 1805 a scenic overlook offers one of the most breathtaking views found anywhere between the Rockies and the Smokey Mountains.

MAPS: The U.S.F.S. Ozark National Forest Map. The Pope and Johnson County road maps. The topographical maps are the Swain, Mt. Judea, Ozone, and Treat, Arkansas quadrangles.

RIVER FLOW INFORMATION: For current flow levels call Moore Outdoors any day between 8:00 AM and 6:00 PM, (501)331-3606, or the Corps of Engineers, Little Rock Office recording (501) 378-5150 for a daily report. Be sure and listen carefully, they give a lot of levels in a hurry. The Little Rock C.O.E. (to talk to a real, live person) (510) 378-5551.

PUT IN: Launch at the Hwy. 123 crossing, west of Pelsor. Alternate put ins for shorter trips are Helton's Farm at 8.6 miles, and the Long Pool Campground at 19.6 miles.

TAKE OUT: Take out at any of the previously mentioned alternate put ins, or Moore Outdoors, immediately downstream from the Hwy. 164 crossing, at the 24.2 mile point.

CAMPING: CANOE CAMPING ON BIG PINEY CREEK IS NOT RECOMMENDED! Long Pool Campground, just north of NFR 1801, makes a good base camp. It is a U. S. Forest Service campground offering primitive camping areas with pit toilets, and well water during the season. Primitive, river front camping is also available, for a fee, at Moore Outdoors, downstream from the Hwy. 164 crossing.

CANOE RENTAL AND SHUTTLE SERVICE: Moore Outdoors, (501) 331-3606, has been renting canoes since 1978. The Helton's run shuttles from their farm, (501) 331-3305.

DISTINGUISHING FEATURES: The Big Piney is a steep-sided, narrow creek with exciting whitewater. Most rapids are Class II's

BUFFALO NATIONAL RIVER
PONCA TO PRUITT
24.0 MILES

PHYSICAL LOCATION: Newton County, northwest Arkansas. Little Rock 175 miles, Memphis 298 miles, Kansas City 290 miles, and Dallas 460 miles.

GENERAL COMMENTS: On March 1, 1972 Congress designated this stream "The Buffalo National River." By this designation the Buffalo is a totally free-flowing stream - no dams or any water obstruction from the headwaters to its juncture with the White River. The bluffs of this section of the river, reaching heights of 500' above the river level, are the highest in the Ozarks. The geology of the river, with its numerous caves, sink holes, waterfalls, springs and rock formations is typical of the Arkansas Ozarks. Allow time to take the side trip to Hemmed-in-Hollow, approximately 5 miles below Steel Creek. This hike is less than one mile. The box canyon ends at the highest waterfall in mid America. It spills water from the bluff top towering over 200' above the canyon floor.

WATER QUALITY: Good to excellent. It will generally have the milky green color unique to the streams of this area. Water temperature ranges from the low 40's in January, to the low 80's in August.

WATER FLOW: This section of the Buffalo is regarded as seasonal and can rarely be floated enjoyably after the end of June. Minimum float level is 3', optimum level is 4½'. Dangerous above 5½'. Gradient is 12' per mile.

PREFERRED SEASONS: Due to extreme low water conditions usually stretching from mid-June to early October, late autumn through early summer are considered the seasons with best weather conditions. March, April and May will generally have optimum flow levels.

HAZARDS: This section will have the most whitewater and rapids, generally in the Class II category. Most of the areas can be negotiated by being careful and using good common sense. Be sure to scout the major rapids and plan a safe route. "Wrecking Rock Rapid" is located less than 2 miles from the Ponca put in. The left channel is usually the best. Just downstream from Sneeds Creek, "S" Turn Rapids primary hazards are the quick, tight turns and overhanging limbs. Although the rapids at Gray Rock can be hazardous, rises in the river have moved the channel away from the rock and lessened the danger. Crisis Curve downstream from Camp Orr (owned by the Boy Scouts of America,) is a narrow channel with a quick left turn. The last recognized

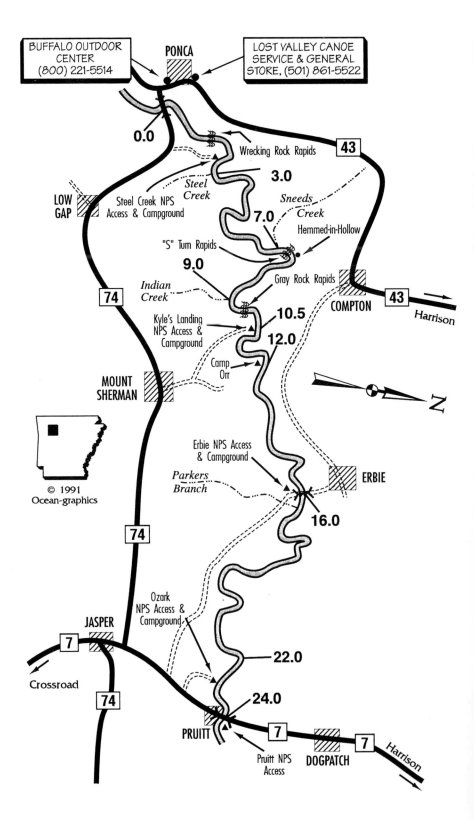

FISHING: Considered a model smallmouth bass stream, the Buffalo has fast, clear, oxygen-rich water with the gravel bottoms and boulder beds which smallmouth love. Of the other 58 species of fresh water fish found in the Buffalo, anglers go after the largemouth and spotted bass, catfish and a wide variety of perch/sunfish. Although smallmouth are occasionally caught weighing 5 pounds and more, the average will be between 1-2 pounds. Smallmouth must be 10" or more to be kept. The fast water areas are always the most productive spots.

AREA ATTRACTIONS: Visit Dogpatch U.S.A., Crystal Dome Caverns and Mystic Caverns all south of Harrison on Hwy. 7. For information on this area contact the Jasper County Chamber of Commerce, P.O. Box 250, Jasper, Arkansas 72641.

MAPS: The Newton County road map. The Ponca, and Jasper, Arkansas topographical quadrangles.

RIVER FLOW INFORMATION: Buffalo Outdoor Center, (800) 221-5514 or (501) 861-5514; Lost Valley Canoe Service and General Store, (501) 861-5522, or Buffalo National River Headquarters in Harrison, (501) 741-5443.

potential hazard is the crossing at Erbie Ford at 16.0 miles. High water levels can create a possible danger here.

PUT IN: Launch at the Highway 74 crossing east of Ponca, or the Steel Creek National Park Service (NPS) access and campground, approximately 2½ miles downriver from the Hwy. 74 crossing. Alternate put in points are at Kyle's Landing, and the NPS access south of Erbie. Allow at least two days for the whole 24 miles. NOTE: the roads leading to access points shown on the adjacent map are representative of direction only. Most of the roads are gravel/dirt with many forks and turn-offs. Check with one of the outfitters before you attempt these access points on your own - they will give you precise directions.

TAKE OUT: The first take out is Kyle's Landing, at 10.5 miles. The second at Erbie Camp/Crossing at 16.0 miles; the third at Ozark NPS access. For the complete 24 mile trip, take out at the Pruitt ,NPS access adjacent to the Hwy. 7 crossing, north of Pruitt.

CAMPING: The NPS has parks at Steel Creek, Kyle's Landing, Ozark and Erbie. These are available at no charge on a first-come first-served basis. For information call (501) 741-5443. The winding roads to Kyle's Landing and Steel Creek are not recommended for large trailers, buses or motor homes.

CANOE RENTAL & SHUTTLE SERVICE: Buffalo Outdoor Center, (800) 221-5514, or Lost Valley Canoe Service and General Store, (501) 861-5522.

DISTINGUISHING FEATURES: Clear water, towering colorful bluffs, wooded hillsides and a myriad of seasonal wild flowers greet the river runner.

Photo courtesy of Buffalo Outdoor Center

BUFFALO NATIONAL RIVER
PRUITT TO GILBERT
49 MILES

PHYSICAL LOCATION: Northwestern Arkansas, Newton and Searcy Counties. Little Rock 160 miles, Memphis 275 miles, Kansas City 270 miles, and Dallas 440 miles.

GENERAL COMMENTS: A trip anyone can enjoy - individuals or groups. This section can be divided into many separate trips. There is considerably less whitewater than on the upper section, and this section generally consists of quiet pools separated by shallow shoals and willow stands. For those interested parties - this section flows through "dry" counties. No beer or liquor is available.

WATER QUALITY: Excellent to good.

WATER FLOW: Not as seasonal as the upper section, but will usually be too shallow for enjoyable floating from early July to late September. Minimum for floating at the Hwy. 65 bridge is 0.5', maximum is 10' (all shoals and river rock are under water at 8.0'). Optimum is between 2' and 6.0'.

PREFERRED SEASON: Early spring and late autumn are optimum. May, June and early July usually offer the best water conditions. August, September and October have fewer people, and generally lower water. Winter trips are also popular for those brave souls who enjoy cold weather canoeing.

HAZARDS: Not as demanding as the upper section although there are numerous whitewater rapids and willow strainers. Areas to exercise caution: A set of tricky rapids known as Woolum Falls or Little Niagara, about one mile below Woolum and directly across from the mouth of Richland Creek., and the rapids in the Calf Creek area. During hot, dry summer months, a two mile section immediately below Jamison Creek (29 miles) will normally go completely dry.

PUT IN: Launch from one of the private camps, adjacent to the river at Pruitt, or the Pruitt Landing National Park Service (NPS) access. Alternate put ins are the NPS Access on the south (right) side of the river downstream from Hasty Bridge, 7.5 miles, the Hwy. 123 crossing, 12 miles, the Carver NPS access, the National Park Service access at Mt. Hersey, 18 miles, the NPS access at Woolum, 27 miles, and Bakers Ford access, 37 miles. NOTE: the roads leading to access points shown on the adjacent map are representative of direction only. Most of the roads are gravel/dirt with many forks and turn-offs. Check with one of the outfitters before you attempt these access points on your own - they will give you precise directions.

TAKE OUT: Depending on your trip length, consider taking out at the NPS access downstream from Hasty Bridge, 7.5 miles, the Hwy. 123 crossing at 12.0 miles, Carver NPS access, Mt. Hersey NPS access, 18.0 miles, the NPS access at Woolum, 27.0 miles, Tyler Bend campground and recreational area at 43.0 miles, the

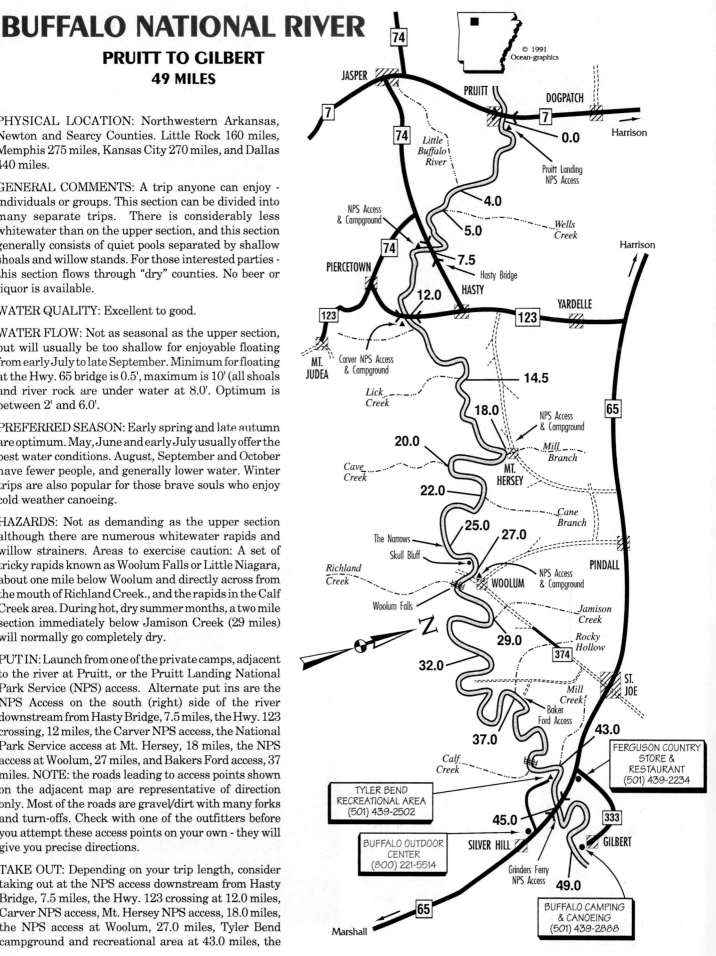

Photo courtesy of Buffalo Outdoor Center

Grinders Ferry NPS access at 45.0 miles, and the gravel bar, adjacent to Buffalo Camping and Canoeing in Gilbert, 49.0 miles.

CAMPING: National Park Service (NPS) camping areas at Hasty Bridge, Carver (Hwy. 123 crossing), Mt. Hersey, Woolum and Gilbert. Tyler Bend National Park, off Hwy. 65 immediately south of the Buffalo River, offers campgrounds, picnic pavilion, hot showers and visitor information center.

CANOE RENTAL & SHUTTLE SERVICE: Buffalo Camping and Canoeing (501) 439-2888., Buffalo Outdoor Center (800) 221-5514 or (501) 439-2244, and Tomahawk Canoe Rental (501) 439-2617.

DISTINGUISHING FEATURES: Approximately 7 miles below Hwy. 7 at Pruitt, you'll see Riggs Bluff towering along the left bank. About 200' above river level is a natural bridge, Chimney Hole. It can be reached from the river. On the right just above the Hwy. 123 crossing is John Eddings Cave (closed to the public.) The unusual "saddle" bluff at The Narrows ("Nars") - this small bluff is about 6' wide and 80' tall. Skull Bluff on the right, just downstream from The Narrows, are good landmarks. Skull Bluff has two holes which make it resemble a skull. At moderate to low water levels you can actually paddle into these cavities.

FISHING: Fish and fishing are the same as for the upper section. Remember a valid Arkansas license is required.

AREA ATTRACTIONS: Ozark Heritage Arts Center in Leslie (20 miles S. of Tyler Bend), features original Ozark historical, musical drama, (501) 447-2500. Hurricane River Cave, 1½ miles off Hwy. 65 between Harrison and Marshall, the Searcy County Museum, off Marshall Square, in Marshall, was originally a jail, built in 1902, and now houses a collection of Indian artifacts. Gilbert General Store is listed in the National Register of Historic Places. Bear Creek Speedway is a ¼ mile, oval dirt track, located on U.S. 65, 7 miles south of Tyler Bend. Also, take the time to visit Tyler Bend Visitors Center. It's definitely worth the trip. For additional information contact the Searcy County Chamber of Commerce, P.O. Box 836, Marshall, Arkansas 72650, (501) 448-5788.

MAPS: The Newton and Searcy County road maps. The topographical maps are the Jasper, Hasty, Mt. Judea, Snowball, Western Grove, and Marshall, Arkansas quadrangles.

RIVER FLOW INFORMATION: Buffalo Camping & Canoeing, (501) 439-2888, Buffalo Outdoor Center, ((800) 221-5514 or 501) 439-2244, and Buffalo National River Headquarters in Harrison, (501) 741-5443.

Photo courtesy of Buffalo Outdoor Center

BUFFALO NATIONAL RIVER
GILBERT TO BUFFALO CITY
54 MILES

PHYSICAL LOCATION: Northwest Arkansas, Marion, Searcy and Baxter Counties. Little Rock 145 miles, Memphis 255 miles, Kansas City 290 miles, and Dallas 420 miles.

GENERAL COMMENTS: Allow enough time for an enjoyable trip especially on the lower portion of this section. This is a trip which can be enjoyed by anyone who has planned well. Expect long, quiet pools bordered by exceptionally scenic river banks, hills and small bluffs. Remember Searcy county is a "dry" county.

WATER QUALITY: Good to excellent.

WATER FLOW: Offers more float opportunities than the upper sections during the hot summer months. It has slowed considerably compared to the upper sections but is not considered as seasonal. Minimum flow for a good trip is 0.9'. The optimum is 1½' - 4.0' measured at the Hwy. 14 bridge.

PREFERRED SEASON: Anytime of the year - weather permitting.

HAZARDS: The gradient has dropped from 9 feet per mile to only 3. This lower portion of the Buffalo is virtually hazard free.

PUT IN: The top most put in is off the gravel bar at Gilbert, adjacent to Buffalo Camping & Canoeing, or the NPS access at Gilbert. Alternate launch points are the National Park Service (NPS) access points at Maumee North, Maumee South, Dillards Ferry NPS access, Buffalo Point, and adjacent to the ghost town of Rush. NOTE: the roads leading to access points shown on the adjacent map are representative of direction only. Most of the roads are gravel/dirt with many forks

Skull Bluff, courtesy of Buffalo Outdoor Center

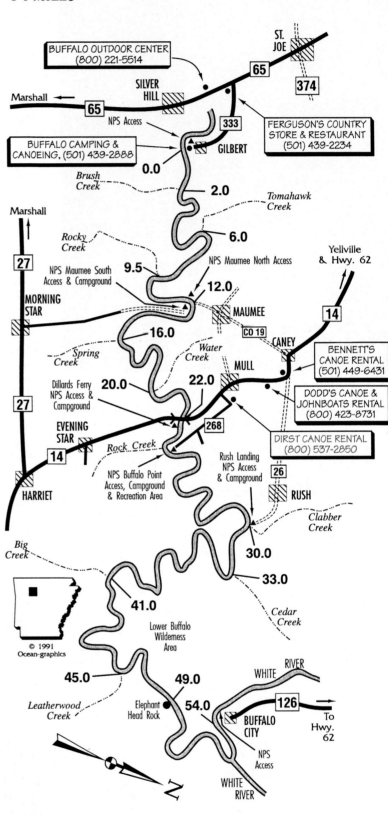

and turn-offs. Check with one of the outfitters before you attempt these access points on your own - they will give you precise directions.

TAKE OUT: Take outs are any of the previously mentioned NPS access points. The last take out is on the right upstream bank at Buffalo City; keep in mind that you must paddle UP the White River for a short distance. This can be tough if the White River is running high with generator release through Bull Shoals Dam.

CAMPING: There are NPS camping areas at Maumee South, Dillards Ferry, Buffalo Point and Rush. The Buffalo Point Concession also boasts trailer hookups and rental cabins - always call for reservations (501) 449-6206. See advertisers for additional camping/rental facilities and phone numbers. If you camp in the Buffalo/White River junction area, ALWAYS camp well above the high water marks. A release of water on the White River creates a FAST rise on this section of the Buffalo.

CANOE RENTAL & SHUTTLE SERVICE: Bennett's Canoe Rental, (501) 449-6431, Buffalo Camping and Canoeing (501) 439-2888; Dirst Canoe Rental (800) 537-2850, or Dodd's Canoe and Johnboats Rental (800) 423-8731.

DISTINGUISHING FEATURES: This section of the Buffalo sustains better flow levels during the summer months than the upper sections. There is considerably less whitewater, the river is wider and the pools are long and deep. A prominent landmark is Elephant Head Rock at 49.0 miles.

FISHING: Same type of fishing and fish as the two upper sections. However, due to the more constant water levels and deeper water, fishing is more pronounced. Guided fishing trips are abundant, and varied, on this section of the Buffalo.

AREA ATTRACTIONS: The Rush Historic District, near Rush Landing. Zinc ore was discovered in the early 1880's and promoted a mining boom along the Buffalo. A smelter was built in 1886. A discovery trail leads to the ghost town of Rush. Entry into old mines, mineral collecting and metal detectors are forbidden.

MAPS: The Marion, Searcy, and Baxter County road maps. The topographical maps for the section are the Marshall, Maumee, Cozahome, Rea Valley, Big Flat, and Buffalo City, Arkansas quadrangles.

RIVER FLOW INFORMATION: Bennett's Canoe Rental, (501) 449-6431; Buffalo Camping and Canoeing (501) 439-2888; Dirst Canoe Rental (800) 537-2850, or Dodd's Canoe and Johnboats Rental (800) 423-8731.

Put in at Gilbert

CADDO RIVER
NORMAN TO HWY. 84
29.0 MILES

PHYSICAL LOCATION: Montgomery, Pike, and Clark Counties in extreme southwest Arkansas. Hot Springs 32 miles, Dallas 285 miles, Houston 430 miles, and Austin 465 miles.

GENERAL COMMENTS: This is a trip which almost everyone can enjoy. The river is testing, yet not hazardous. It has retained enough of its remote charms to remain scenic and picturesque. Trips can easily be planned to fit a specific time frame or the ability and fitness of the paddlers.

WATER QUALITY: Clean and unpolluted. Good to excellent.

WATER FLOW: The flow from Norman to Caddo Gap, on the upper 7 miles, is considered seasonal. The water may be too low during the summer months for enjoyable canoeing. However, the flow from Caddo Gap down to the Hwy. 84 crossing, a 22 mile section, can sustain enjoyable float trips year round.

PREFERRED SEASONS: Late spring, early summer and autumn are the optimum float periods on the Caddo.

HAZARDS: There are no major hazards in this area. Numerous Class I and Class II rapids can be found along this section, but generally nothing which can be considered hazardous under normal flow conditions.

PUT IN: The first launch site is on the south side of the bridge crossing, adjacent to the Norman Town Square. The alternate put in is the crossing at 7 miles, west of Caddo Gap, just off Hwy. 8.

TAKE OUT: The take out for the upper trip is at 7 miles, the crossing west of Caddo Gap. Alternate take out points are the Highway 70/ Hwy. 27 crossing, west of Glenwood, at 15.8 miles; the highway crossing north of Amity at the 24.4 mile mark, or the old highway crossing, just north of the Hwy. 84 crossing, at 29.0 miles.

CAMPING: Abundant sand and gravel bars offer excellent camp sites all along the river. Arrowhead Cabin and Canoe Rentals, (501) 356-2944, and Wright Way Canoe Rentals,

© 1991
Ocean-graphics

ARROWHEAD CABIN & CANOE RENTALS, (501) 356-2944

WRIGHT WAY CANOE RENTAL (501) 356-2055

Norman 0.0
5.5
Cottier Creek
7.0
CADDO GAP
Hooper 240
Gap Creek
South Fork Caddo 8.8
10.5
12.6
Five Mile Cr.
Salem 15.8
13.4
GLENWOOD
16.5
Lick Creek
Hot Springs
18.8
ROSBORO
Power Line
23.6
84
24.4 27.3
Sugarloaf Creek
AMITY
29.0
Old Highway
Arkadelphia and IH-30

(501) 356-2055. Both offer cabins and full facilities on the river. The Crystal Recreational Area, northeast of Norman on FS 177, three miles off Hwy. 27, offers camping facilities.

CANOE RENTAL & SHUTTLE SERVICE: Arrowhead Cabin and Canoe Rentals, Inc. (501) 356-2944, and Wright Way Canoe Rental (501) 356-2055.

DISTINGUISHING FEATURES: Under normal conditions the water is a translucent green and is ideal for fishing and swimming. There is an abundance of rounded gravel in the river bed.

FISHING: Many sport fish are native to the Caddo, including large and smallmouth bass, spotted bass, white bass, walleye, crappie, and channel, flathead and blue catfish. The smallmouth is the main fish attraction, however. The Caddo is an excellent stream for fly fishing, ultra light and light spinning tackle. For the most fun and fish, stay with light, low visibility lines and light tackle.

AREA ATTRACTIONS: The fun of Hot Springs is just 32 miles away. You can attend the pari-mutuel horse racing or relax in the soothing hot springs. You can search for diamonds at the Diamond Head Mine at Lake Catherine State Park.

MAPS: The topographical maps are the Norman, Caddo Gap, Glenwood and Amity, Arkansas quadrangles.

RIVER FLOW INFORMATION: Arrowhead Cabin and Canoe Rentals, Inc. (501) 356-2944, and Wright Way Canoe Rental (501) 356-2055, or the Caddo Ranger District (501) 356-4186.

Fred, Has Something Gone Out of Our Marriage?

LITTLE MISSOURI RIVER

ALBERT PIKE CAMPGROUND TO HWY. 70
19.0 MILES

PHYSICAL LOCATION: Pike and Montgomery Counties in extreme southwest Arkansas. Hot Springs 50 miles, Arkadelphia 75 miles, Little Rock 110 miles, and Dallas 275 miles.

GENERAL COMMENTS: For intermediate to expert boaters only. Dangerous for any novice or group unfamiliar with "big" whitewater. Decked canoes or kayaks should be used. Tie in and waterproof all gear. Be in good physical condition. To determine the flotability of the river, check the flow over the old low water crossing, below the new Hwy. 84 crossing. Four to six inches of water over the old crossing ensures a decent trip. If there is a foot or more over the crossing, expect the river to be high, dangerous, and demanding. This is a true whitewater gem of Arkansas.

WATER QUALITY: Excellent to good.

WATER FLOW: Probably the most seasonal in Arkansas. Adequate flow conditions exist only after local rains.

PREFERRED SEASONS: All, except the hot dry months.

HAZARDS: Heavy whitewater due to the steep gradient. The river drops approximately 25 feet per mile for the first five miles. Rapids will reach the Class IV category at high water levels. "Keyhole Rapid," a Class II, is a long rapid and terminates where Blaylock Creek meets the river. The first real boat bender is "Winding Stairs Rapid," Class III-IV, at 3.8 miles. The river forks above the rapid. Take the left. "Winding Stairs Rapid" is located where these two forks rejoin. Approximately a mile below "Winding Stairs" is "Edgar's Surprise Rapid," Class II. The true danger here is the large ledge running parallel to the current in mid-stream. This ledge creates a hydraulic current, which is very dangerous, along the left bank of the river. Approximately 2 miles below "Edgar's Surprise" is a dangerous willow jungle. There is no easily identified course, but the best route is generally to the right. Immediately below the willow jungle are some of the largest waves on the river. The river narrows and the waves reach heights exceeding four feet as it flows into "Acceleration Rapid."

PUT IN: Launch at the Albert Pike Campground, adjacent to the NFS 106 crossing. Access is good and the parking area adequate.

TAKE OUT: It is possible to take out at the Hwy. 84 crossing, at 8.3 miles, or continue on to the crossing at Hwy. 70. Take out adjacent to the Hwy. 70 crossing at the Star of the West Use Area.

CAMPING: Albert Pike Campground, and the Star of the West Use Area offer camping. Facilities are limited. Most of the land adjacent to the river is owned by large lumber companies and camping is permitted. Just leave the property clean and extinguish all campfires.

CANOE RENTAL AND SHUTTLE SERVICE: None.

DISTINGUISHING FEATURES: Heavy whitewater reaching the Class IV level. Narrow, twisting, rocky channel. Very steep gradient, especially the upper section. Remote and unpolluted. Low during dry periods.

FISHING: Smallmouth and spotted bass, green sunfish, and longears can be caught all year. Thousands of rainbow trout are stocked in the stream annually. The best place for trout fishing is near the Albert Pike Rec. Area (you will need a trout stamp). Due to the fast currents, it is sometimes best to beach and wade fish. Light spinning tackle and fly fishing equipment get the best results. Avoid the summer months due to low flow levels.

AREA ATTRACTIONS: The Little Missouri Falls area, off Hwy. 25, east of the Hwy. 43/Hwy. 25 junction, northwest of Albert Pike.

MAPS: Pike and Montgomery County maps. The topographical maps are the Athens and Center Point N.E., Arkansas quadrangles.

RIVER FLOW INFORMATION: Little Rock C.O.E. (501) 378-5551 or their recording at (501) 378-5150.

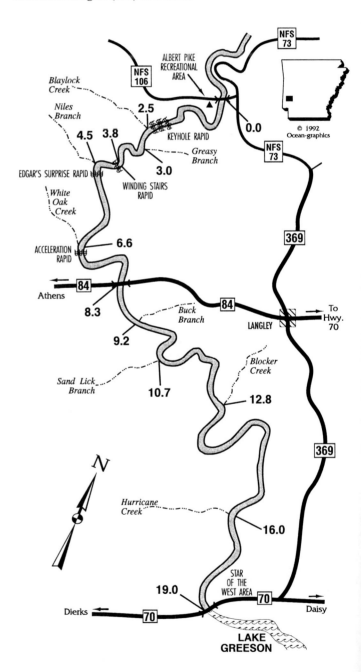

112

MULBERRY RIVER
WOLF PEN REC. AREA
TO HWY. 23
15.6 MILES

PHYSICAL LOCATION: Extreme northwest Arkansas in Franklin and Johnson counties. Little Rock 125 miles, Memphis 255 miles, Oklahoma City 245 miles, Kansas City 235 miles, and Dallas 350 miles.

GENERAL COMMENTS: A very demanding river at good flow levels. Definitely not a trip for the novice, the ill equipped or anyone in poor physical condition. Most rapids fall in the Class II or Class III categories and require some skill. Life jackets should be worn at all times, and warm clothing or wetsuits are necessary during the cooler seasons. Tie in and waterproof all gear and equipment. Check with any of the local outfitters for what to expect on each trip at a specific flow level.

WATER QUALITY: Excellent.

WATER FLOW: Normally the Mulberry is considered seasonal and should be floated from mid-October through mid-June. Check river levels with one of the outfitters if in doubt of the safe flow levels. The gauge reading and corresponding ability levels are as follows:

Below 1.8' - very low; lots of dragging.

1.8 - 2.0' - same dragging and very little whitewater.

2.1-2.4' - no dragging; good float with mild whitewater.

2.5 - 2.9' - intermediate skill required.

3.0 - 3.9' - prime whitewater; intermediate to advanced skills required; canoes should have extra flotation.

4.0 - 4.9' - advanced river runners only.

5.0' and up - plan a trip somewhere else.

PREFERRED SEASONS: Mid March through mid June offer the best water and weather conditions.

HAZARDS: The rapids in this section are exceptionally tough and demanding. Sharp, twisting turns, downed trees and large, canoe-swamping waves are ever present hazards. As the river level rises above 4.0' it spreads out into the trees. Always stay in the main channel. This section has a gradient ranging from 12' to 15' per mile.

PUT IN: The top put in is the Hwy. 103 crossing, south of Oark. However, it is not recommended because of numerous log jams downstream from the crossing. The first recommended put in is at the Wolf Pen Recreational Area, off Hwy. 215, approximately 2 river miles west of Hwy. 103. Alternate launch sites are the High Bank access at 4.0 miles, Byrd's Canoe Rental and Campground at

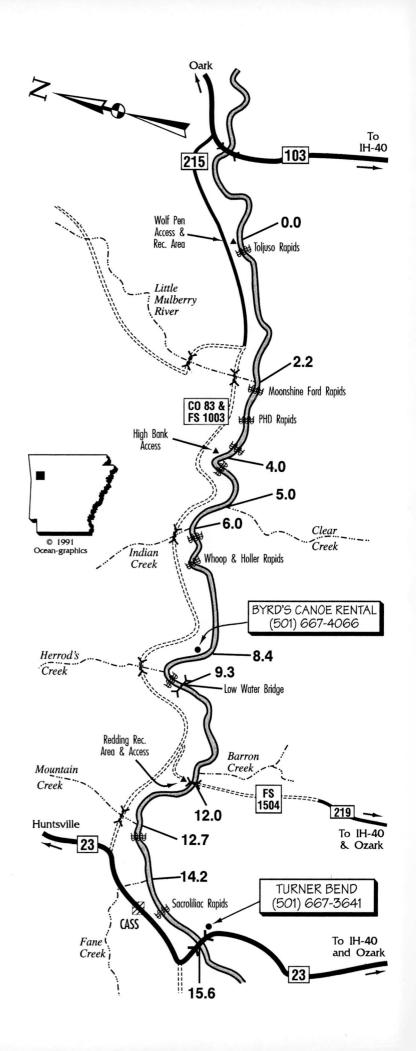

114

8.4 miles, the low water bridge at 9.3 miles, and the Redding Recreational Area access at 12.0 miles.

TAKE OUT: Any of the alternate put ins can also be used as take outs. The final take out for this section is at Turner Bend Canoe Rental and Campground, on the left bank at 15.6 miles.

CAMPING: Because it is necessary to float with as little weight as possible, canoe camping is not recommended. Public camping is available at the Forest Service sites of Wolf Pen, and the Redding Recreational area. Private camping is offered at Byrd's Canoe Rental and Turner Bend Canoe Rental.

CANOE RENTAL & SHUTTLE SERVICE: Byrd's Canoe rental, (501) 667-4066 and Turner Bend Canoe Rental, (501) 667-3641.

DISTINGUISHING FEATURES: Possibly the best, and most popular, whitewater river in Arkansas. Many Class I and Class II rapids which increase to Class IV's at high water levels. Abundant willow stands in the river. Beautiful rock formations and boulder gardens. Clean, clear water. A true gem of the Ozarks.

FISHING: Generally very good at low to normal water levels, ranging from 1.8' to 2.8'. The Forest Service consistently stocks the river with channel cat and smallmouth bass. Although considered second to the smallmouth, there are many largemouth bass taken from the Mulberry each year.

AREA ATTRACTIONS: The rugged and beautiful Ozark Highlands Trail passes within a couple of miles of the Mulberry. This trail stretches the full length of the Ozark National Forest. Its numerous access points offer great hiking opportunities, except during the hot summer months. Visit White Rock Mountain in the heart of the Ozark National Forest. Rustic cabins and a campground are available. Contact the U.S. Forest Service at (501) 667-2191 for information on White Rock Mountain facilities, or data on the Ozark Highlands Trail. Visit the wineries in Altus, only 20 miles from the Mulberry. They all feature tours and wine tasting.

MAPS: The Johnson and Franklin County road maps. The topographical maps are the Yale and Cass, Arkansas quadrangles.

RIVER FLOW INFORMATION: Byrd's Canoe Rental, (501) 667-4066 and Turner Bend Canoe Rental, (501) 667-3641.

MULBERRY RIVER
HWY. 23 TO MILL CREEK
22.3 MILES

PHYSICAL LOCATION: Extreme northwest Arkansas in Franklin County. Little Rock 125 miles, Memphis 265 miles, Oklahoma City 235 miles, Kansas City 225 miles, and Dallas 340 miles.

GENERAL COMMENTS: A very demanding river at good flow levels. Definitely not a trip for the novice, the ill equipped, or anyone in poor physical condition. Most rapids fall in the Class II or Class III categories and require some skill. Life jackets should be worn at all times, and warm clothing or wetsuits are necessary during the cooler seasons. Tie in and waterproof all gear and equipment. Check with any of the local outfitters for what to expect on each trip at a specific flow level.

WATER QUALITY: Excellent.

WATER FLOW: Generally the same as the upper section. The gradient on this section will average about 11' per mile.

PREFERRED SEASONS: Mid March through mid June offer the best water and weather conditions.

HAZARDS: Downed trees generally present problems on the upper portion of this section. One of the toughest runs on the river, Ham Falls, is approximately half a mile above Campbell Cemetery. This is a long, treacherous rapid. Start to the right and work gradually to the left when running it. Hell Roaring Falls, approximately 3 miles below Campbell Cemetery, is a 3' drop which should be run straight on. There are a number of testy rapids between Hurricane Creek, 15.5 miles, and the take out at Mill Creek.

PUT IN: The first put in for this section is at Turner Bend. Alternate put ins are at Milton Ford, 8.3 miles, and Campbell Cemetery at 10.2 miles. Both of these alternates are on "dirt" roads and not easy to find. Check with one of the local outfitters for directions.

Moonshine Ford, map page 114

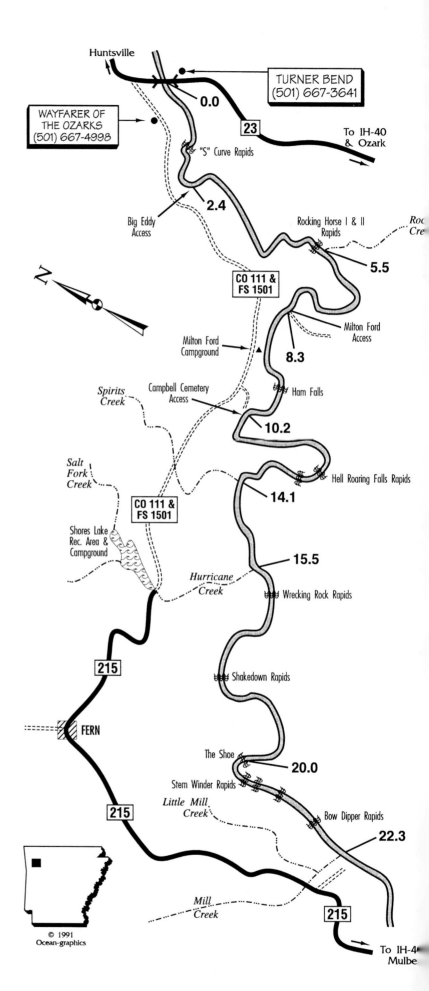

Trail passes within a couple of miles of the Mulberry. This trail stretches the full length of the Ozark National Forest. Its numerous access points offer great hiking opportunities, except during the hot summer months. Visit White Rock Mountain in the heart of the Ozark National Forest. Rustic cabins and a campground are available. Contact the U.S. Forest Service at (501) 667-2191 for information on White Rock Mountain facilities, or data on the Ozark Highlands Trail. Visit the wineries in Altus, only 20 miles from the Mulberry. They all feature tours and wine tasting.

MAPS: The Franklin County road map and Cass, Watalula, and Cravens Arkansas topographical quadrangles.

RIVER FLOW INFORMATION: Turner Bend Canoe Rental, (501) 667-3641 and Wayfarer of the Ozarks, (501) 667-4998.

Rapid just below Ham Falls

TAKE OUT: Either of the alternate put ins will also serve as take out points for short trips. For a longer trip, the most popular take out is Mill Creek, at 22.3 miles. To identify the Mill Creek take out, look for a cable with a trolley chair which crosses over the river. The Mill Creek access is a mile down river, on the right bank. If you want an even longer trip, you can take out at the Old Silver Bridge, another 3.5 miles downstream.

CAMPING: Because it is necessary to float with as little weight as possible, canoe camping is not recommended on this section either. Public camping is available at the Forest Service sites at Milton Ford and Shores Lake Recreational Area. Private camping is offered at Turner Bend Canoe Rental and Campground and by Wayfarer of the Ozarks..

CANOE RENTAL & SHUTTLE: Turner Bend Canoe Rental, (501) 667-3641 and Wayfarer of the Ozarks, (501) 667-4998.

DISTINGUISHING FEATURES: The gradient is not quite as steep as on the upper section. The river takes on a more "long pool and drop" characteristic. Although not numerous, the rapids are big, with steep drops and large standing waves. Large boulders such as the "house-size" rock at The Shoe add character to this section. At The Shoe, the boulder sits in the middle of a left hand bend; it's approximately 2.3 miles above Mill Creek. The lower portion of the river is beautiful, remote and seldom floated.

FISHING: Generally very good at low to normal water levels, ranging from 1.8' to 2.8'. The Forest Service consistently stocks the river with channel cat and smallmouth bass. Although considered second to the smallmouth, there are many largemouth bass taken from the Mulberry each year.

AREA ATTRACTIONS: The rugged and beautiful Ozark Highlands

OUACHITA RIVER
PINE RIDGE TO HWY. 270
19.6 MILES

PHYSICAL LOCATION: Montgomery County, West Central Arkansas. Mena 25 miles, Hot Springs 55 miles, Fort Smith 60 miles, and Dallas 290 miles.

GENERAL COMMENTS: An exceptionally scenic trip as the river winds its way along towering rock bluffs. Flowering wild beauty decorates the river channel at every bend. Truly a year round scenic adventure. This is a trip which everyone can enjoy . Don't try to make the full 19.6 miles in one day, you'll miss too much of the beauty! The river offers excellent fishing.

WATER QUALITY: Clean and unpolluted.

WATER FLOW: Series of small to medium size rapids alternating with long quiet pools. The water speed averages about one mile per hour. This section of the Ouachita River should be considered borderline seasonal because of extreme low water levels during the summer months.

PREFERRED SEASONS: Spring and fall offer more consistent water levels, and tolerable temperatures,

HAZARDS: Very few except at high water levels, however, the narrow crooked channel combined with the rocky terrain may prove disastrous after heavy rains.

PUT IN: Launch at the river crossing southeast of Pine Ridge, off Hwy. 88. The turn off to the crossing is approximately 1 mile east of Pine Ridge on Hwy. 88. For a shorter trip, put in at the Hwy. 379 crossing, south of Oden.

TAKE OUT: For the 10.2 mile upper section, take out at the Hwy. 379 crossing, south of Oden. The second take out is the campground at Rocky Shoals Rec. Area, at the Hwy. 270 crossing, southeast of Pencil Bluff, 19.6 miles.

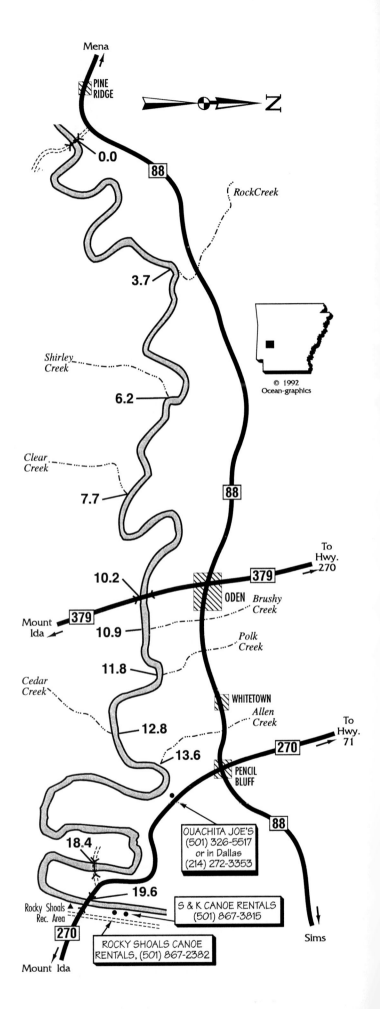

CAMPING: There are nine U.S. Forest Service Camps and landings above Lake Ouachita. Both road and river signs mark these areas. Note: some of these signs are very poor.

CANOE RENTAL AND SHUTTLE SERVICE: Ouachita Joe's Canoe Rental, Pencil Bluff, (501) 326-5517, Rocky Shoals Canoe Rentals, Mount Ida, (501) 867-2382 or (501) 326-4710, and S & K Canoe, Mt. Ida, (501) 867-3815.

DISTINGUISHING FEATURES: Noisy shoals, quick turns, and a tunnel of overhanging trees characterize this section of the Ouachita. Here you'll find some of the best scenery on the river, including a towering bluff a few miles above the Hwy. 270 take out. Deep pools, fun rapids, and shady banks create an ever-changing panorama of river beauty.

FISHING: The Ouachita has been a favorite fishing spot of sportsmen for years. Smallmouth and spotted bass are caught year-round. The best time for the big bass, four pounders are fairly common, is during the cooler months from October to March. You will also find large quantities of green and longear sunfish, plus a few walleye, largemouth bass, catfish and bluegill.

AREA ATTRACTIONS: Primarily, just a lot of beautiful country.

MAPS: The topographical maps are the Oden, and Mount Ida Arkansas 15' quadrangles.

RIVER FLOW INFORMATION: Ouachita Joe's Canoe Rental, Pencil Bluff, (501) 326-5517, Rocky Shoals Canoe Rentals, Mount Ida, (501) 867-2382 or (501) 326-4710, and S & K Canoe, Mt. Ida, (501) 867-3815.

OUACHITA RIVER

HWY. 270 TO HWY. 27

23.5 MILES

PHYSICAL LOCATION: Montgomery County, West Central Arkansas. Mena 32 miles, Hot Springs 40 miles, Fort Smith 76 miles, and Dallas 290 miles.

GENERAL COMMENTS: An exceptionally scenic trip as the river winds its way along towering rock bluffs. Flowering wild beauty decorates the river channel at every bend. Truly a year round scenic adventure. The river offers excellent fishing. Ideally suited for family outings. Numerous access points allow you to plan a trip to suit your time, and conditioning.

WATER QUALITY: Clean and unpolluted. Good to excellent.

WATER FLOW: Series of small to medium-size rapids, alternating with long quiet pools. Generally considered a year-round trip.

PREFERRED SEASONS: Spring and Autumn because of more constant water levels, and tolerable daytime temperatures.

HAZARDS: Very few except at high water levels. Caution should be exercised in the tight turns and narrow channels due to overhanging limbs and brush.

PUT IN: The initial launch is from the campground at Rocky Shoals Rec. Area, just off Hwy. 270..

TAKE OUT: The first take out is Sims Bridge (3.8 miles). Other good take out points are Fulton Branch (Fulton Campground) at 8.0 miles, Drag Over at 9.2 miles, and River Bluff at 12.5 miles. The last take out is the Hwy. 27 crossing at 23.5 miles, south of Washita.

CAMPING: Camping facilities ranging from fair to excellent are available at Rocky Shoals Campground, Sims Campground (downstream from the bridge at 3.8 miles), Fulton Branch, Drag Over and River Bluff. There are also numerous Forest Service campgrounds here

CANOE RENTAL AND SHUTTLE SERVICE: Ouachita Joe's Canoe Rental, Pencil Bluff (501) 326-5517, Rocky Shoals Canoe Rentals, Mount Ida (501) 867-2382 or (501) 326-4710, or S & K Canoe, Mt. Ida (501) 867-3815.

DISTINGUISHING FEATURES: Just about the same as the previous section. However, this section is somewhat slower and has more long deep pools.

FISHING: Same species of fish as the upper section, but will also include rock bass, channel, blue and yellow catfish. Although, the Ouachita is a prime smallmouth stream, white bass are very popular in the early spring. From late March through early April, white bass make their spawning run up from Lake Ouachita. Some of these are quite large, many weighing in the 3 to 4 pound class. Small jigs, spinners, spoons and crankbaits will all catch whites.

AREA ATTRACTIONS: Hot Springs is the nearest metroplex. Here you can enjoy a number of activities and attractions. For more information, contact the Hot Springs Convention and Visitors Bureau, (800) 543-BATH (2284).

MAPS: Montgomery County map. Topographical map is the Mount Ida, Arkansas quadrangle.

RIVER FLOW INFORMATION: Ouachita Joe's Canoe Rental, Pencil Bluff (501) 326-5517, Rocky Shoals Canoe Rentals, Mount Ida (501) 867-2382 or (501) 326-4710, or S & K Canoe, Mt. Ida (501) 867-3815.

Oden

PENCIL BLUFF

OUACHITA JOE'S (501) 326-5517 or In Dallas (214) 272-3353

270

88

Rock Creek

Hackberry Creek

Rocky Shoals Rec. Area

0.0

ROCKY SHOALS CANOE RENTALS, (501) 867-2382

1.2

3.1

SIMS

S & K CANOE RENTALS (501) 867-3815

298

3.8

Craft Creek

270

4.7

5.9

8.0

Fulton Branch

Fulton Branch Rec. Area

Rainy Creek

270

8.3

88

379

9.2

MOUNT IDA

West Spring Creek

11.0

Drag Over Rec. Area

12.5

GIBBS

River Bluff Rec. Area

Haw Creek

15.3

Wheat Creek

16.2

17.8

18.3

Big Creek

21.5

88

27

23.5

LAKE OUACHITA

27

WASHITA

© 1992 Ocean-graphics

120

SOUTH FORK OF THE SPRING RIVER
SADDLE TO HARDY
18.3 MILES

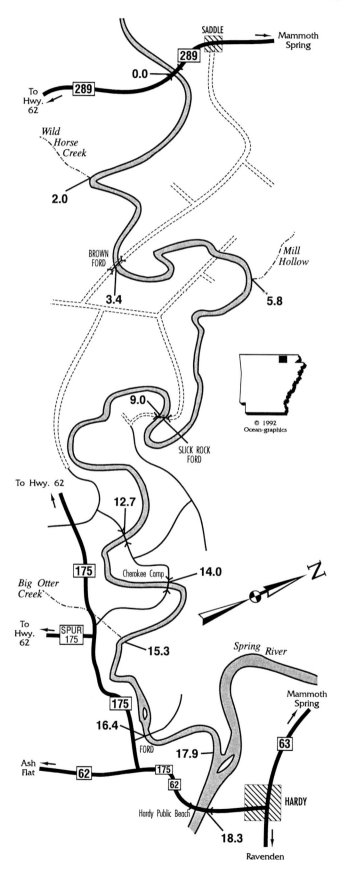

PHYSICAL LOCATION: Fulton and Sharp counties in extreme North Central Arkansas, between Saddle and Hardy.

GENERAL COMMENTS: The South Fork of the Spring is scenic and remote as it winds its way between the densely shrouded banks of Ozark hardwoods. Its majestic bluffs, twisting channels, and rocky shoals offer an ever changing panorama to the lucky river runner, or outdoorsman. This area is generally remote and wild, with few signs of civilization. If in doubt about safe or comfortable river levels, check the distance between the river level and the old bridge piers at Cherokee Camp, 14.0 miles. If the distance is more than a foot, the river is too low to be enjoyable; if the distance is half a foot or less, the river is high and dangerous.

WATER QUALITY: Excellent. Clear and cold as the river flows over rocky shoals and clean gravel.

WATER FLOW: Optimum during spring months. Should be considered seasonal at other times. Almost totally dependent on run off for flow volume.

HAZARDS: Due to the time of year best suited to floating on the South Fork, air and water temperature should be prime considerations when planning or making the trip. Although the river is characterized by sharp turns, narrow chutes, and rocky shoals, none of these present extremely hazardous conditions, except at high water levels. The Ford at 16.4 miles should definitely be considered dangerous. Portage on the right bank. Extreme caution should be exercised at the low water bridges at Brown Ford, Slick Rock, and Cherokee Camp.

PUT IN: The Hwy. 289 bridge crossing, south of Saddle.

TAKE OUT: Take out at Cherokee Camp after 14 miles, or at Hardy Public Beach on the right bank at 18.3 miles. Both are easy take outs.

CANOE RENTAL AND SHUTTLE SERVICE: Many Islands Camp, (501) 856-3451. See Spring River map for Many Islands Camp location.

CAMPING: Many excellent natural campsites. Also, there is a good camping area at Many Islands Camp with all needed facilities. Expect to pay a fee for the use of any commercial camp facilities.

DISTINGUISHING FEATURES: The South Fork is characterized by sharp turns, narrow chutes, rocky shoals, and large gravel bars.

FISHING: The smallmouth is the primary game fish in the river. However, largemouth and spotted bass, rock bass, catfish, warmouth, and longear sunfish are regularly caught. During the colder months, rainbow trout (stamp required), and walleye make their way up from the Spring River, and can be caught along the lower section of the South Fork.

AREA ATTRACTIONS: See the summary of the Spring River for the attractions in this area.

MAPS: The Agnos and Stuart, Arkansas topographical quadrangles.

RIVER FLOW INFORMATION: Available from Many Islands Camp, (501) 856-3451.

SPRING RIVER
DAM #3 AT HWY. 342 TO HARDY BEACH
15.0 MILES

Map labels:

Thayer, Missouri

MAMMOTH SPRING

© 1992 Ocean-graphics

9 — Salem

289

342

63

Dam #3

0.0

Field Creek

1.0

Saddle

Public Access

Cottonwood Hollow

3.5

Big Creek

Brush Creek

3.9

SADDLER FALLS

5.0 COTTONWOOD FALLS

English Creek — 5.5

5.8 HORSESHOE FALLS

8.0

MANY ISLANDS CAMP (501) 856-3451

Myatt Creek

Gut Creek

9.4 — 9.9

Scrabble Creek

10.3

11.7

Ray Hollow

12.6

FORD

12.4

13.0

Dry Creek

Stillhouse Hollow

13.7

N

14.6 HIGH FALLS

HARDY

South Fork Spring River

63

Hardy Beach — 15.0

175

62

Ravenden

To Hwy. 62

Ash Flat

PHYSICAL LOCATION: Fulton and Sharp counties in extreme North Central Arkansas, north of Hardy.

GENERAL COMMENTS: Due to the continuous flow from Mammoth Springs, approximately 9 million gallons per hour, the Spring River is one of the most popular streams in the Ozarks. Water comes from the spring at a constant 58 degrees - it's cold any time of the year. The river is a staircase of many small and medium waterfalls, framed in the natural beauty of the Ozark wilderness. This is an excellent trip for the photographer, and fisherman. The trip is a little tricky and does require good common sense, but is one which those with minimal experience can enjoy. Elderly people or families with small children might want to consider tamer waters.

WATER QUALITY: Excellent. Almost totally spring fed. Flowing clear, and cold.

WATER FLOW: Due to the continuous flow from Mammoth Spring, the river maintains a constant year round flow.

PREFERRED SEASONS: Generally any time of the year the weather or seasonal conditions will permit.

HAZARDS: Approximately 5½ miles from the put in is Saddler Falls, a series of fast, narrow channels, and a double waterfall. Saddler Falls Camp is on the left bank immediately above the falls. Approach and run the first small fall on the left. Stay left and line up just left of center to drop over the larger falls. A smaller, but more tricky, fall is immediately below. If necessary, this second fall can be portaged on the left. Downstream at 5.8 miles is Horseshoe Falls. This is a 4-5 foot fall which can be run. If you want to keep your powder dry, take the channel leading off to the left above the falls. This channel bypasses the falls. The are a number of tricky rapids between Many Islands, at

8.0 miles, and Gut Creek at 9.9 miles. At 11.7 miles is another difficult fall. The river narrows here and the constriction creates fast water and large standing waves. At 12.4 miles is a dangerous low water crossing which must be portaged on the right. Beach well above the crossing to avoid the possibility of being swept under the bridge. The largest fall, High Falls, is located at the junction of the Spring River and the South Fork of the Spring River, 14.6 miles. This is a drop of 5-6 feet and can be run with caution. Line up and run the groove to the left of the main fall.

PUT IN: The east side of Dam #3 where Hwy. 342 meets the river. To reach the launching area, take Arkansas 342, west off U.S. 63, for slightly less than a mile.

TAKE OUT: For a short trip, take out on the left at Many Islands Camp after 8 miles. To go the 15 mile distance, take out at Hardy Beach, a public park on the stream's southwest (right) bank below the Hwy. 62 crossing.

CAMPING: Excellent facilities including all conveniences at Many Islands Camp. Also there are many natural camp sites.

CANOE RENTAL AND SHUTTLE SERVICE: Both available at Many Islands Camp, (501) 856-3451.

DISTINGUISHING FEATURES: A consistent high volume of cold water which makes the Spring a year round float stream, and allows the annual stocking of rainbow trout. Numerous waterfalls and rapids make this an exciting trip.

FISHING: Rainbow trout (stamp required), rank at the top of the list, and brown trout take a close second. One to three pounders are not uncommon in the area around, and above, Many Islands Camp. The best spots for catching trout are immediately below falls, in the fast whitewater. In addition to trout, the Spring offers high quality fishing for smallmouth bass, walleye (two species), channel and flathead catfish, spotted bass, rock bass, warmouths, and longear sunfish. Light weight spinning and fly fishing tackle are preferred for this area. Any of the locals will tell you what they're hitting at the time.

AREA ATTRACTIONS: Don't miss viewing one of the largest springs in the country at Mammoth Springs State Park. Next door to the State Park is the Mammoth Spring National Fish Hatchery, the nations's leading producer of smallmouth bass. Visitors are welcome to take a self-guided tour of the hatchery. Also, you might want to check out the historic sites, shops and buildings in Hardy.

MAPS: The topographical maps are the Mammoth Spring, Stuart, and Hardy, Arkansas quadrangles.

RIVER FLOW INFORMATION: Available from Many Islands Camp, (501) 856-3451.

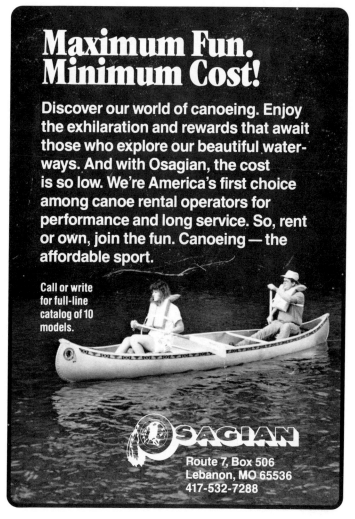

OKLAHOMA

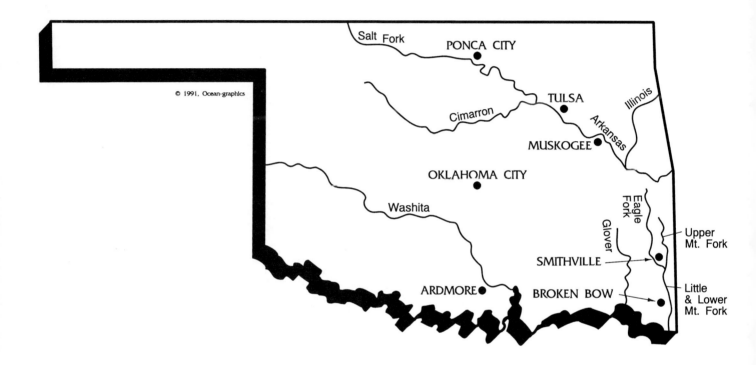

© 1991, Ocean-graphics

Oklahoma is blessed with many beautiful, "fun to run" streams and rivers. Most are nestled in the Oklahoma Ozark hills, in extreme southeastern Oklahoma, or along the Oklahoma-Arkansas border. You can just about "pick and choose" your own special type of stream in this state. Whether your prime interest is wild whitewater, scenic remote beauty or fantastic fishing, you can find it all, and more, in the rivers and streams of the "Sooner" state.

Oklahoma has realized the trememdous potential of its rivers, and has wisely seen fit to put many of them into the Oklahoma Scenic River system. This guaran-

tees greater protection for the natural environment of the river while, at the same time, making more information available to the public. Oklahoma's Scenic River Commission recently began publishing the "Oklahoma Floater's Guide" starting with the Illinois River. The Commission will gradually assemble a floaters guide for the majority of the Scenic Rivers. Each guide will be an individual write up covering a specific stream. Request the guide from the Oklahoma Scenic River Commission, P.O. Box 292, Tahlequah, OK 74465, (800) 299-3251.

ILLINOIS RIVER
WATTS PUBLIC ACCESS AREA TO HANGING ROCK
30.5 MILES

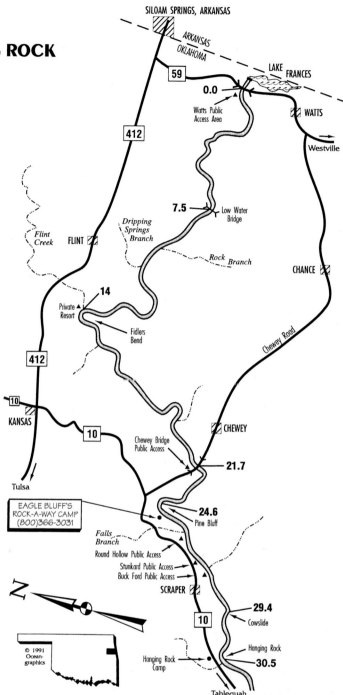

PHYSICAL LOCATION: Northeastern Oklahoma, Adair, Delaware and Cherokee Counties. Oklahoma City 195 miles, Tulsa 75 miles, Dallas 260 miles and Austin 450 miles.

GENERAL COMMENTS: The Illinois is highly developed for canoe traffic. Campgrounds and canoe rentals are numerous and adequate. An excellent, clean, clear flowing stream with few hazards; a stream anyone can enjoy! Get an Oklahoma fishing license if you plan to wet a hook. All private canoes are required to display a trip sticker on the starboard bow. IT IS LAW - no glass containers allowed on the river.

WATER QUALITY: Excellent to good.

WATER FLOW: Always adequate, especially on the lower 8.8 miles. During excessively dry periods the 21.7 mile section above Chewey bridge will be too low for enjoyable canoeing.

PREFERRED SEASONS: Anytime of the year offers enjoyable canoeing on some section of the Illinois. May 1st through October 1st, however, is considered the "canoeing season."

HAZARDS: The low water crossing at 7.5 miles should be considered dangerous at high water levels.

PUT IN: The initial put in is the public access point at Watts Public Access Area, off Hwy. 59, north of Watts.

TAKE OUT: The first take out is the low water crossing at 7.5 miles, the next is the Private Resort at 14.0 miles. Chewey Bridge Public Access is next at 21.7 miles. Public access areas, camps, road crossings, and canoe liveries offer unlimited take out/launch points below Chewey Bridge. The last take out for this section is adjacent to Hanging Rock Camp, at 30.5 miles. Many of these areas offer fine access, but the private camps will charge a nominal fee for put in, take out, or parking.

CAMPING: Camp sites, both public and private, are abundant.

CANOE RENTAL & SHUTTLE SERVICE: Eagle Bluff's Rock-A-Way Camp (800) 366-3031 or (918) 456-3031, and Hanging Rock Camp (800) 375-3088, or (918) 456-3088.

DISTINGUISHING FEATURES: The Illinois is scenic and beautiful as it runs from the dam at Lake Frances to the headwaters of Tenkiller Reservoir. It has several stretches of mild rapids. Some of the sharp turns and overhanging limbs may pose minor hazards for the novice or unwary.

FISHING: Although there are 68 other species of fish in the Illinois, the smallmouth bass is the most prominent.

AREA ATTRACTIONS: See the Cherokee Heritage Center and the Tsa-La-Gi Ancient Village, southeast of Tahlequah. Other places of interest are the historic Murrell Mansion, and Fort Gibson, one of the first forts in the West (1824), restored to its original condition. Pari-mutuel horse racing is featured at Blue Ribbon Downs, located between Sallisaw and Vian, south of Tahlequah.

MAPS: The Adair and Cherokee County road maps. The AR-OK-MO 1:100,000 topographical quadrangle.

RIVER FLOW INFORMATION: See Canoe Rental & Shuttle Service, or the Oklahoma Scenic Rivers Commission (800) 299-3251 or (918) 456-3251.

125

ILLINOIS RIVER

HANGING ROCK TO HIGHWAY 62

26.1 MILES

PHYSICAL LOCATION: Northeastern Oklahoma, immediately north of Tahlequah, in Cherokee County. Oklahoma City 185 miles, Tulsa 65 miles, and Dallas 250 miles.

GENERAL COMMENTS: Very similar to the upper section, with highly developed canoe and campground facilities. As the river meanders downstream, it becomes slower, deeper, and wider. An abundance of access points offer a wide variety and selection of trips.

WATER QUALITY: Excellent to good.

WATER FLOW: Always adequate. Will always have better year-round flow levels than the upper section.

PREFERRED SEASONS: Floating the Illinois is enjoyable anytime of the year. However, the primary canoeing "season" extends from May through September.

HAZARDS: This lower section is virtually hazard free.

PUT IN: Launch at Hanging Rock Camp. Alternate put ins are available at the numerous private facilities, the public access areas, or Comb's bridge, 4.1 miles. Expect to pay a fee at the private camps for launching and parking.

TAKE OUT: Take out at any of the alternate put ins. The last take out point for this trip is the Riverside Park Public Access at 26.3 miles.

CAMPING: The private and public access points offer a wide variety of camping facilities.

CANOE RENTAL AND SHUTTLE: Check with any of the camps and rental agencies listed on the map. Most offer complete rental and shuttle services.

DISTINGUISHING FEATURES: The Illinois is Oklahoma's best known scenic river. Bordered by an ever-changing oak and hickory forest, it flows clear and clean. Some small rapids still show up along the river, although it gradually becomes slower, deeper and wider than the previous section.

FISHING: Including smallmouth, largemouth and rainbow trout (stamp required), there are 69 species of fish in the Illinois. The smallmouth is the dominant game fish, but large numbers of the others are caught annually. The smallmouth and the trout will hold close to, or in, the faster currents,

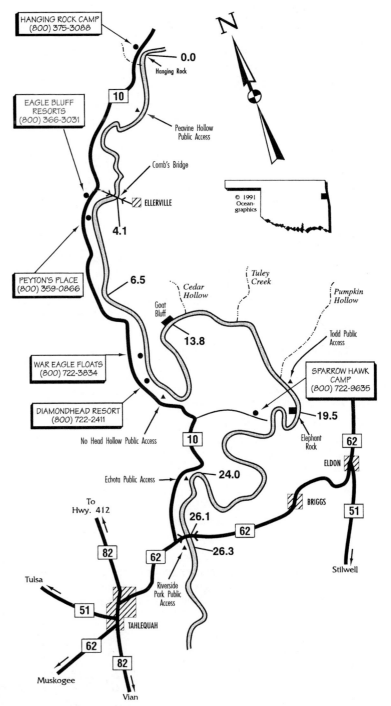

while the largemouth will be caught in the deeper, slower pools. For best results, stay with light tackle, low visibility lines, and small baits resembling the natural foods of the area and season.

AREA ATTRACTIONS: Same as the previous section. However, for additional information, contact the Lake Tenkiller Association (918) 457-4403, the Tahlequah Chamber of Commerce (918) 456-3742, or the Oklahoma Scenic Rivers Commission (800) 299-3251.

MAPS: The Cherokee County road map and the Chewey, Moodys, Tahlequah, and Proctor, Oklahoma topographical quadrangles.

RIVER FLOW INFORMATION: Any of the listed rental or camping facilities on the river. Tulsa C.O.E. (918) 581-7666 or Oklahoma Scenic Rivers Commission (800) 299-3251 or (918) 456-3251.

GLOVER RIVER
EAST & WEST FORK JUNCTION
TO GLOVER
27.5 MILES

PHYSICAL LOCATION: Extreme southeastern Oklahoma in McCurtain County. Dallas 200 miles, Oklahoma City 175 miles, and Shreveport 150 miles.

GENERAL COMMENTS: Plan on short trips. The upper section will require some walking around rocks and rapids. Some short portages may also be necessary. Travel light and waterproof all gear. An ultra scenic, and exciting trip, especially in the spring. Five digit highway numbers designate forest company roads - many of these roads are unmarked, so do not hesitate to ask for directions.

WATER QUALITY: Good; flowing over solid rock and gravel shoals.

WATER FLOW: Due to the river bed terrain, the upper section may require some walking. Unless there has been an exceptionally dry season, the lower section will have adequate water for an enjoyable trip.

PREFERRED SEASONS: March through July, and September to mid November.

HAZARDS: There are many small falls, rock gardens, and outcroppings which can prove hazardous. At low levels, portages may be required to get around some of these obstacles. Stay off the river at high levels, unless you're outfitted for heavy whitewater, and have adequate experience. Super slippery rocks can be hazardous, especially at low water levels - beware! The low water bridges at 7.2 miles, and 16.3 miles, can be extremely dangerous at high levels. Portage if there is any doubt.

Cossatot's Washing Machine Rapid, map page 101

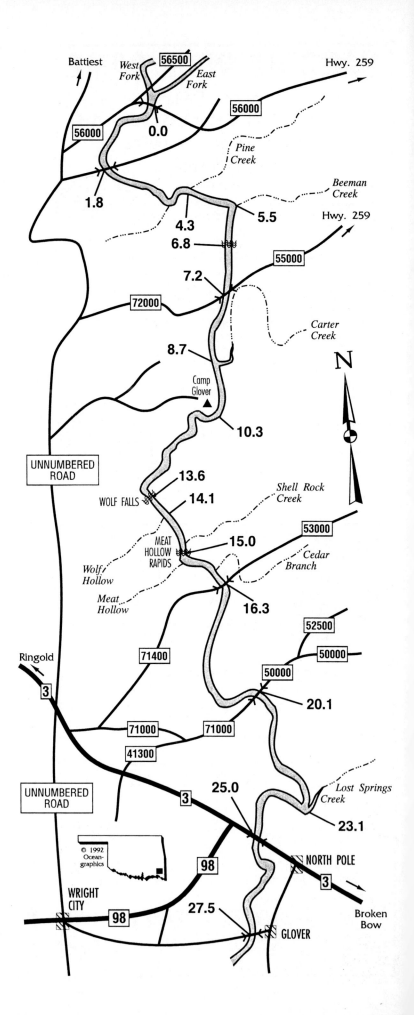

128

Wolf Falls, 13.6 miles, and Meat Hollow Rapids, 15.0 miles, fall into the extremely hazardous category. Portage or plan your route carefully.

PUT IN: Launch at the low water bridge, on forest road #56000, immediately below the West and East Fork Junction. The forks are visible approximately ¼ mile upstream.

TAKE OUT: The first take out is the #72000/#55000 crossing at 7.2 miles. Camp Glover, 10.3 miles, can be used as an emergency take out point, but permission must be obtained from the camp caretaker. There is a locked gate at the camp entrance. The next exit point from the river is the forest road #53000/#71400 crossing at 16.3 miles. Alternate take outs are the low water crossing at 20.1 miles, the Hwy. 3 bridge, at 25.0 miles and the low water bridge, approximately half a mile west of Glover, at 27.5 miles. Parking at this crossing is very limited.

CAMPING: The best camping facility is Lost Rapids Camp at Pine Creek Lake, 7 miles west on Hwy. 3 from the junction of Hwy. 3 and Hwy. 98. There are primitive camping areas at Meat Hollow and the crossing at 16.3 miles. Natural camp sites are abundant, especially since most of the land bordering the river belongs to the Weyerhaeuser Company. For more information on the recreation areas offered by Weyerhaeuser, contact any of their Dierks Division offices or forestry stations in the Glover area.

CANOE RENTAL AND SHUTTLE SERVICE: None on the river at this printing.

DISTINGUISHING FEATURES: Solid bedrock, ledges, outcroppings, and boulders create fun rapids, chutes, and natural dams. Miles of unbroken forest line and dense vegetation cover each bank. Many of the roads in this area are rough.

FISHING: Fishing in the slower areas is generally good. To fish the upper section, it's best to beach the boat and wade fish the protected areas. Smallmouth, largemouth, and a variety of perch can all be taken on the Glover. Light tackle, low visibility lines,

small lures, and short accurate casts will consistently catch fish.

AREA ATTRACTIONS: In Idabel, south of Broken Bow, visit the Magnolia Mansion and the Museum of the Red River. In the Broken Bow area, see the Forest Heritage Center in Beavers Bend State Park, or the Gardner Mansion, the 1880 home of Choctaw chief, Jefferson Gardner. For more information, contact the Idabel Chamber of Commerce (405) 286-3305, or the Broken Bow Chamber of Commerce (405) 584-3393

MAPS: The Bethel and Golden, Oklahoma topographical maps are the best available covering this area.

RIVER FLOW INFORMATION: Oklahoma River information recording, in Tulsa (918) 581-7662, or the Oklahoma Scenic Rivers Commission (800) 299-3251 or (918) 456-3251. In Carrollton, Texas contact North Texas Canoes (214) 245-7475.

The Last Trip!

UPPER MOUNTAIN FORK RIVER

HWY. 246 TO "THE NARROWS"
28.6 MILES

PHYSICAL LOCATION: South Oklahoma/Arkansas state line. Polk County, Arkansas and McCurtain County, Oklahoma. Texarkana 80 miles, Shreveport 150 miles, and Dallas 240 miles.

GENERAL COMMENTS: A scenic trip offering excitement and adventure. Can be divided into a one, two, or three day trip. Good fishing, but be sure to have an Arkansas *and* Oklahoma fishing license.

WATER QUALITY: Good to excellent.

WATER FLOW: This section generally has adequate flow for an enjoyable float trip.

PREFERRED SEASONS: Anytime of the year, weather permitting. Due to the scenic color changes of the seasons, and better river flow, spring and fall are the optimum seasons.

HAZARDS: There are numerous small rapids which will be a problem if not run properly. The first considered dangerous is located approximately 6.5 miles from the put in. Another hazardous rapid is located approximately ¼ mile below the Hwy. 4 bridge. Between the Hwy. 4 crossing and the takeout point there are numerous rapids, falls, and ledges which will require some scouting. When in doubt, look them over.

PUT IN: Launch under the west end of the Hwy. 246 crossing. There is a primitive campground here and access to the river.

TAKEOUT: The first take out point is the crossing at 8.3 miles. This is an easy one day float. The next is the Hwy. 4

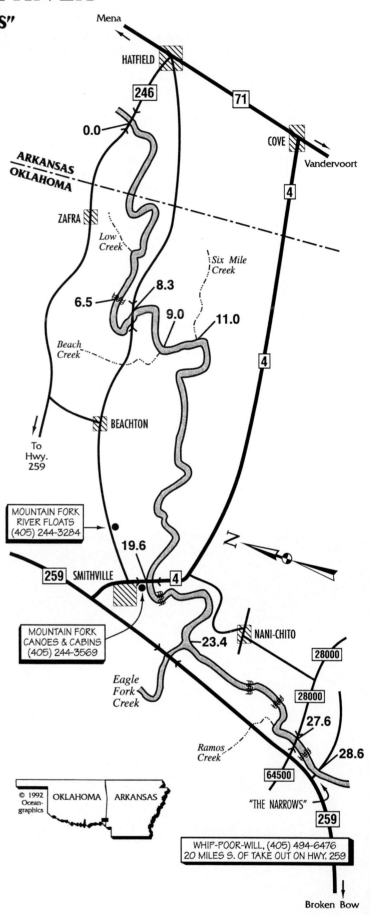

© 1992 Oceangraphics — OKLAHOMA ARKANSAS

WHIP-POOR-WILL, (405) 494-6476
20 MILES S. OF TAKE OUT ON HWY. 259

crossing at 19.6 miles, and the last at "The Narrows," at 28.6 miles. The old bridge is washed out here. This section can be easily divided into three one day trips or stretched into a single trip of three days.

CAMPING: Mountain Fork Canoes and Cabins (405) 244-3569, and Whip-Poor-Will (405)494-6476. There are primitive camp sites and parking areas at the Hwy. 246 crossing, and the crossing at 8.3 miles. There is a small park at an old road crossing approximately 0.1 mile below the Hwy. 4 crossing. There are numerous natural camping areas, both in the river bed, and along the banks. Obtain permission to camp on private property.

CANOE RENTAL AND SHUTTLE SERVICE: Mountain Fork Canoes and Cabins (405) 244-3569, and Whip-Poor-Will Canoe Rental (405) 494-6476.

DISTINGUISHING FEATURES: Clear clean water. Some scattered rock bluffs alternating with high banks and sloping shorelines. Many large, deep holes of water ending in rapids, rock shoals, or small falls. Numerous gravel bars with backgrounds of pine forested slopes.

FISHING: The Upper Mountain Fork is regarded as Oklahoma's best smallmouth stream. The fast, clear water and rocky gravel bottom offer an excellent environment for smallmouth. Spinning lures, plastic grubs, plastic worm-jig combinations, small crank baits, and small to medium topwaters will all catch fish. Fish the fast waters, but concentrate on the slower, protected water for largemouth.

AREA ATTRACTIONS: Not many in this area unless you take the drive south to Broken Bow. This area is extremely scenic, but remote. Here, it's just great to enjoy the beauty of the countryside.

MAPS: Polk, Arkansas and McCurtain, Oklahoma county maps. The Cove and Zafra, Arkansas topographical quadrangles.

RIVER FLOW INFORMATION: Mountain Fork Canoes and Cabins (405) 244-3569, and Whip-Poor-Will Canoe Rental (405) 494-6476. Oklahoma River Information recording in Tulsa (918) 581-7662. Oklahoma Scenic Rivers Commission, (800) 299-3251 or (918) 456-3251.

LOWER MOUNTAIN FORK AND LITTLE RIVER

REREGULATION DAM TO ASHALINTUBBI
16.8 MILES

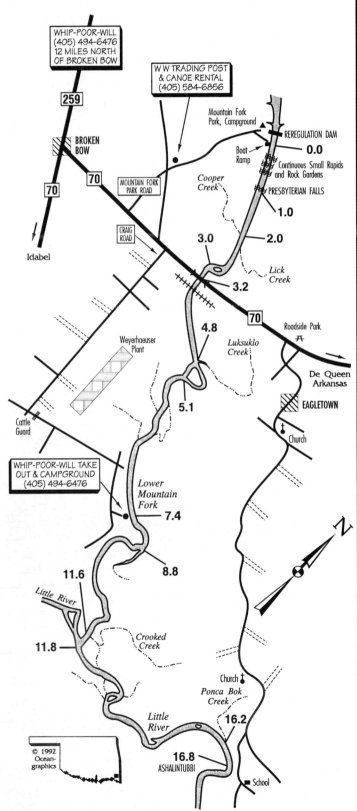

WHIP-POOR-WILL
(405) 494-6476
12 MILES NORTH
OF BROKEN BOW

259

BROKEN BOW

70

70

Idabel

MOUNTAIN FORK
PARK ROAD

CRAIG
ROAD

W W TRADING POST
& CANOE RENTAL
(405) 584-6856

Mountain Fork
Park, Campground

Cooper
Creek

REREGULATION DAM

Boat
Ramp

0.0

Continuous Small Rapids
and Rock Gardens

PRESBYTERIAN FALLS

1.0

3.0   2.0

Lick
Creek

3.2

70   Roadside Park

4.8

Weyerhaeuser
Plant

Luksuklo
Creek

De Queen
Arkansas

5.1

EAGLETOWN

Cattle
Guard

Church

WHIP-POOR-WILL TAKE
OUT & CAMPGROUND
(405) 494-6476

Lower
Mountain
Fork

7.4

N

8.8

11.6

Little River

Crooked
Creek

11.8

Church
Ponca Bok
Creek

16.2

Little
River

© 1992
Ocean-
graphics

16.8
ASHALINTUBBI

School

132

PHYSICAL LOCATION: Extreme southeastern Oklahoma, McCurtain County. Texarkana 70 miles Shreveport 140 miles, and Dallas 230 miles.

GENERAL COMMENTS: This can be an exciting and adventuresome trip, however, some of the roads in this area are unmarked and we recommend that you check with one of the rental agencies for directions.

WATER QUALITY: Good to excellent - swift and clear.

WATER FLOW: Flow is determined by release from Broken Bow Reservoir. Conditions are generally ideal for canoeing, even during the summer months when the Upper Mountain Fork is too low for float trips.

PREFERRED SEASONS: Overall water conditions generally make for enjoyable canoeing anytime of the year - weather permitting. The Spring and Autumn are especially beautiful along the Lower Mountain Fork.

PUT IN: Launch immediately below the Reregulation Dam, located north of Hwy. 70, on Mountain Fork Park Road. There is a sign at the turn "Reregulation Dam and Primitive Camping 3 miles."

TAKE OUT: For a short trip, take out on the left at the Hwy. 70 crossing, at 3.2 miles. There is a parking area here, but be sure to park above the generating level. The next take out is on the right at Whip-Poor-Will's Campground, 7.4 miles. The Ashalintubbi take out is 5 miles below the confluence of the Little River, at the 16.8 mile mark.

HAZARDS: The river should be considered dangerous if both generators are running. Check the red beacon below the dam. If it's on, the generators are running. DO NOT try to run the Reregulation Dam; it's an 18 foot drop with a very bad hydraulic current. There are continuous small rapids and falls extending from the dam to Presbyterian Falls. The numerous rock outcroppings can be rough on equipment if you're not careful.

CAMPING: Mountain Fork Park and Campground, beside the Reregulation Dam, has tables, restrooms, RV and tent camping. Whip-Poor-Will Canoe Rental offers furnished cabins at their location 12 miles north of Broken Bow, on Hwy. 259, and camping at the 7.4 mile take out. There are also numerous natural camping

areas along the river, however, you must obtain permission to camp on private property.

CANOE RENTAL AND SHUTTLE SERVICE: Whip-Poor-Will Canoe Rental (405) 494-6476, and W W Trading Post and Canoe Rental (405) 584-6856.

DISTINGUISHING FEATURES: The river flows clear and clean over numerous rock ledges which have created fun, skill-testing rapids and fast chutes. The area is very scenic, especially in the spring and fall months.

FISHING: Due to the abundance of rapids in the section above the Hwy. 70 crossing, the majority of the fishing is done further downstream. Smallmouth, largemouth and rainbow trout (stamp required), are the primary game fish caught on the Lower Mountain Fork. Due to the current, many sections of the river may be better if you wade fish, rather than trying to fish from a fast moving boat. Fish the protected areas, just off, or directly in the current for the trout and smallmouth. Naturally, fly tackle works best for the trout. Small floating/diving plugs, spinner/trailer combinations, and small topwaters will catch both largemouth and smallmouth bass, as well as a variety of perch and sunfish.

AREA ATTRACTIONS: Northeast of Broken Bow, visit the Forest Heritage Center in Beavers Bend State Park. In Broken Bow, tour the Gardner Mansion, the 1880 home of Choctaw chief, Jefferson Gardner. For more information, call the Broken Bow Chamber of Commerce (405) 584-3393.

MAPS: McCurtain county map, and the Broken Bow, Eagle Town, and Good Water, Oklahoma topographical quadrangles.

RIVER. FLOW INFORMATION: Whip-Poor-Will Canoe Rental at (405) 494-6476, or W W Trading Post and Canoe Rental at (405) 584-6856.

EAGLE FORK CREEK
OCTAVIA TO 0.2 MILES BELOW HWY. 259
12.5 MILES

PHYSICAL LOCATION: Southeast Oklahoma in McCurtain and LeFlore Counties. The River runs along Hwy. 259, north of Hwy. 4, and empties into the Upper Mountain Fork River. Dallas 220 miles, Texarkana 80 miles, Oklahoma City 185 miles, and Tulsa 185 miles.

GENERAL COMMENTS: The Eagle Fork is fed only by run off after rains in the Kiamichi Mountains, so put off planning a trip if there have been no rains. This is a remote area with metropolitan areas nearby. The stream is characterized by narrow channels, and quick, twisting turns. At above normal levels, some canoeing experience is essential.

WATER QUALITY Clean, unpolluted and cold.

WATER FLOW: If water is flowing about a foot over low water bridge #1, above Octavia, there will be plenty of water for a good trip. Two feet over the bridge the river becomes dangerous. When the flow is at road level, or lower, the river is too low for enjoyable canoeing.

PREFERRED SEASONS: Spring and Fall, after adequate rains.

HAZARDS: There are two low dams, below low water bridge #1, with strong hydraulic currents. They are both killers and should be portaged on the left. At the 4.5 mile mark there is a "hidden" waterfall with a 4 to 5 foot drop. This will appear to be just another rapid from upstream, it isn't! It can be portaged on the left, or run on the right, but only after scouting.

PUT IN: The first launch point is 1½ miles above the Octavia turn off, west of Hwy. 259. The next put in is low water bridge #2, west of Octavia. Then low water bridge #3 (7.6 miles), west of Hwy. 259 and north of Hwy. 4. Do not confuse this low water bridge with the one suggested as a gauge (low water bridge #1).

TAKE OUT. The last take out is the old bridge, 0.2 miles below the Hwy. 259 crossing, 12.5 miles.

CAMPING: Whip-Poor-Will, located 12 miles north of Broken Bow on Hwy. 259, offers furnished log cabins (405) 494-6476. Mountain Fork Canoes and Cabins, located on Hwy. 4 in Smithville, has cabins, showers, restrooms, and tent camping area (405) 244-3569. Primitive camp sites are located at each low bridge crossing.

CANOE RENTALS AND SHUTTLE SERVICE: Mountain Fork Canoes and Whip-Poor-Will listed above.

DISTINGUISHING FEATURES: Beautiful, remote hill country terrain. Rocky shoals and numerous small falls empty into the river.

FISHING: Smallmouth, largemouth, rainbow trout (stamp required), and an assortment of sunfish and perch can all be taken from Eagle Fork Creek. Lightweight spinning gear and fly tackle constitute the best fish catching combinations.

AREA ATTRACTIONS: Primarily just a lot of beautiful scenery. Situated between the Ouachita National Forest and the McCurtain County Wilderness Area, this part of Oklahoma offers miles of remote, natural beauty.

MAPS: Topographical maps are the Octavia and Smithville, Oklahoma quadrangles.

RIVER FLOW INFORMATION: See listings under "Camping."

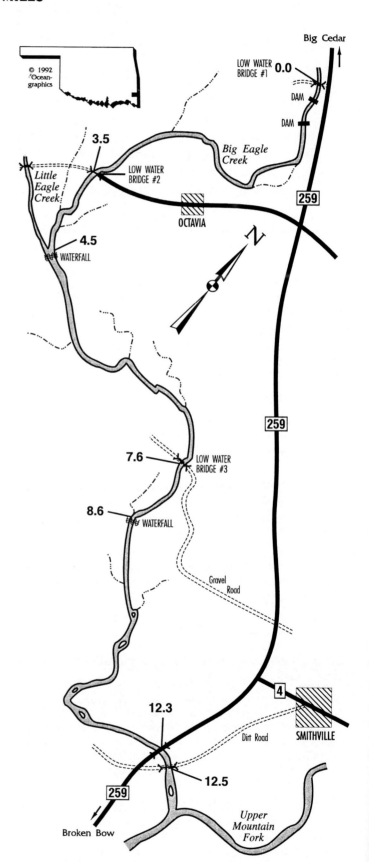

134

WASHITA RIVER
HWY. 77 TO HWY. 53
21.9 MILES

PHYSICAL LOCATION: Murray and Carter Counties in South Central Oklahoma. Dallas 110 miles, Ardmore 15 miles, Oklahoma City 95 miles, and Tulsa 175 miles.

GENERAL COMMENTS: Nice short float. Can be enjoyed by family groups. This is a scenic area with lots to do.

WATER QUALITY: Water quality is good, but generally dingy to muddy dependent on recent rainfalls.

WATER FLOW: The river is usually floatable at any season, but will be low during extended dry periods.

PREFERRED SEASONS: Spring and fall are the preferred seasons because the rainfall keeps the river at an optimum float level. If there has been adequate rainfall, the summer also offers good conditions for float trips.

HAZARDS: High flow rates due to heavy rainfall run off will create standing waves, reaching heights of 6 feet in Big Canyon. Other than logs and some brush, there are few hazards encountered on this trip.

PUT IN: Launch sites are located at either the Hwy. 77 crossing or Dougherty Bridge, 7.5 miles, depending on the length of the trip desired.

TAKE OUT: Take out at the Dougherty Bridge, 7.5 miles, or further downstream at the bridge on Hwy. 53, 21.9 miles.

CAMPING: There are adequate camp sites in the Arbuckle Lake Area, east of Hwy. 177. Turner Falls Park, just off IH-35 has camping, electrical hookups, and a picnic area.

CANOE RENTAL AND SHUTTLE SERVICE: Washita Canoe Sales, Ardmore, Oklahoma, (405) 223-4862.

FISHING: Although bass and a variety of perch and sunfish can be caught on the Washita, it has not been considered one of the better fishing streams as its flow is totally dependent upon rainfall. This is more a fun float trip than a fishing trip.

AREA ATTRACTIONS: Turner Falls, just off IH-35, offers many activities which include swimming and water slides. To the south in Ardmore visit the Carter County Historical and Genealogical Society, the Charles B. Goddard Center for Visual and Performing Arts, and the Eliza Cruce Hall Doll Museum. South of Sulphur is the Travertine Nature Center.

MAPS: The Murray and Carter County road maps.

RIVER FLOW INFORMATION: Washita Canoe Sales, (405) 223-4862.

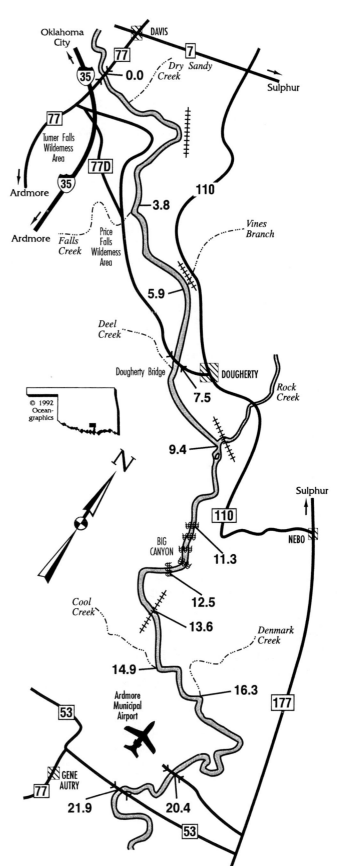

RESTAURANTS

TEXAS

ANGELINA RIVER
KOUNTRY KITCHEN, Hwy. 96 North, Jasper
CATFISH HUT, Hwy. 63 West, Jasper

ARMAND BAYOU
FRANK'S SHRIMP HUT, 1818 Nasa Road 1, Seabrook
MONTEREY'S TEX-MEX CAFE, 914 Nasa Road 1, Webster

BRAZOS RIVER (Below Possum Kingdom)
JACK'S FAMILY RESTAURANT, Weatherford, (817) 594-6464

BRAZOS RIVER (Below Lake Granbury)
HAMMOND'S, Glen Rose, (817) 897-3321
WESTERN KITCHEN, Glen Rose, (817) 897-2310

BRAZOS RIVER (Below Lake Whitney)
LONE STAR TAVERN STEAKHOUSE, 4713 Bellmead Dr., Waco
GEORGE'S, 1525 Circle, Waco

CADDO LAKE
WATERFRONT RESTAURANT, Hwy. 43 N. Bridge, Karnack
FLY N FISH RESTAURANT, Cypress Dr., Uncertain

COLORADO RIVER (Above Austin)
SMOKEHOUSE BAR B CUE, Hwy. 281 S., Lampasas
SONIC DRIVE-IN, 702 S. Key, Lampasas

COLORADO RIVER (Austin Area)
MATT'S EL RANCHO, 2613 S. Lamar, Austin
RUTH'S STEAKHOUSE, 3010 Guadalupe, Austin

COLORADO RIVER (Columbus Area)
COLUMBUS INN & RESTAURANT, 2208 Hwy. 71, Columbus
HICKORY HILL DRIVE-IN, Hwy. 71 W., Columbus

FRIO RIVER
KEN'S KOUNTRY KITCHEN, Hwy. 83, Concan
NEAL'S VACATION LODGE & CAFE, Concan, Texas, (512) 232-6118. Memorial Day to Labor Day 3 Meals, country style menu, daily groups, catering, BBQ, open by demand other months.

GUADALUPE RIVER (Kerrville)
LAFOUR'S SEAFOOD, 1129 Junction Hwy., Kerrville
MENCIUS' GOURMET CHINESE, 208 Cully Drive, Kerrville

GUADALUPE RIVER (Above Canyon Dam)
ANTLER RESTAURANT, Corner of 281 & Hwy. 46
TEXAS 46, Corner Hwy. 46 & Sun Valley Drive

GUADALUPE RIVER (Below Canyon Dam)
NEW BRAUNFELS SMOKEHOUSE, IH-35 & Hwy. 46, New Braunfels
GRIST MILL RESTAURANT, Gruene

LLANO & SOUTH LLANO RIVER
DAYS INN RESTAURANT, 111 S. Martinez, Junction
ISAACK'S RESTAURANT, 1606 Main St., Junction, (915) 446-2629. Open 7 days, 6 am - 10 pm. Full Service, Groups catered by reservation, daily lunch specials.

MEDINA RIVER
HARVEY'S OLD BANK STEAK HOUSE, 309 Main St., Bandera, (512) 796-8486. Specializing in steaks, pizza and seafood. Lunch and dinner 7 days a week, Daily lunch specials.
HORSESHOE INN, 2½ miles from Bandera on Hwy. 173N., (512) 796-3105. Down-home country cooking in a laid back atmosphere. Daily lunch specials.
OLD SPANISH TRAIL, 305 Main St., Bandera, (512) 796-3836. Specializing in Mexican Food, full meal service, daily lunch buffet, open 7 days a week.

NECHES RIVER
BIG JIM'S BAR-B-Q & BURGERS, Hwy. 418 W., Silsbee
EMMA'S CHUCK WAGON, 2256 Hwy. 96 S., Silsbee

RED RIVER (Above Lake Texoma)
DENNY'S, 1938 N. IH-35, Exit 499, Gainesville
CATFISH LOUIE'S, 2105 N. IH-35, Gainesville

RED RIVER (Below Lake Texoma)
SOUTH AUSTIN GRILL, 1530 South Austin, Denison

RIO GRANDE RIVER
DESERT DELI DINER, Ghost Town, Terlingua
LA KIVA, Hwy. 170, Terlingua

SABINE RIVER
GLORY BEE BAKING CO., Gladewater
UPPER CRUST GOURMET BAKERY, Gladewater

SAN MARCOS RIVER
IMPERIAL GARDEN CHINESE RESTAURANT, 1104-L Thorpe Lane, San Marcos
SIRLOIN STOCKADE STEAKHOUSE, San Marcos

VILLAGE CREEK (East Texas)
PILGRIM HOUSE, Kountze
TOP HALF DRIVE-IN, N. Hwy. 69, Kountze

ARKANSAS

BUFFALO NATIONAL RIVER (Upper Section)
CLIFF HOUSE INN RESTAURANT, Hwy. 7 S., Jasper
POINT OF VIEW FAMILY DINING, Just off Hwy. 7 on Hwy. 74W. in Jasper, (501) 446-2992, Home-style cooking in a family atmosphere, very affordable prices, great desserts!

BUFFALO NATIONAL RIVER (Middle Section)
FERGUSON'S COUNTRY STORE AND RESTAURANT, St. Joe, (501) 439-2234. Home cooked meals with a flavor of the past.
SUNSET RESTAURANT, Hwy. 65 & Hwy. 27, Marshall

BUFFALO NATIONAL RIVER (Lower Section)
HILLTOP FAMILY RESTAURANT, Yellville
CHASTAIN'S RESTAURANT, Yellville

MULBERRY RIVER
TURNER BEND COUNTRY STORE, Hwy. 23 & Mulberry River

OUACHITA RIVER
HARTLEY'S CHARBROILIN WILLIES, Junction Hwy. 88 & 270, Pencil Bluff

SPRING & SOUTH FORK SPRING RIVER
BEACH CLUB BBQ, Hardy
KITCHEN'S CUPBOARD RESTAURANT, Hardy

OKLAHOMA

ILLINOIS RIVER
AUNT NELLIE'S FAMILY RESTAURANT, 1006 E. Downing, Tahlequah
DEL RANCHO RESTAURANT, 4800 S. Muskogee Ave., Tahlequah

UPPER & LOWER MOUNTAIN FORK RIVERS
BEAVERS BEND RESTAURANT, Broken Bow
CHARLES WESLEY RESTAURANT, Broken Bow

WASHITA RIVER
JOHN KELLY'S RESTAURANT, Old Hwy. 77 S., Ardmore
WESTERN SIZZLIN STEAKHOUSE, 2610 W. Broadway, Ardmore

ACCOMMODATIONS (HOTELS, MOTELS, R.V. PARKS/CAMPGROUNDS)

TEXAS

ARMAND BAYOU
AMERICAN HOST HOTEL, 2020 Nasa Road 1, (713) 332-3551
MOTEL6/NASA, 1001 Nasa Road 1, (713) 332-4581
BRAZOS RIVER (Below Possum Kingdom)
ROCHELLE'S, Graford, (817) 659-3341
BRAZOS RIVER (Below Lake Granbury)
INN ON THE RIVER B & B, Glen Rose, (817) 897-2101
KELLER'S CAMP, Cleburne, (817) 897-2314
OAKDALE'S CAMP 'N' FISH, Glen Rose, (817) 897-2321
YE OLE' MAPLE INN B & B, Glen Rose, (817) 897-3456
BRAZOS RIVER(Below Lake Whitney)
BRAZOS RIVER RV PARK & REDDELL'S CAMP, Gholson, (817) 826-3018
HEART COTTAGE B & B, Clifton, (817) 675-3189
COLORADO RIVER (Above Austin)
BAREFOOT CAMP, (915) 628-3394 or (915) 628-3395
COLORADO BEND STATE PARK, (915) 628-3240
SULPHUR SPRINGS CAMP, Bend, (915) 628-3252
COLORADO RIVER (Below Austin)
BASTROP STATE PARK, (512) 321-2101
BUESCHER STATE PARK, (512) 237-2241
DEVILS RIVER
BAKER'S CROSSING CAMPGROUND, (915) 292-4503
FRIO RIVER
Please Note: In November, 1992 the "512" Area Code for all Frio River listings will change to "210."
NEAL'S VACATION LODGES, Concan, (512) 232-6118
RIO FRIO BED & BREAKFAST & LODGING, Ranch Rd. 1120, Rio Frio, TX 78879, (512) 232-6633, Secluded cabins along the Frio, Open year around, Spanish style homes & log homes that sleep 2 - 12.
RIVER HAVEN COURTS, Box 510, Leakey, TX 78873, (512) 232-5400. Rustic river cabins & log cabins with air, heat, fireplaces.
YEARGAN'S RIVER BEND CAMP, Concan, (512) 232-6616.
GUADALUPE (Above Canyon Dam)
Please Note: In November, 1992 the "512" Area Code for all Guadalupe River listings will change to "210."
KERRVILLE-SCHREINER STATE PARK, Kerrville, (512) 257-5392
BERGHEIM CAMPGROUND & R.V. PARK, (512) 336-2235
GUADALUPE RIVER (Below Canyon Dam)
ABBOTT'S CAMPGROUND, River Road, (512) 964-2685
HILL COUNTRY R. V. RESORT, New Braunfels, (512) 625-1919
MARICOPA LODGE, Canyon Lake, (512) 964-3600
RIO RAFT CO./RIVER VALLEY COTTAGES & R.V. PARK, P.O. Box 2036, Canyon Lake, TX 78130, (512) 964-3613. A/C cottages, river front along the Guadalupe below Canyon Dam, 4th crossing bridge. RV hookups, grocery store.
WHITEWATER SPORTS, Canyon Lake, (512) 964-3800
LLANO RIVER & SOUTH LLANO RIVER
DAYS INN, 111 S. Martinez, P.O. Box 384, Junction, TX 76849, (915) 446-3730. 48 rooms, meeting room, free continental breakfast, pool, hot tub, BBQ grills, picnic tables, river access, cable TV.
THE HILLS MOTEL, 1520 N. Main, Junction, TX 76849, (915) 446-2567. Triple AAA Motel, 27 rooms, queens, king & doubles, full cable TV, A/C, pool, movies, all credit cards. Curt & Sandy Olsen.
MEDINA RIVER
Please Note: In November, 1992 the "512" Area Code for all Medina River listings will change to "210."
ECONO LODGE, 1900 Hwy. 16S., Bandera, TX 78003, (512) 796-3093. 43 beautiful rooms, color TV, pool, full service restaurant & lounge, Medina River frontage, meeting rooms.

HORSESHOE INN, Rt. 3, Box 300, Bandera, TX 78003, (800) 352-3810. Fun Country Inn, breakfast included, picnic areas, equipment storage available.
YOGI BEARS JELLYSTONE PARK, Bandera, (512) 796-3751. River front camping, full service RV park, pool, game room, store.
NECHES RIVER (Alto area)
RATCLIFF LAKE, Ratcliff, (409) 544-2046
MISSION TEJAS STATE HISTORICAL PARK, Alto, (409) 687-2394
RIO GRANDE RIVER
CHISOS MINING MOTEL, Terlingua, (800) 343-1640
DESERT AIR, Sanderson, (915) 345-2572
SABINE RIVER
CAROUSEL HOUSE B & B, Gladewater, (903) 845-6830
HONEYCOMB SUITES, Gladewater, (800) 594-2253
SAN MARCOS RIVER
PECAN PARK RETREAT, Martindale, (512) 392-6171
SHADY GROVE CAMPGROUNDS, Martindale, (512) 357-6113

ARKANSAS

BUFFALO NATIONAL RIVER (Upper Section)
BUFFALO OUTDOOR CENTER, Ponca, (800) 221-5514
LOST VALLEY LODGING, Ponca, (501) 861-5522,
BUFFALO NATIONAL RIVER (Middle Section)
BUFFALO CAMPING & CANOEING, Gilbert, (501) 439-2888
BUFFALO RIDGE MOTEL, St. Joe, (501) 439-2653
TYLER BEND RECREATION AREA, St. Joe, (501) 439-2502
BUFFALO NATIONAL RIVER (Lower Section)
BENNETT'S CANOE RENTAL, Yellville, (501) 449-6431
DIRST CANOE RENTAL, Yellville, (800) 537-2850
CADDO RIVER
ARROWHEAD CABINS, Caddo Gap, (501) 356-2944
MULBERRY RIVER
BYRD'S CAMPGROUNDS, Ozark, (501) 667-4066
THE BUNKHOUSE, Mulberry Ranch, Oark, AR 72852, (501) 292-3725. Bunkhouse with 2 bedrooms, kitchen, greatroom and sleeps 7. Bed & breakfast on a working cattle ranch. Doug & Susan Pfeifler.
TURNER BEND CAMPGROUND, Ozark, (501) 667-3641
WAYFARER'S CAMPGROUND, Ozark, (501) 667-4998
OUACHITA RIVER
ROCKY SHOALS CANOE RENTALS, Mount Ida, (501) 867-2382
SPRING RIVER & SOUTH FORK OF THE SPRING
MANY ISLANDS CAMP, Mammoth Spring, (501) 856-3451

OKLAHOMA

EAGLE FORK CREEK
MOUNTAIN FORK CABINS, Smithville, (405) 244-3569
WHIP-POOR-WILL CABINS, Broken Bow, (405) 494-6476
ILLINOIS RIVER
DIAMONDHEAD RESORT, Tahlequah, (800) 722-2411
EAGLE BLUFF RESORTS, Tahlequah, (800) 366-3031
HANGING ROCK CAMP, Tahlequah, (800) 375-3088
PEYTON'S PLACE, Tahlequah, (800) 359-0866
SPARROW HAWK CAMP, Tahlequah, (800) 722-9635
WAR EAGLE RESORT, Tahlequah, (800) 722-3834
UPPER MOUNTAIN FORK RIVER
MOUNTAIN FORK CABINS, Smithville, (405) 244-3569
WHIP-POOR-WILL CABINS, Broken Bow, (405) 494-6476
LOWER MOUNTAIN FORK RIVER
WHIP-POOR-WILL CABINS, Broken Bow, (405) 494-6476

RIVER FLOW INFORMATION

C.O.E. - Corps of Engineers

TEXAS

FOR ALL INCLUDED STREAMS:
National Weather Service Forecast Office:
Fort Worth (817) 429-2631
San Antonio (512) 826-4679, after 11-1-92 (210) 826-4679

ANGELINA RIVER (Below Sam Rayburn Reservoir)
Fort Worth: C.O.E. (817) 334-2214 or 2196

ARMAND BAYOU
Seabrook: A to Z Action Sports (713) 474-3079

BRAZOS RIVER (Below Lake Possum Kingdom)
Possum Kingdom: Brazos River Authority (817) 779-2422
Fort Worth: C.O.E. (817) 334-2214 or 2196
Graford: Rochelle's Canoe Rental (817) 659-3341 or (817) 659-2581
Mineral Wells: Castle Canoe Rental (800) 234-7116 or (817) 659-3313
Mineral Wells: Rio Brazos Canoes (800) 222-1418 or (817) 325-9354

BRAZOS RIVER (Below Lake Granbury)
Ft. Worth: C.O.E. (817) 334-2214 or 2196
Waco: Brazos River Authority (817) 776-1441
Cleburne: Rhodes Canoe Rental (817) 897-4214
Cleburne: Keller's Camp & Tube Rental (817) 897-2314 or
(817) 897-4003
Glen Rose: Oakdale's Camp 'N' Fish (817) 897-2321 or (817) 897-2478
Nemo: Low Water Bridge Canoe Rental (817) 897-3666
Hurst: Double "M" Canoe Sales & Rental (817) 282-3135

BRAZOS RIVER (Below Lake Whitney)
Waco: Brazos River Authority (817) 776-1441
Ft. Worth: C.O.E. (817) 334-2214 or 2196
Laguna Park: The Outpost & Dick's Place (817) 622-8364
Gholson: Reddell's Camp (817) 829-1470 or 826-3018

BRAZOS RIVER (Hidalgo Falls)
Houston: The Whitewater Experience (713) 522-2848

CADDO LAKE
Karnack: Caddo Lake State Park (903) 679-3351

COLORADO RIVER (Above Colorado Bend State Park)
Bend: Colorado Bend State Park (915) 628-3240

COLORADO RIVER (Below Austin, TX)
Columbus: Colorado River Longhorn Canoes (409) 732-3723

DENTON CREEK
Ft. Worth: C.O.E. (817) 334-2214 or 2196
Carrollton: North Texas Canoes (214) 245-7475
Dallas: Trinity River Expeditions (214) 941-1757

DEVILS RIVER
Baker's Crossing (915) 292-4503
Devils River State Park (915) 395-2133
Comstock: High Bridge Adventures (915) 292-4462 or (915) 292-4495

FRIO RIVER
**Please Note: In November, 1992 the "512" Area Code
for all Frio River listings will change to "210."**
Leakey: River Haven Courts (512) 232-5400
Concan: Yeargan's River Bend (512) 232-6616
Concan: Neal's Vacation Lodges (512) 232-6118
Concan: Garner State Park (512) 232-6132

GUADALUPE RIVER (Above Canyon Dam)
**Please Note: In November, 1992 the "512" Area Code
for all Guadalupe River listings will change to "210."**
Bergheim: Bergheim Campground & R.V. Park (512) 336-2235
Canyon Lake: Bigfoot Canoes (512) 885-7106 or 438-4617
Spring Branch: Guadalupe Canoe Livery (512) 885-4671 or 964-3189
Canyon Dam: C.O.E. Recording (512) 964-3342 or C.O.E.
(512) 964-3341
Ft. Worth: C.O.E. (817) 334-2214 or 2196

GUADALUPE RIVER (Below Canyon Dam)
**Please Note: In November, 1992 the "512" Area Code
for all Guadalupe River listings will change to "210."**
Canyon Dam: C.O.E. Recording (512) 964-3342 or C.O.E.
(512) 964-3341
Ft. Worth: C.O.E. (817) 334-2214 or 2196
New Braunfels: Abbott's River Outfitters (512) 625-4928 or
(512) 964-2685 or (512) 964-2625
New Braunfels: Whitewater Sports (512) 964-3800
Canyon Lake: Rio Raft Co. (512) 964-3613
Spring Branch: Guadalupe Canoe Livery (512) 885-4671
or (512) 964-3189
New Braunfels: Texas Canoe Trails (512) 625-1919 or (512) 625-3375
New Braunfels: Bezdek's Rentals (512) 964-2244
New Braunfels: Molly's Raft Rental (512) 629-4422

LLANO RIVER
Junction: Coleman Canoes (915) 446-3540

SOUTH LLANO RIVER
Junction: Coleman Canoes (915) 446-3540

MEDINA RIVER
**Please Note: In November, 1992 the "512" Area Code
for all Medina River listings will change to "210."**
Bandera: Fred Collins Workshop (512) 796-3553
Bandera: Bandera Watersports (512) 796-3021 or (512) 796-3022
Bandera: Jellystone Park (512) 796-3751

NECHES RIVER
Crockett: Davy Crockett National Forest Park Ranger - Neches
District (409) 544-2046
Kountze: Piney Woods Canoe Company (409) 274-5892
B.A. Steinhagen Lake: C.O.E (409) 429-3491

PECOS RIVER
Comstock: High Bridge Adventures (915) 292-4462 or
(915) 292-4495
Comstock: Pecos River District Ranger (915) 292-4544

RED RIVER (Above Lake Texoma)
Gainesville: David Claunch (817) 668-6207
Denison Dam C.O.E. Recording (903) 465-1491 or (903) 465-4990
Tulsa: C.O.E. (918) 581-7811

RED RIVER (Below Lake Texoma)
Denison: J.W. Canoe Rental (903) 465-5771
Tulsa: C.O.E. (918) 581-7811
Ft. Worth: C.O.E. (817) 334-2214 or 2196
Denison Dam: C.O.E Recording (903) 465-1491 or (903) 465-4990

RIO GRANDE RIVER (Big Bend Area)
Panther Junction Park Headquarters: (915) 477-2251
Terlingua: Far Flung Adventures (800) 359-4138 or (915) 371-2489
Terlingua: Lajitas Trading Post (915) 424-3234
Terlingua: Outback Expeditions (800) 343-1640 or (915) 371-2490
Terlingua: Desert Sports (800) 523-8170 or (915) 424-3366
Marathon: Scott Shuttle Service (915) 386-4574

RIO GRANDE RIVER (Lower Canyons)
Persimmon Gap Ranger Station: (915) 477-2393
Marathon: Scott Shuttle Service (915) 386-4574

SABINE RIVER
Gilmer: Sabine River Trips (903) 734-5305

SAN MARCOS RIVER
Martindale: T.G. Canoe Livery (512) 353-3946
Martindale: Pecan Park Retreat (512) 392-6171
Martindale: Spencer Canoes (512) 357-6113

TRINITY (CLEAR FORK)
Ft. Worth: C.O.E. (817) 334-2214 or 2196
Hurst: Double "M" Canoe Sales & Rental (817) 282-3135

TRINITY RIVER (ELM FORK)
Ft. Worth: C.O.E. (817) 334-2214 or 2196
Carrollton: North Texas Canoes (214) 245-7475
Dallas: Trinity River Expeditions (214) 941-1757
Garland: High Trails Co. (214) 2-Paddle or (214) 272-3353

TRINITY RIVER (Below Livingston Dam)
Houston: Canoesport (713) 660-7000
Kountze: Piney Woods Canoe Company (409) 274-5892

VILLAGE CREEK (Arlington, TX)
Hurst: Double "M" Canoe Sales & Rental (817) 282-3135

VILLAGE CREEK (Big Thicket Area)
Kountze: Piney Woods Canoe Company (409) 274-5892
Village Creek State Park: (409) 755-7322

WHITE ROCK CREEK
Garland: High Trails Co. (214) 2-PADDLE or (214) 272-3353
Carrollton: North Texas Canoes (214) 245-7475

ARKANSAS
FOR ALL INCLUDED STREAMS:
C.O.E. Recording (501) 378-5150
Water Levels - Buffalo National River Headquarters
(501) 741-5443 or (501) 449-4311
Arkansas Lakes and Rivers: Recording (501) 348-5100
Little Rock: C.O.E. (501) 378-5551

BIG PINEY CREEK
Dover: Moore Outdoors (501) 331-3606

BUFFALO NATIONAL RIVER (Upper Section)
Ponca: Buffalo Outdoor Center (800) 221-5514 or (501) 861-5514
Ponca: Lost Valley Canoe Service (501) 861-5522

BUFFALO NATIONAL RIVER (Middle Section)
Gilbert: Buffalo Camping and Canoeing (501) 439-2888 or
(501) 439-2386
St. Joe: Buffalo Outdoor Center, Inc. (501) 439-2244 or
(800) 221-5514
St. Joe: Tomahawk Canoe Rental (501) 439-2617

BUFFALO NATIONAL RIVER (Lower Section)
Yellville: Bennett's Canoe Rental (501) 449-6431
Yellville: Dodd's Canoe & Johnboat Rental (800) 423-8731 or
(501) 449-6619
Yellville: Dirst Canoe Rental (800) 537-2850 or (501) 449-6636

CADDO RIVER
Caddo Gap: Arrowhead Cabin & Canoe Rental (501) 356-2944
or (501) 767-5326
Glenwood: Wright Way Canoe Rental (501) 356-2055

COSSATOT RIVER
Cossatot Weather Observer (501) 394-2321
Caddo Gap: Arrowhead Cabin & Canoe Rental (501) 356-2944
or (501) 767-5326
Glenwood: Wright Way Canoe Rental (501) 356-2055
Mount Ida: Rocky Shoals Canoe Rental (501) 867-2382
or (501) 326-4710

LITTLE MISSOURI RIVER
Caddo Gap: Arrowhead Cabin & Canoe Rental (501) 356-2944 or
(501) 767-5326
Glenwood: Wright Way Canoe Rental (501) 356-2055
Mount Ida: Rocky Shoals Canoe Rental (501) 867-2382 or
(501) 326-4710

MULBERRY RIVER
Ozark: Byrd's Canoe Rental & Campgrounds (501) 667-4066
Ozark: Turner Bend, Inc. (501) 667-3641
Ozark: Wayfarer of the Ozarks (501) 667-4998 or (501) 667-4066

OUACHITA RIVER
Pencil Bluff: Ouachita Joe's (501) 326-5517
Mount Ida: Rocky Shoals Canoe Rentals (501) 867-2382 or
(501) 326-4710
Mount Ida : S & K Canoe (501) 867-3815

SPRING RIVER
Mammoth Spring: Many Island Camp (501) 856-3451

SOUTH FORK OF THE SPRING RIVER
Mammoth Spring: Many Islands Camp (501) 856-3451

OKLAHOMA
FOR ALL INCLUDED STREAMS :
Oklahoma River Information recording: (918) 581-7662
Oklahoma Scenic Rivers Commission (800) 299-3251 or (918) 456-3251

EAGLE FORK CREEK
Broken Bow: Whip-Poor-Will (405) 494-6476

GLOVER RIVER
Carrollton, Texas: North Texas Canoes (214) 245-7475

ILLINOIS RIVER
Oklahoma Scenic Rivers Commission (800) 299-3251 or (918) 456-3251
Tulsa: C.O.E. (918) 581-7666
Tahlequah: Eagle Bluff Resorts (800) 366-3031 or (918) 456-3031
Tahlequah: Hanging Rock Camp (800) 375-3088 or (918) 456-3088
Tahlequah: Peyton's Place (800) 359-0866 or (918) 456-3847
Tahlequah: War Eagle Resort (800) 722-3834 or (918) 456-6272
Tahlequah: Diamondhead Resort (800) 722-2411 or (918) 456-4545
Tahlequah: Sparrow Hawk Camp (800) 722-9635 or (918) 456-8371

LOWER MOUNTAIN FORK and LITTLE RIVER
Broken Bow: Whip-Poor-Will (405) 494-6476
Broken Bow: W W Trading Post (405) 584-6856

UPPER MOUNTAIN FORK RIVER
Tulsa: C.O.E. (918) 581-7811
Smithville: Mountain Fork Canoes & Cabins (405) 244-3569
Smithville: Mountain Fork River Floats (405) 244-3284
Broken Bow: Whip-Poor-Will (405) 494-6476

WASHITA RIVER
Ardmore: Washita Canoe Sales & Rentals (405) 223-4862

LET'S TRY IT FIRST
RENTAL AND GUIDE SERVICE
TEXAS RIVERS

BRAZOS RIVER (Below Lake Possum Kingdom)

ROCHELLE'S CANOE RENTAL
Rt. 1, Box 119 (Brazos River and Hwy. 4)
Graford, Texas 76449
(817) 659-3341 or (817) 659-2581
Canoe rentals and shuttles, camping and parking
Joyce or Buddy Rochelle

CASTLE CANOE RENTAL
P. O. Box 1174
Mineral Wells, Texas 76067
(800) 234-7116 or (817) 659-3313
Rentals, shuttles, camping
Ted Ray

RIO BRAZOS CANOES
Rt. 3, Box 335
Mineral Wells, Texas 76067
(800) 222-1418 or (817) 325-9354
Canoe rentals, shuttles, parking, primitive camping
Steve and Cenna Smith

HIGH TRAILS
3610 Marquis Drive
Garland, Texas 75042
(214) 2-PADDLE or (214) 272-3353
Sales and rentals; canoes, rafts, kayaks, river accessories, booking agent for canoe rentals on Texas, Arkansas and Oklahoma Rivers
Bob Narramore (Dallas, Texas area)

BRAZOS RIVER (Below Lake Granbury)

KELLER'S CAMP & TUBE RENTAL
Rt. 9, Box 495
Cleburne, Texas 76031
(817) 897-2314 or (817) 897-4003
Tube rentals, camping, RV hookups, picnic supplies, shuttles, hot showers
Charles and Rebecca Keller

OAKDALE'S CAMP 'N' FISH & RENTAL
P. O. Box 548
Glen Rose, Texas 76043
(817) 897-2478 or (817) 897-2321
Canoe and tube rental and shuttle service
Scott May

RHODES CANOE RENTAL
Rt. 9, Box 600
Cleburne, Texas 76031
(817) 897-4214
Canoe rental, shuttles, group discounts
Max and Luella Rhodes

LOW WATER BRIDGE CANOE RENTAL
P. O. Box 420
Nemo, Texas 76070
(817) 897-3666
Canoe and tube rentals, shuttles, camping, guided tours
Jack Cathey

DOUBLE "M" CANOE SALES & RENTAL
Hurst, Texas
(817) 282-3135
Canoe trips, catering to large groups, Old Town canoes
Max and Madeline Armstrong

BRAZOS RIVER (Below Lake Whitney)

THE OUTPOST - DICK'S PLACE
P. O. Box 5408
Laguna Park, Texas 76634
(817) 622-8364
Canoe rentals, parking, shuttles for our canoes only
Dick and Jeanne Weinkauf

COLORADO RIVER

COLORADO RIVER LONGHORN CANOES
P. O. Box 871
Columbus, Texas 78934
(409) 732-3723
Rentals, shuttles, lodging, hot showers
Jim McGee

DALLAS, Texas (Metropolitan Area)

HIGH TRAILS
3610 Marquis Drive
Garland, Texas 75042
(214) 2-PADDLE or (214) 272-3353
Sales and rentals; canoes, rafts, kayaks, river accessories, river information. Booking agent for rentals and guided river tours in Texas, Arkansas and Oklahoma.
Bob Narramore

"DOC" BAKER'S CANOE RENTAL
2910 Maryland
Dallas, Texas 75216
(214) 371-0434, John Baker
or (214) 2-PADDLE or 272-3353, High Trails

GUADALUPE RIVER (Above Canyon Dam)

Please Note: In November, 1992 the "512" Area Code for all Guadalupe River listings will change to "210."

BERGHEIM CAMPGROUND & R.V. PARK
Guadalupe River at Hwy. 3160
Rt. 2, Box 60
Bergheim, Texas 78004
(512) 336-2235
Camping, rentals; canoes, rafts, tubes, shuttles, R. V. hookups
Jim and Dianne Irie

BIGFOOT CANOES
Guadalupe River below FM 311
Rt. 5, Box 815-X
Canyon Lake, Texas 78130
(512) 885-7106 or Bigfoot II (512) 438-4617
Rental canoes, rafts, tubes, shuttle service, camping
Wendall and Debbie Lyons

GUADALUPE CANOE LIVERY
Guadalupe River at Hwy. 281
P. O. Box 8
Spring Branch, Texas 78070
(512) 885-4671 or 964-3189
Rentals, sales; canoes, rafts, kayaks, tubes, shuttles, R.V. hookups, guide service
Mike and Linda Clark

GUADALUPE RIVER (Below Canyon Dam)

Please Note: In November, 1992 the "512" Area Code for all Guadalupe River listings will change to "210."

ABBOTT'S 306, RIVER OUTFITTERS, INC.
1st Hwy. 306 crossing, below Canyon Dam
HCR 4, Box 74H
Canyon Lake, Texas 78133
(512) 964-2625 or (512) 625-4928
Canoes, kayaks, rafts, tubes, shuttles, retail store, river front camping
Steve and Jane Abbott

WHITEWATER SPORTS
Hwy. 306 at Guadalupe River
HC-3, Box 22
New Braunfels, Texas 78132-2201
(512) 964-3800
Canoes, kayaks, rafts, tubes, shuttles, camping, RV hookups, cabins and restaurant
Ellen Posey or Edward Martin

RIO RAFT CO./RIVER VALLEY COTTAGES & R.V. PARK
4th crossing on River Road
P. O. Box 2036
Canyon Lake, Texas 78130
(512) 964-3613
Canoes, rafts, tubes, camping, cabins, RV hookups, hot showers, shuttles and parking
John Guenzel or William Perkins

GUADALUPE CANOE LIVERY
Below 3rd crossing on River Road
P. O. Box 8
Spring Branch, Texas 78070
(512) 885-4671 or 964-3189
Rental and sales: canoes, rafts, kayaks, tubes, shuttles, RV hookups, guide service
Mike or Linda Clark

TEXAS CANOE TRAILS, INC.
Between 3rd & 2nd Crossings on River Road
131 Ruekle Rd.
New Braunfels, Texas 78130
(512) 625-3375 or 625-1919
Rentals and sales: canoes, rafts, kayaks, tubes, shuttles, camping, fishing
Ben Schumacher

BEZDEK'S RENTALS
Between 3rd & 2nd crossings on River Road
Star Route 3, Box 854
New Braunfels, Texas 78130
(512) 964-2244
Rafts, canoes, tubes, camping, Bar-B-Q, shuttles
Johnnie Bezdek

ABBOTT'S CAMPGROUND
Between 3rd and 2nd crossings on River Road
HCR 3, Box 854B
New Braunfels, Texas 78132
(512) 964-2685 or (512) 625-4928
Rentals, shuttles, hot showers, restrooms, electrical hookups, river front campground.
Steve and Jane Abbott

ABBOTT'S RIVER OUTFITTERS, INC.
Between 2nd and 1st crossings on River Road
HCR 3, Box 871
New Braunfels, Texas 78132
(512) 625-4928
Canoes, tubes, rafts, kayaks, inflatables, shuttles, retail store. River trips from 4-14 days in Mexico.
Steve and Jane Abbott

MOLLY'S RAFT RENTAL & GENERAL STORE
Hueco Springs Road at River Road
P. O . Box 134
New Braunfels, Texas 78131
(512) 629-4422
Tube, canoe & raft rentals, shuttles, parking, camping supplies, groceries
Molly Armstrong

HOUSTON, Texas (Metropolitan Area)

A TO Z ACTION SPORTS
1505 Hwy. 146
Seabrook, Texas 77586
(713) 474-3079
Sales, Rentals, Service and Boating Accessories
Billy Fuller

SUMMIT TOURS
P. O. Box 6516 (Loop 494 & Kingwood Drive)
Kingwood, Texas 77325
(800) 228-4185 or (713) 359-2499
Guide service, instruction, sales, rentals, outdoor and educational programs
Corkey Lucas

THE WHITEWATER EXPERIENCE
6005 Cypress
Houston, Texas 77074
(713) 522-2848
Wilderness expeditions, rentals, sales, canoes, rafts, kayaks
Don Greene

MEDINA RIVER

Please Note: In November, 1992 the "512" Area Code for all Medina River listings will change to "210."

FRED COLLINS WORKSHOP
P.O. Box 1869 (½ mile north of Bandera on Hwy. 16)
Bandera, Texas 78003
(512) 796-3553
Canoe and tube rentals, shuttles
Fred Collins

BANDERA WATERSPORTS
403 Main Street (General Delivery)
Bandera, Texas 78003
(512) 796-3021 or (512) 796-3022
Scrambler fun boats, watersports equipment rental, tubes, shuttles
Jim Bob & Rita Cox

YOGI BEAR'S JELLYSTONE PARK
P. O. Box 1687 (Hwy. 173S at the Medina River)
Bandera, Texas 78003
(512) 796-3751
Canoe rentals, tubes, shuttles, river front camping, full service R.V. Park
Bob Abbey

RENTAL AND GUIDE SERVICE
TEXAS RIVERS (CONTINUED)

MIDLAND, Texas

SKI SKELLER
3325 West Wadley
Midland, Texas 79707
(915) 697-0427
Canoe and raft rentals, camping and backpacking accessories
Dick Ragan

PECOS RIVER

HIGH BRIDGE ADVENTURES
Box 816
Comstock, Texas 78837
(915) 292-4462 or (915) 292-4495
Rentals, shuttles, scenic tours, pontoon boats
Manuel and lnez Hardwick

RED RIVER (Below Lake Texoma)

J. W. CANOE RENTAL, INC.
Route 1, Box 220-A
Denison, Texas 75020
(903) 465-5771 (Day or Night)
Canoe rentals and shuttles
J. W. and Reba Collins

RIO GRANDE RIVER

FAR FLUNG ADVENTURES
P.O. Box 377
Terlingua, Texas 79852
(915) 371-2489 or (800) 359-4138
Expeditions in Big Bend, New Mexico, Mexico, Colorado and Arizona
Steve Harris or Patrick Brown
LAJITAS TRADING POST
Star Route 70, Box 436
Terlingua, Texas 79852
(915) 424-3234
Raft rentals and shuttles, groceries, supplies
Bill C . Ivey
OUTBACK EXPEDITIONS
P. O. Box 229 - Hwy. 170
Terlingua, Texas 79852
(800) 343-1640 or (915) 371-2490
Canoeing, rafting, backpacking, motel and curio shop
B. C. Small
DESERT SPORTS
P. O. Box 584
Terlingua, Texas 79852
(915) 424-3366 or (800) 523-8170
Rentals, sales, repairs, camping, hiking supplies
Elizabeth Gay Blashill
SCOTT SHUTTLE SERVICE
P. O. Box 477 (Hwy. 90 E. and 385 S.)
Marathon, Texas 79842
(915) 386-4574
Canoe rentals, shuttles and equipment
Mike and Sharan Scott

SABINE RIVER

SABINE RIVER TRIPS
Rt. 1, Box 968
Gilmer, Texas 75644
(903) 734-5305
Rentals, sales, shuttles
Jerry Gumm

SAN MARCOS RIVER

T. G. CANOE LIVERY
P. O. Box 177
Martindale, Texas 78655
(512) 353-3946
Rentals, sales, shuttles, repairs
Duane or Evelyn TeGrotenhuis
PECAN PARK RETREAT
P. O. Box 219
Martindale, Texas 78655
(512) 392-6171
Guided river trips, camping, cabins, outfitting
Tom and Paula Goynes
SPENCER CANOES /SHADY GROVE CAMPGROUND
Rt. 1, Box 55-R
Martindale, Texas 78655
(512) 357-6113
Canoes, kayaks, sales, rentals, repairs, instruction, shuttles, riverside camping, custom boat building
Pat and Mike Spencer

SOUTH LLANO RIVER

COLEMAN CANOES
P. O. Box 25
Junction, Texas 76849
(915) 446-3540
Rentals and shuttles
Gene and Donnie Coleman

TRINITY RIVER (Elm Fork)

NORTH TEXAS CANOES
1325 Whitlock Lane, Ste. 316
Carrollton, Texas 75006
(214) 245-7475
Canoes, kayaks, rentals, shuttles, sales, instruction
Rich Manning
TRINITY RIVER EXPEDITIONS
(214) 941-1757
Canoe rental and shuttle service
Charles Allen

VILLAGE CREEK

PINEY WOODS CANOE COMPANY
P. O. Box 1994
Kountze, Texas 77625
(409) 274-5892
Canoe rentals, shuttles, sales, camping, Big Thicket permits
Nick Rodes

WHITE ROCK CREEK (Dallas, Texas)

HIGH TRAILS
3610 Marquis Drive
Garland, Texas 75042
(214) 2-PADDLE or (214) 272-3353
Sales, rentals, canoes, rafts, kayaks, river accessories
Bob Narramore

ARKANSAS RIVERS

BIG PINEY CREEK

MOORE OUTDOORS
Rt.2, Box 303 M (At Twin Bridges)
Dover, Arkansas 72837
(501) 331-3606
Canoe and raft rentals, sales, supplies, whitewater instruction
Kerry and Debbie Moore

BUFFALO NATIONAL RIVER (Upper Section)

BUFFALO OUTDOOR CENTER
P. O. Box 1
Ponca, Arkansas 72670
(800) 221-5514 or (501) 861-5514
Rentals, sales, canoes, rafts, shuttles, log cabins
Mike Mills

LOST VALLEY CANOE SERVICE AND GENERAL STORE
Hwy. 43
Ponca, Arkansas 72670
(501) 861-5522
Canoes, rafts, rentals, shuttles, lodging, camping, hot showers
Michael and Larry Olesen

BUFFALO NATIONAL RIVER (Middle Section)

BUFFALO CAMPING AND CANOEING
P. O. Box 504
Gilbert, Arkansas 72636
(501) 439-2888 or (501) 439-2386
Rentals, shuttles, campgrounds, RV hookups, hot showers, cabins, general store
Ben and Cynthia Fruehauf

BUFFALO OUTDOOR CENTER
Route 1, Box 56
St. Joe, Arkansas 72675
(800) 221-5514 or (501) 439-2244
Rentals, sales, canoes, rafts, shuttles, log cabins
Tom Aston

TOMAHAWK CANOE RENTAL
Rt. 1, Box 11-A
St. Joe, Arkansas 72675
(501) 439-2617
Canoe rentals and shuttles
Bobby or Elain Younger

BUFFALO NATIONAL RIVER (Lower Section)

BENNETT'S CANOE RENTAL
HCR 66, Box 331
Yellville, Arkansas 72687
(501) 449-6431
Rentals, shuttles, log cabins, craft shop
Joe and Dale Bennett

DIRST CANOE RENTAL
HCR 66, Box 385
Yellville, Arkansas 72687
(800) 537-2850 or (501) 449-6636
Canoe rentals, shuttles, log cabins, deli, grocery store
Russell and Mildred Dirst

DODD'S CANOE AND JOHNBOATS RENTAL
HCR 66, Box 365
Yellville, Arkansas 72687
(800) 423-8731 or (501) 449-6619
Canoe and johnboat rental, shuttle, guide service
Leslie, Julie and Josey Dodd

CADDO RIVER

ARROWHEAD CABIN & CANOE RENTALS, INC.
209 E. Portia Terrace
Hot Springs, Arkansas 71913
(501) 356-2944, Caddo Gap, Arkansas
(501) 767-5326 off season
Rentals, guide service, sales, camping, RV hookups, bunkhouse
John Carter and Phil Ward

WRIGHT WAY CANOE RENTAL
P. O. Box 180
Glenwood, Arkansas 71943
(501) 356-2055
Rentals, shuttles, guide service, sales, cabins
Steve Wright

MULBERRY RIVER

BYRD'S CANOE RENTAL & CAMPGROUND
HCR 61, Box 131
Ozark, Arkansas 72949
(501) 667-4066
Canoe, raft, tube rentals, shuttles, camping, hot showers, electrical hookups, grocery store
Barbara Byrd

TURNER BEND
HC 63, Box 216 (Hwy. 23 at River)
Ozark, Arkansas 72949
(501) 667-3641
Canoe rentals, shuttles, campground, groceries
Brad Wimberly or Lloyd Schlicker

WAYFARER OF THE OZARKS
HCR 61, Box 131
Ozark, Arkansas 72949
(501) 667-4998 or (501) 667-4066
Canoe, raft, tube rentals, shuttles, camping, hot showers
Pam and Tammy Byrd

OUACHITA RIVER

OUACHITA JOE'S CANOE RENTAL SERVICE
P. O. Box 65
Pencil Bluff, Arkansas 71965
(501) 326-5517
Canoe rentals, shuttles, fishing accessories
Patsy and Harrold (Joe) Little

ROCKY SHOALS CANOE RENTALS
Rt. 2, Box 200
Mount Ida, Arkansas 71957
(501) 326-4710 or 867-2382
Rentals, shuttles, camping, electrical hookups, showers, cottage
Tim and Sandy Williamson

S & K CANOE
HC 67, Box 177-A
Mount Ida, Arkansas 71957
(501) 867-3815
Rentals, shuttles, guided trips, camping, catering
Steve and Kris Roberts

SPRING RIVER

MANY ISLANDS CAMP
Rt. 2, Box 75
Mammoth Spring, Arkansas 72554
(501) 856-3451
Canoe and kayak rentals, camping, cabins
Bob Wood

ILLINOIS RIVER

EAGLE BLUFF RESORTS
HC 61, Box 230
Tahlequah, Oklahoma 74464
(800) 366-3031 or (918) 456-3031
Canoe, raft rentals, camping , RV sites, hot showers, A/C motel,
supplies, parking
Jeff and Vicki Bennett

HANGING ROCK CAMP
HC 61, Box 199
Tahlequah, Oklahoma 74464
(800) 375-3088 or (918) 456-3088
Canoe, raft rentals, camping, cabins, motel, cafe, RV hookups,
showers, supplies
Carl and Shirley Ragsdale

PEYTON'S PLACE
HC 61, Box 231
Tahlequah, Oklahoma 74464
(800) 359-0866 or (918) 456-3847
Canoe, raft rentals, camping, cabins, bathhouse, deli, grocery
store
Archie Peyton

WAR EAGLE RESORT
HC 61, Box 263
Tahlequah, Oklahoma 74464
(800) 722-3834 or (918) 456-6272
Canoe, raft rentals, camping, motel, RV hookups, hot showers,
pool, miniature golf
L. D. Stephens

DIAMONDHEAD RESORT
HC 61, Box 264
Tahlequah, Oklahoma 74464
(800) 722-2411 or (918) 456-4545
Canoe, raft rentals, camping, motel, hot showers, electrical hookups,
groceries
Tom and Joyce Eastham

SPARROW HAWK CAMP
HC 61, Box 392
Tahlequah, Oklahoma 74464
(800) 722-9635 or (918) 456-8371
Canoe, raft rentals, campground, shuttles, RV hookups, supplies,
showers, instruction
Carl George

Shuttle Service on the Devils River

Shuttle "Tow" Service on the Pecos River

LOWER MOUNTAIN FORK RIVER

WHIP-POOR-WILL CANOE RENTALS
Star Route, Box 38
Broken Bow, Oklahoma 74728
(405) 494-6476
Canoe rentals, float trips, log cabins, riding stables, trail rides
Cecil or Barbara Hicks

W W TRADING POST & CANOE RENTAL
Rt. 1, Box 532
Broken Bow, Oklahoma 74728
(405) 584-6856
Canoe rental, shuttles, groceries, bait, tackle, licenses
Neil and Lesley Wood

UPPER MOUNTAIN FORK RIVER

MOUNTAIN FORK CANOES AND CABINS
P. O. Box 128 (Hwy. 4 at River)
Smithville, Oklahoma 74957
(405) 244-3569
Canoes, jon boats, cabins, RV hookups, camping, showers, shuttles
George Fell

THE WHIP-POOR-WILL CANOE RENTALS
Star Route, Box 38
Broken Bow, Oklahoma 74728
(405) 494-6476
Canoe rentals, float trips, log cabins, riding stables, trail rides
Cecil or Barbara Hicks

WASHITA RIVER

WASHITA CANOE SALES AND RENTALS
P. O. Box 5156
Ardmore, Oklahoma 73403
(405) 223-4862
Canoe, raft sales, rentals, instruction
Robert Sweeten